GREAT DECISIONS

GREAT DECISIONS IS A TRADEMARK OF THE FOREIGN POLICY ASSOCIATION.

© COPYRIGHT 2021 BY FOREIGN POLICY ASSOCIATION, INC., 551 FIFTH AVENUE, NEW YORK, NEW YORK 10176.

All rights reserved.

No part of this book may be reproduced in any form, or by any means, without permission in writing from the publisher.

PRINTED IN THE UNITED STATES OF AMERICA BY DARTMOUTH PRINTING COMPANY, HANOVER, NH.

LIBRARY OF CONGRESS CONTROL NUMBER: 2020919618

ISBN: 978-0-87124-275-4

Researched as of November 22, 2020.

The authors are responsible for factual accuracy and for the views expressed.

FPA itself takes no position on issues of U.S. foreign policy.

The Foreign Policy Association has moved office!

Our new address is:
551 Fifth Avenue, 30th Floor, New York, NY 10176.

IN MEMORIAM

Ann R. Monjo

1929–2020

This issue of GREAT DECISIONS is dedicated
to Ann R. Monjo, who devoted her life to the
Foreign Policy Association. An editor's editor,
Ann ensured that FPA's publications, including GREAT
DECISIONS, met the highest editorial standards. Over a
64-year career at FPA, Ann's enthusiasm for FPA's mission
never flagged. To the contrary, her conviction that FPA's
mission mattered only grew. She toiled in the vineyard of
international affairs education that we may have a more
informed public and a more vibrant democracy.

Rebuilding Trust, Domestic Renewal and U.S. Foreign Policy

We take great pride at the Foreign Policy Association in presenting the Foreign Policy Association Medal to the Honorable George P. Shultz, who served as the 60th Secretary of State from 1982 to 1989. Reflecting on a life of public service and, coinciding with his one-hundredth birthday, Secretary Shultz has written a remarkable essay, On Trust, in which he sets out his thoughts for meeting foreign policy challenges facing the United States.

At the Foreign Policy Association, we fully endorse the clarion call by Secretary Shultz for a broad national consensus on U.S. foreign policy. Returning to the time-honored tradition of bipartisanship in defining America's role in the world has never counted for more. Partisan politics should once again end at the water's edge.

To forge such a consensus and to sustain American leadership in the world will require protracted attention to domestic challenges. This is a theme we will emphasize in our programing at the Foreign Policy Association in 2021. U.S. global leadership hinges upon domestic renewal.

The hollowing out of the U.S. middle class can and should be reversed. Stagnant household incomes over the past fifteen years and the coronavirus pandemic pose a real threat to U.S. capacity to play a leadership role in the world.

The Carnegie Endowment for International Peace convened a bipartisan task force to explore what a middle-class focused foreign policy might look like. The Carnegie task force concluded: *Administrations of both parties have not done enough to adapt to the changing needs of and stresses on the middle class. What the American public seems to want more than anything else is enlightened international leadership by Washington that is anchored by more and smarter investments at home and a domestic economy that provides more Americans with opportunity and hope for a better future.*

The Carnegie task force advocates significantly scaling up public investment in science, worker training, and research and development, and adopting a National Competitiveness Strategy. It is proposed that the Commerce Department lead this mission. Given the many cross-cutting policies that must be shaped and coordinated, perhaps an interagency body would be better suited for this task.

Ways to reignite partnerships among governments, at all levels, universities and the private sector will generate rich programming. At the outset, FPA plans to convene thought leaders to consider how New York City and other urban centers can be reinvented in a post-Covid world.

U.S. national competitiveness can be further enhanced if we engage with our neighbors, Canada and Mexico, to promote a North American competiveness strategy. As the world moves increasingly in the direction of trading blocs, such as the recent Regional Comprehensive Economic Partnership among the Asia-Pacific nations, we must work assiduously to foster North American cooperation. Too often, we have taken our neighbors for granted, and the opportunity costs for them and for us have been lamentably high.

Noel V. Lateef
President and Chief Executive Officer
Foreign Policy Association

The following is excerpted from "On Trust" by former Secretary of State George P. Shultz*:

Now in my hundredth year, I am impelled by recent events to offer my thoughts about what I have come to believe is as crucial an element in public life as it is in private life. I am thinking about trust. We all instinctively, or from personal experience, know that good neighborly relations thrive when neighbors trust one another, and that life can become miserable if trust is replaced with suspicion and doubt. Trust is perhaps a more complex factor in life between communities and nations, but it is just as critical in determining whether cooperation or conflict—or even war or peace—will dominate the relationship.

I have become deeply concerned in these last few years that distrust has become a common theme in our domestic life. It is now accepted as normal that our two great political parties rarely find common ground and that legislation to advance the well-being of American citizens can be achieved only under the pressure of a great life-or-death crisis like the COVID-19 pandemic. It has taken a nationally circulated video of a Black man's atrocious murder by a police officer--whose duties included training newcomers to a major American city's police department—to reveal the depths of racial distrust that exist in our country.

Our relations with much of the rest of the world also have become characterized by distrust bordering on hostility, even in the way Washington deals with close allies in Europe and Asia. We are nearing a Cold War II situation in our relations with China and Russia. Reliance on military threats, with little or no effort at diplomacy, is the most prominent feature of our relations with nations that we associate with anti-American sentiments and actions.

Trust among nations or between those who represent their nations in official discourse with other nations should not be equated with burgeoning friendship or a change in fundamental beliefs on either side. The idea implies a belief that what a nation or a public official commits to do will, in fact, be done. That means not only honesty has become the accepted norm but also that what a nation or its official says will happen is, in fact, capable of being done; that is, the commitment is precise enough to measure its implementation, and the authority to carry out the commitment is assured....

I see a need in the coming years to rebuild trust where now it is absent, based on polices that defend and advance American interests and ideals. The international system is constantly being reshaped; right now, trends in technology and economics, and even the pandemic, are having a major impact on how our country interacts with the rest of the world. With skillful diplomacy and visionary leadership, we can influence these trends and help to create an international system consistent with our values. Our partners in this effort will have to regain trust that we do, indeed, share the same democratic values, and that we really are working for an international system of nations that benefits all of us. Even our adversaries will have to regain the trust that we can work together to mange global threats to humanity's very existence even when we disagree on other issues.

* Reprinted from November 2020 issue of *The Foreign Service Journal*

Global supply chains and U.S. national security

by Jonathan Chanis

Amid the coronavirus outbreak an employee works on the production line of surgical masks at Yilong Medical Instruments Co., Ltd, on April 16, 2020, in Zunyi, Guizhou Province of China. (QU HONGLUN/CHINA NEWS SERVICE/GETTY IMAGES)

The Covid-19 pandemic has painfully reminded Americans that their access to vital medical supplies depends on foreign, especially Chinese, manufacturers. Critical provisions including facemasks, gloves, gowns, ventilators, and generic pharmaceutical drugs such as antibiotics were in desperately short supply. U.S. manufacturers were unable to increase production and compensate for foreign supplies that stopped arriving, or satisfy the surge in demand due to the higher Covid-19 case load.

The lack of adequate personal protective equipment (PPE) and other supplies revealed a strategic vulnerability in America's medical supply chain. The intentional withholding by China of products previously shipped to the U.S. illustrated not only the extent of this vulnerability, but also how foreign governments manipulate these vulnerabilities.

It is this foreign government manipulation that primarily distinguishes a strategic supply chain vulnerability from a commercial vulnerability. Commercial vulnerabilities tend not to occur through government actions, and their purpose tends to be profit oriented, not political.

JONATHAN CHANIS *has worked in investment management, emerging markets finance, and commodities trading for over 25 years. Currently he manages New Tide Asset Management, a company focused on global and resource trading. He previously worked at Citigroup and Caxton Associates where he traded energy and emerging market equities, and commodities and currencies. He has taught graduate and undergraduate courses on political economy, public policy, international politics, energy security and other subjects at several higher education institutions including Columbia University.*

The U.S. medical supply chain struggle with China and a few other states is part of a larger conflict involving many other supply chains across a range of products and sectors. These include defense-related products, semiconductors and computers, telecommunications and aerospace equipment, passenger railcars, and automobiles. From a national security perspective, there are several relevant aspects to global supply chain (GSC) vulnerability:

1. The transformation of the supply chain over the last 30 years led to the *relative* deindustrialization of America, particularly in comparison to China. The U.S. produces fewer defense products, weakening its defense industrial base (DIB), and the U.S. military and government struggle to purchase a range of civilian products. Continued relative deindustrialization also, by definition, undermines the U.S. non-defense manufacturing sector's ability to innovate and develop emerging products and technologies.

2. As China sells more products to U.S. consumers and the U.S. military, the nation becomes more vulnerable to espionage, economic and military sabotage, and large-scale data thefts or misuse.

3. A range of economic policy options targeting GSC vulnerability can be deployed for undermining national adversaries.

At least three policy options for dealing with GSC vulnerability have emerged; they are: renewed engagement, decouplement, and industrial policy adoption. How the U.S. attempts to reconfigure the GSC to minimize its strategic vulnerability or maximize that of other countries raises fundamental questions about the use

Before you read, download the companion **Glossary** that includes definitions, a guide to acronyms and abbreviations used in the article, and other material. Go to **www.fpa.org/great_decisions** and select a topic in the Resources section. (Top right)

of economics as an instrument of international power. It also raises sensitive questions about the relationship between the U.S. government and the private sector. Decisions about strategic GSC vulnerability will profoundly affect U.S. economic security, U.S.-China relations, and the overall standing of the U.S. in the world.

Economics as an instrument of power

U.S.-China tension over GSCs is a manifestation of an intensifying power conflict caused by China's rise over the last 20 years. China's 2001 World Trade Organization (WTO) entry allowed it to transform its economy by increasing inbound direct foreign investment and the outbound sale of manufactured goods. This economic transformation then financed China's substantial and continuing military modernization, and allowed it to create webs of economic dependencies throughout the world. Such a radical transformation in the global balance of power can only alarm the U.S., if it wishes to avoid Asia being dominated by China.

As China's ambitions increase and the rivalry with the U.S. intensifies over issues such as China's actions in the South China Sea, takeover of Hong Kong and designs on Taiwan, it becomes extremely difficult for this struggle to avoid pushing the economic relationship from cooperation to competition. Economic power, like military, diplomatic, or cultural power, is just another instrument used by states in their competition to survive.

While much attention focuses on the U.S. use of economic power, China also uses its growing economic might to damage other states when it feels its interests challenged. Among countries targeted since 2010 were Australia, Japan, Norway, the Philippines, and South Korea, and the goods and services utilized included agricultural products, fish, entrainment programing, tourism, and rare earth metals. The pretext for these actions ranged from displeasure over military deployments and territorial claims, to human rights criticism and a request for an investiga-

tion into the origin of the coronavirus.

The difficulty with using economics as an element of power in the U.S.-China relationship is that globalization and the growth of GSCs has knitted the two economies together in ways that are costly for either side to undo. Moreover, some sections of the American elite still think China is either not a threat to the U.S., or that it can be brought into a new American-managed international economic order on terms advantageous to the U.S.

The ability of the U.S. to utilize effectively economic power against China depends on: finding a durable domestic consensus on the nature and scope of China's challenge to U.S. interests; the costs it is willing to bear to use economic power; and how well it can control the actions of its own and other countries' multinational corporations (MNCs).

Global supply chain basics

A supply chain describes the steps necessary to bring a product or service to a customer, and it usually includes procuring raw materials, transforming these materials first into intermediate goods and then a final product, and then selling and delivering the finished product to a customer. Supply chains coordinate the actions of multiple companies and industries, and when these actions cross national borders they are global. The chain metaphor is useful because the entire operation is only as strong as its weakest link.

Between each step in a supply chain, many activities occur including: defining all concerned parties' expectations of others through documentation, contracts, and information exchanges; physically moving intermediate and final goods between locations or organizations; and storing goods until needed. Logistics refers to the latter two activities of moving and storing goods, and its purpose is to ensure that there are no delays between steps and that costs are minimized.

In the production of a good or service, innumerable events can disrupt the process and threaten sales and

Chinese factory workers assemble motorcycles on the assembly line at the plant of Sundiro Honda Motorcycle Co., Ltd. in Taicang City, China. (CYNTHIA LEE/ALAMY)

profits. "Just-in-time" inventory management increases supply chain vulnerability by reducing inventory along the chain. Increasing complexity also makes current GSCs more fragile since there are often multiple supplier levels, many of whom are unknown to the organizing company. Given the tendency for single product suppliers, there also often are many "single points of failure." Consequently, if a particular item is delayed or fails to arrive, the entire production process may stop. The high and increasing dependence of GSCs on information technology also places them at greater risk since they are more easily disrupted by competitors, cyber-criminals, random malicious actors, and even foreign governments. Global supply chains are an essential feature of contemporary business strategies to maximize corporate profits. Poor supply chain management can result in higher material and labor costs, expensive delays, manufacturing quality

problems, missed sales, and ultimately lower profits or even losses. Improving supply management can represent small but repeated advancements that cumulatively, by making the production and sales process ever more efficient, contribute mightily over the long run to corporate profits.

The phenomenal change to the global supply chain since the 1990s reflects both the search by MNCs for greater profitability and China's opening to the world. Major improvements in information and communication technology (ICT) in the 1980s and 1990s allowed MNCs to move production elsewhere. China, with its extremely low-cost labor force and improving infrastructure, provided the ideal ground for a factory location. As a result, hundreds of thousands of manufacturing operations were established in China. This "offshoring" of production was accompanied by "outsourcing" whereby corporations shed entire parts of the pro-

Chart I

A TYPICAL SUPPLY CHAIN

RAW MATERIALS

CONSUMERS

SUPPLIERS

MANUFACTURER

RETAILERS

DISTRIBUTERS

LUCIDITY INFORMATION DESIGN, LLC

duction process and began purchasing components or products from others. MNCs were central to manufacturing relocation because they provided or facilitated vast flows of foreign direct investment for financing these factories.

The increased share of intellectual property contained in manufactured products also accelerated the shift toward outsourcing, since manufacturing itself usually is not highly profitable. Apple is the quintessential example of this. While over 3 million people now work in Apple's China supply chain, only 13,600 people were reported in 2018 to be directly employed by Apple. The actual manufacturing of an iPhone, for example, is primarily handled by Foxconn of Taiwan.

iPhones illustrate how a disproportionate part of a product's profitability often comes upstream from manufacturing, from research, development, and design, and downstream, from marketing, sales and service. This was first described by Acer's co-founder Stan Shih in 1994 as the "Smile Curve." The assembly and manufacture of most goods tend to be a low profit margin business, and most U.S., European and Japanese corporations were eager to have foreign companies take over this part of the process. This also exemplifies the MNC's greater concern for the "value chain," rather than the supply chain. The former focuses more on where in the process a company makes its money; the latter focuses more on how and where it physically makes its products.

As Chart 2 shows, the profitability of the upstream and downstream parts of the GSC increased substantially after the 1970s with offshoring and outsourcing. As global corporations got better at shifting low profitability, midstream work to foreign manufacturers, they became even more profitable.

Chinese supply chain dominance

The relocation of so many manufacturing facilities out of the U.S., Europe, and Japan completely reconfigured global supply chains. This reconfiguration made China not only the assem-

Chart 2

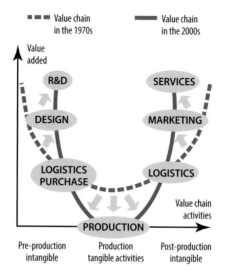

THE SMILE CURVE
Value distribution along the global value chain

SOURCE: "INTERCONNECTED ECONOMIES BENEFITING FROM GLOBAL VALUE CHAINS", OECD 2013.

bly and manufacturing workshop of the world, but also a manufacturing superpower. If one excludes North American automobile manufacturing, China basically dominates the global manufacturing supply chain.

According to a study by BCG, China produced more real manufacturing value in 2017 than the U.S., Germany, South Korea, and the UK combined. It dominates vast global industries such as: textiles and apparel; furniture and bedding; toys and sports equipment; active pharmaceutical ingredients for generic drugs; optical instruments; machine tool building; ship building; electronic equipment including flat-panel display manufacturing; computer and other media device assembly; and; telecommunications equipment including phone manufacturing and assembly.

A number of economists, including Arvind Subramanian and Martin Kessler at the Peterson Institute for International Economics (PIIE), label China's rise to supply chain dominance between the 1990s and 2008 as a period of "hyperglobalization." Compared to previous globalization experiences, the growth in global trade since the 1990s vastly outpaced the growth in global

(or U.S.) Gross Domestic Product (GDP). This super-sized international trade growth made it impossible for most all developed countries, including the U.S., to adapt to the surge of manufactured goods coming out of China. As a result, entire American industries, including furniture and bedding, toys and sports equipment, apparel and shoes, and a range of light manufacturing products such as televisions and washing machines were just destroyed by Chinese imports.

Subramanian and Kessler also labeled China a "mega-trader" in order to differentiate it from all other contemporary countries since its export capacity relative both to its own and the global economy were so immense. As a share of its GDP, China's exports are almost 50%, and at its peak year 2008, China's trade-to-GDP ratio, i.e., imports and exports of goods and services, was 62.2%. (See Graph 1.) No country including the U.S., Japan, or Singapore at their peaks came close to these figures. The nearest any other country came to this global trade dominance was Britain in the heyday of its empire before World War I.

Graph 1

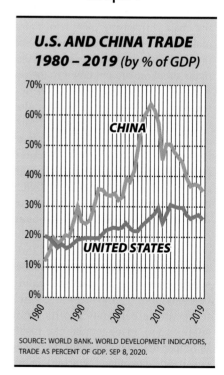

U.S. AND CHINA TRADE 1980 – 2019 *(by % of GDP)*

SOURCE: WORLD BANK. WORLD DEVELOPMENT INDICATORS, TRADE AS PERCENT OF GDP. SEP 8, 2020.

Relative deindustrialization

As some point out, the U.S. still is a manufacturing powerhouse, and based on value added in 2017 it manufactured $2.2 trillion of goods. But while the U.S. remains a manufacturing powerhouse, China is a manufacturing superpower. Beginning in 2010, China's manufacturing output surpassed that of the U.S. and the gap between the two has grown ever since. (See Graph 2.)

In 2017, China manufactured $3.5 trillion of goods, or almost 60% more than the U.S. As a share of GDP, U.S. manufacturing has been declining for over a decade (see Graph 3), and when properly measured the U.S. in the 2000s lost more manufacturing output as a share of GDP than almost any other developed nation. This decline is starkly evident when comparing the U.S. and China share of global manufacturing output the over time. The U.S. share declined from almost 30% in 2002, to 17% in 2018; China's share rose from less than 10%, to 28%. According to the U.S. Census' Statistics of U.S. Businesses, during this time over 60,000 U.S. factories (out of approximately 350,000) closed.

Empirically, there is little doubt that free trade was incredibly beneficial to the U.S. According to a calculation by the Peterson Institute, international trade and investment since 1945 raised real U.S. household incomes by $10,000 annually. But the reality since around the year 2000 gets more complicated, and many ardent, past supporters of free trade including Alan Blinder and Paul Krugman are asking if the unabashed enthusiasm for free trade went too far. In particular, they ponder if there was a connection between decades of increasing China trade with America's manufacturing decline and the growth of U.S. income inequality.

In its contemporary form, the economic argument for free trade emphasizes that a country is better off with the maximal amount of global specialization and trade because goods and services are produced more efficiently and this lowers prices and increases consumer purchasing power. Employ-

Graph 2

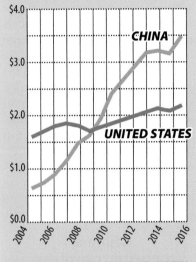

U.S. AND CHINA MANUFACTURING OUTPUT, 2004 – 2016
(VALUE ADDED IN CURRENT U.S.D. TRILLIONS)

SOURCE: WORLD BANK. WORLD DEVELOPMENT INDICATORS, MANUFACTURING, VALUE ADDED (CURRENT US$). SEP. 8, 2020.

Graph 3

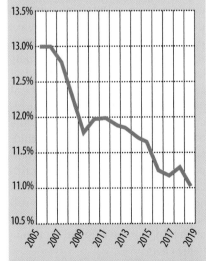

U.S. MANUFACTURING
(as a percentage of GDP)

SOURCE: FEDERAL RESERVE BANK OF ST. LOUIS. VALUE ADDED BY PRIVATE INDUSTRIES: MANUFACTURING AS A % OF GDP, PERCENT, ANNUAL, NOT SEASONALLY ADJUSTED. JULY 6, 2020

ment losses from trade are dismissed as "transition costs" since workers will find other well-paying jobs to replace those lost through imports. Everyone is better off since consumers have lower-priced products and displaced workers are absorbed back into the labor force at sufficiently high incomes.

However, in "The China Shock," David Autor and his fellow researchers summed up the impact of Chinese exports on the U.S. as follows:

"Alongside the heralded consumer benefits of expanded trade are substantial adjustment costs and distributional consequences. These impacts are most visible in the local labor markets in which the industries exposed to foreign competition are concentrated. Adjustment in local labor markets is remarkably slow, with wages and labor-force participation rates remaining depressed and unemployment rates remaining elevated for at least a full decade after the China trade shock commences. Exposed workers experience greater job churning and reduced lifetime income. At the national level, employment has fallen in the US industries more exposed to import competition... but offsetting employment gains in other industries have yet to materialize."

"The China Shock" rebutted the notion that automation was the principal driver of U.S. manufacturing job losses and that China had little to do with stagnating U.S. manufacturing output. The study found that "import growth from China between 1999 and 2011 led to an employment reduction of 2.4 million." (See Graph 4 on next page.) This represents almost half the manufacturing jobs lost in the U.S. during this period. And this estimate is conservative. Other studies find large, or larger, China-induced job losses.

The non-defense sector and a declining defense industrial base

The defense industrial base is the private and public capabilities that design, produce, and maintain the platforms and systems on which U.S. warfighters depend. It is a parallel supply chain dedicated to U.S. military needs, it also

Graph 4

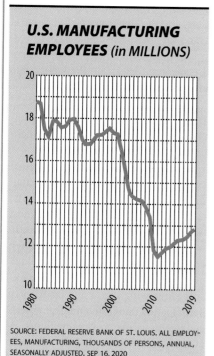

U.S. MANUFACTURING EMPLOYEES *(in MILLIONS)*

SOURCE: FEDERAL RESERVE BANK OF ST. LOUIS. ALL EMPLOYEES, MANUFACTURING, THOUSANDS OF PERSONS, ANNUAL, SEASONALLY ADJUSTED. SEP 16, 2020

interacts with and depends on non-defense supply chains for a variety of skills and products.

In a 2018 DoD report *Assessing and Strengthening the Manufacturing and Defense Industrial Base and Supply Chain Resiliency of the U.S.*, "the decline of U.S. manufacturing capabilities and capacity," and the industrial policies of competitor nations, "notably the economic aggression of China," were two of the five greatest risks weakening the DIB. Quoting from a *National Security Strategy* report, it said:

"The ability of the military to surge in response to an emergency depends on our Nation's ability to produce needed parts and systems, healthy and secure supply chains, and a skilled U.S. workforce. The erosion of American manufacturing over the last two decades, however, has had a negative impact on these capabilities and threatens to undermine the ability of U.S. manufacturers to meet national security requirements."

A vibrant manufacturing sector develops workforce and managerial skills and knowledge. Spillover of this devel-opment into other sectors can increase the productivity of other industries and make everyone better off. Conse-quently, the declining domestic manu-facturing base degrades the country's industrial process and manufacturing capabilities makes it difficult for de-fense manufactures to hire and retain workers with requisite skills from other sectors when needed.

Instead, defense procurement also increasingly relies on single suppliers and even suppliers from adversarial countries for critical defense items. The location of manufacturing research and development centers in other countries, especially China, also undermines fu-ture U.S. innovation since these juris-dictions and the foreign nationals that staff the centers are subject to differ-ent intellectual property laws that, ac-cording to the Department of Defense (DoD), "will impede U.S. access" to this research.

Chinese neo-mercantilism

While the tone of the DoD assessment is blunt and alarming, many other as-sessments from the private sector also concluded that Chinese actions under-mine U.S. economic security. After 1945, the U.S. designed and supported an increasingly open global trading system that was primarily interested in reducing protectionism and other neo-mercantilist practices among like-minded countries. But China came into this system and rejected these rules. As a 2016 U.S. Trade Representative report (issued before Donald Trump came to office) described it, China "... seeks to limit market access for im-ported goods, foreign manufacturers and foreign service suppliers, while offering substantial government guid-ance, resources, and regulatory sup-port to Chinese industries. The prin-cipal beneficiaries of these policies are state-owned enterprises, as well as other favored domestic companies attempting to move up the economic value chain."

China selectively places all the resources of the state behind compa-nies and industries that it deems stra-tegically important. It then supports them in ways that ignore traditional market mechanisms, especially the need to earn a profit. For over two decades, China grossly undervalued its exchange rate in order to subsidize exports and tax imports. It also used domestic regulations and policies to favor its own companies through loan subsides, land grants and permitting preferences, and hobbled the growth of American firms in its domestic mar-ket by erecting discriminatory regula-tory barriers.

One of the most potent Chinese strategies for technologically surpass-ing the U.S. is civilian-military "fu-sion." This strategy seeks to facilitate the transfer of technological knowl-edge between the Chinese civilian and defense sectors in support of defense-related science and technology ad-vancements. It effectively mobilizes all Chinese companies, state or pri-vate, in support of the State's military and economic objectives.

In 2015, China took its state-cap-italist model to a new level with the development of a comprehensive pol-icy for economic, and eventually mili-tary, dominance. The "Made in China 2025" (MIC 2025) program detailed a comprehensive masterplan for eco-nomic and industrial modernization. Specifically, it seeks to create eco-nomic dominance in ten critical areas including: next-generation informa-tion technology; aerospace and avia-tion equipment; maritime vessels and engineering equipment; advanced rail equipment; energy-saving and new energy vehicles; and biopharmaceu-ticals and high-performance medical devices.

The plan subsidizes uncompetitive industries until they gain competi-tiveness, acquires foreign technology through intellectual property theft, extortion, and espionage, and places market and non-market barriers to en-try on U.S. firms wishing to operate in China. China eventually realized how provocative MIC 2025 was and it stopped using the term. However, there is no indication that any of the policies changed.

Existing supply chain strategic vulnerability

As China sells more products to U.S. consumers and the U.S. military, the U.S. becomes increasingly vulnerable to espionage, economic and military sabotage, and large-scale data theft and its attendant misuse. Below are brief sketches of these vulnerabilities, as well as examples.

■ According to many corporate and U.S. government sources, China raised the art of espionage, or the process of obtaining military, political, commercial, or other secrets to a new level. While espionage in the military realm is to be expected, the degree to which China uses state assets, including the Peoples Liberation Army, in support of its corporations and engages in economic espionage against U.S. corporations and the public is shocking.

■ The "2020–2022 National Counterintelligence Strategy" highlighted China's use of the global supply chain "to gain access to critical infrastructure, and steal sensitive information, research, technology, and industrial secrets." It specifically noted that China, is "attempting to access our nation's key supply chains at multiple points—from concept to design, manufacture, integration, deployment, and maintenance—by inserting malware into important information technology networks and communications systems." One of the greatest threats from Chinese produced products concerns the installation of "trojan" chips or infiltration of viruses that alter product performance. This is especially relevant for power generation equipment and transportation products.

■ The connection between Chinese companies and illicit data acquisition is indisputable. Leaving aside the great lengths China goes to acquire economic and personal data through outright theft and espionage, there are many known examples of Chinese corporations surreptitiously collecting, or setting themselves up to collect, large amounts of customer data. TikTok,

for example, defeated a privacy safeguard in Google's Android operating system and collected unique identifiers from millions of mobile devices. Vodafone, one of the world's largest telecommunication companies disclosed that it found a "backdoor" in equipment manufactured by Huawei Technologies. According to an analysis by software security firm Finite State, Huawei's telecommunications equipment is more likely to contain exploitable flaws for malicious use than equipment from rival companies.

Below is a sampling of specific GSC related national security threats.

Bulk Power Supply Equipment: The U.S. acknowledged in 2014 that China possessed the capacity to shut down the U.S. power system. According to the more recent "2020–2022 National Counterintelligence Strategy," this capacity is achieved not only through traditional spying, economic espionage, and cyber operations, but also through the manipulation of the supply chain. Specifically, it cites "increasing reliance on foreign-owned or controlled hardware, software, or services as well as the proliferation of networking technologies, including those associated with the Internet of Things..." Since 2009, ap-

proximately 85% of all newly purchased transformers by U.S. power operators were manufactured abroad, including more than 200 in China. Before 2009, none were imported from China. The threat is not just Chinese manufacturers, but also non-Chinese companies such Germany's Siemens and Switzerland's ABB Group that manufacture in China and then sell into the U.S.

Surveillance Cameras: The DoD purchased large numbers of Chinese surveillance cameras and the accompanying software and installed them on domestic and overseas military bases. This equipment endangers U.S. security by potentially providing China with a detailed window into U.S. military activities across the globe.

Small Drones: The problem with surveillance cameras is duplicated with small drones. Beside battlefield applications, in the civilian world small drones are popular for structural and physical monitoring of bridges, pipeline, and electric transmission lines, and for surveying wildfires and animal life. The Chinese company DJI is the world's dominant producer of small drones with 74% of the market in 2019. DoD and other government purchases of Chinese drones were prohibited in 2019, but finding U.S. suppliers able to produce similar products is problematic.

Employees work on a mobile phone assembly line at a Huawei Technologies Co. production base in Dongguan, China, on March 6, 2019. (QILAI SHEN/BLOOMBERG/GETTY IMAGES)

China and the U.S. Automotive Industry

The U.S. automobile industry is by far the largest and most important manufacturing sector in the U.S., and it is critical for the economic health and prosperity of the country. There are close to one million people directly employed in vehicle and parts manufacturing. When other jobs such as auto dealership employees are included, the industry supports approximately 10 million workers, or 1 in 20 domestic jobs. This economic output equals roughly 6% of U.S. GDP.

Although U.S. consumer acceptance of electric vehicles (EV) is tepid, China and Europe have embraced this technology as an alternative to the internal combustion engine. China included EVs in its MIC 2025 program and sees EV development as a way to leapfrog over the U.S. and dominate mobility in the 2030s.

U.S. vehicle manufactures are acutely aware of the China threat. However, they are disadvantaged in responding because they face an extremely powerful state that both manipulates markets against them, and uses a large array of non-market, coercive, state-backed policies and strategies to undermine their response. As a result, American vehicle manufacturers potentially may go the way of shipbuilding or passenger railcar manufacturing. There will be no need to employ Americans in this industry, if China builds all the cars.

Although China exported just under 700,00 passenger vehicles in 2019, many auto companies are expanding manufacturing in China in anticipation of selling into the global market. China-produced vehicles would then represent a serious threat, not only to American jobs, but also to privacy and cyber security. The Chinese government could collect huge amounts of data on Americans or place backdoor devices in vehicles or components sold to Americans.

While the U.S. government is aware of the economic and industrial threat posed by China in areas like artificial intelligence, quantum computing, and 5G, it largely ignores the emerging and accelerating danger along the vehicle supply chain. If it continues to do so, it may concede what is one of the most, if not the most, important manufacturing sector of the U.S. economy.

This photo taken on April 11, 2019, shows employees working on the JAC (Anhui Jianghuai Automobile Group) Motor assembly line at JAC's factory in Hefei in China's eastern Anhui province. (KELLY WANG/AFP/GETTY IMAGES)

Railcars: Chinese Railway Rolling Stock Corp (CRRC) is the beneficiary of the full array of helpful China state policies. As a result, CRRC undercuts its competitor's prices and sold approximately $2.7 billion of railcars to four American cities (Boston, Chicago, Los Angeles and Philadelphia). For several years, before being prohibited by Congress, the Washington, D.C. Metro also sought to purchase CRRC railcars. With the scores of thousands of U.S. defense and national security personnel using the Washington D.C. Metro to commute to work every day, the espionage, sabotage, and data theft risk were obvious. The U.S. no longer manufactures passenger railcars and now it is the U.S. doing the low profitability assembly work. It is telling how China advanced up both ends of the "Smile Curve" with this product and how the economic roles have been reversed.

Rare Earth Elements (REE): REE such as dysprosium and europium are used in many civilian products such as cell phones, computers, flat-screen televisions, and high-strength magnets used by alternative energy technologies, e.g., wind turbine generators and batteries of hybrid and electric vehicles. Military applications include components of jet engines, missile guidance systems, antimissile defense systems, satellites, and communication systems. According to the U.S. Geologic Survey, between 2011 and 2017, China produced approximately 84% of the world's REEs and it also has a near-monopoly on the processing of these elements. Since the U.S. has no capacity to separate rare earths elements, produce metal, alloys or magnets it is effectively 100% import dependent on China for these products. In 2010 China curtailed shipments of REEs to Japan over a maritime dispute. Since that time, the U.S. military has been seriously concerned about its own access to REE. In response, the U.S. government has helped fund the development of the single major REE mine, Mountain Pass, in the U.S.

Drugs: Before generic drugs are processed into finished products, they start as active pharmaceutical ingredients (APIs). According to the U.S. Food and Drug Administration, approximately 80% of API generic drug manufacturers are located outside of the U.S., and Chinese companies are a significant and growing share of these manufactures. For some of the drugs Americans consume, such as antibiotics and blood pressure medication, Chinese manufacturers have a virtual monopoly on API production. This high dependence is dangerous because if tensions with China were to rise and supplies interrupted, the withholding of APIs could seriously and negatively affect the health of millions of Americans. And even if China chose not to totally restrict API sales, they could create shortages or cause prices to escalate rapidly.

What the above examples all have in common is the inability or difficulty of avoiding Chinese-made products. There are no, or few alternative American or even allied country suppliers, and those that may exist often are inferior or more costly. The inability or extreme difficulty of avoiding Chinese-made products is a direct result of how MNCs and China have reconfigured the GSC.

Using GSCs to advance U.S. national security

While media attention focused largely on the GSC threat to the U.S., the GSC also provides the U.S. with opportunities to enhance its national security and weaken adversaries, particularly China. Indeed, the Trump administration increasingly attempts to use GSC related measures to advantage America. As Adam Segal of the Council on Foreign Relations described this new "high-tech Cold War," the Trump Administration is "restricting the flow of technology to China, restructuring global supply chains, and investing in emerging technologies at home." Below are specific examples:

Semiconductors: One of China's greatest supply chain vulnerabilities concerns advanced semiconductor chips. Semiconductors are electric components that go into products such as memory chips, microprocessor, and integrated circuits. They are essential to almost all electronic products from consumer phones and computers, to missile and jet fighter. In 2019, imported chips represented over 80% of the computer chips China used, and the import bill, in excess of $300 billion, substantially exceeded that for crude oil. China is extremely dependent on American sourced semiconductors, whether purchased outright from U.S. suppliers, or manufactured under license. Continued and increasing disruption of the semiconductor flow would severely undermine China's ability to advance many of its most important technology programs such as Huawei's 5G network. After a series of increasingly prohibitive measures, the Trump administration in August 2020 finally restricted the sale of U.S. produced or designed semiconductors to Chinese entities.

Satellites: Surprisingly, U.S. corporations such as Boeing, Maxar Technologies and the investment firm Carlyle Group all have assisted China in deploying advanced U.S. satellite communications in support of their military and security services. While the Chinese government and its companies are barred from directly purchasing U.S.-made satellites, they have skillfully found ways to use offshore companies to purchased advanced U.S. satellites and then lease back bandwidth to their military and security organizations. The U.S. government is still wrestling with how to close the legal loopholes that make this possible.

Basic Scientific Research: A large area of vulnerability for the Chinese GSC concerns access to advanced research in the U.S. Basic research is the foundation upon which most all advanced manufacturing rests, and as noted, China is extremely aggressive in acquiring the best American scientific ideas to support its industrialization. Among other methods, China developed programs to attract top U.S. scientific talent by targeting U.S. college and university researchers and paying them generously. In many cases, it even brought the researchers to China to establish parallel labs to those operating in the U.S. Much of this cutting-edge research includes some with direct military applications, and it was conducted with the cooperation of many U.S. universities. After the extent of this threat became clear, the Federal Bureau of Investigation investigated and indicted several prominent scientists. A number of institutions also paid multimillion-dollar fines to settle charges. While final rules for China's relationship with U.S. research institutions are being designed, the most threatening practices have stopped. But given the potential benefits from this activity, China is unlikely to reduce its efforts in this area.

Policy options

In response to GSC vulnerability and China's abuse of the international trading system, three policy options emerge. These are: renewed engagement, decouplement, and industrial policy adoption. While the difference between engagement and the other two perspectives is stark, i.e., cooperation or competition, there often is overlap between decouplement and industrial policy. The difference between the two tends to be where one places the central emphasis, i.e., limiting the U.S.-China relationship, or rebuilding America's industrial capacity.

Renewed engagement

The ranks of those advocating for renewed engagement with China have thinned considerably since 2016. Supporters of this position tend to come from an older generation of businessmen, diplomats, policy advocates, and academics. At its top, the group is largely populated by people who had very successful careers building the U.S.-China relationship, or who have become wealthy off it. These advocates want to avoid conflict, minimize competition, and build cooperation with China. Engagement and globalization are still seen as a win-win for both sides.

Engagers think too antagonistic a response to China would be counterproductive, especially if it is really trying to push China into an econom-ic or political crisis. In a prominent *Washington Post* op-ed from July 2019, more than 100 engagers, including Stapleton Roy, Susan Thornton, and Ezra Vogel argued that an alternative policy risks losing decades of hard-built relationships, unnecessarily elevates the risk of military confrontation, and may even lead to a new era of McCarthyism in America. On the GSC they wrote:

"U.S. efforts to treat China as an enemy and decouple it from the global economy will damage the U.S.' international role and reputation and undermine the economic interests of all nations. U.S. opposition will not prevent the continued expansion of the Chinese economy, a greater global market share for Chinese companies and an increase in China's role in world affairs....If the U.S. presses its allies to treat China as an economic and political enemy, it will weaken its relations with those allies and could end up isolating itself rather than Beijing."

Noticeably absent from this group are many U.S. manufacturing businesses that pioneered the GSC relocation to China, and that previously were ardent supporters of engagement. The cause of this change is found in the declining profitability of many U.S. operations in China. The unmooring of the U.S.-China relationship from its business foundation seriously weakened U.S. support for an accommodative policy. In particular, there is less of a counterbalance to deflect or defeat longstanding China critics among the labor and defense communities.

The last major bastion for pro-engagement policies among the U.S. business community is financial service companies, especially the large banks, asset managers, and private equity firms. Since these firms had less in-country exposure to China, they have not had the same punishing experience as U.S. manufacturers. Also, chimera or otherwise, many of these companies think they still can become fabulously wealthy by engaging with China. Undoubtedly and regardless of its national security implications, some of them will be correct.

Decouplement

Derek Scissors, a policy scholar at the American Enterprise Institute, is a prominent advocate of decoupling from China. Scissors sees decoupling as a third way between doing nothing to counter China's harmful economic actions, and punitive polices built around sanctions and other aggressive measures. Scissors wants to restrict and shrink "the economic relationship for an indefinite period because parts of it are harmful" to the U.S. The purpose of decoupling is not to destroy bad Chinese actors, but to stop enriching them.

Scissors proposes an array of measures including better use of countervailing and antidumping duties, stricter and more efficient use of export controls, continued restrictions on Chinese inbound investment, and new, stricter restrictions on U.S. investment, including portfolio investment in China. Decoupling supports relocating strategic supply chains, like PPE, into the U.S. or friendly countries. In many cases, it will be necessary to outlaw the use or consumption of Chinese products or materials. Particularly during the beginning of decoupling, Scissors says only a small number of supply chains should be relocated. This will avoid unjustified protectionism and allow the U.S. government and industry to learn how best to undertake these transfers. Coordination and sharing relocated supply chains with like-minded countries also is important.

Large scale U.S.-China decoupling will impose economic costs on both China and the U.S. However, the precise impact on U.S. inflation, innovation, and the standard of living is hard to know. Some critics of decoupling argue that it can cost trillions of dollars and that it is therefore not possible. However, this is a strawman argument since no serious advocate is arguing for a total decoupling.

According to Scissors, even a limited decoupling would need tens of billions of dollars of U.S. government support and it would have to contend with Chi-

Technicians monitor a machine that manufactures 300mm silicon wafers at the Applied Materials Inc. Maydan Technology Center in Santa Clara, California, U.S., on Sept. 1, 2011. Applied Materials Inc. develops, manufactures, markets, and services semiconductor wafer fabrication equipment and related spare parts for the worldwide semiconductor industry. (DAVID PAUL MORRIS/BLOOMBERG/GETTY IMAGES)

nese retaliation. The gains, however, will be "impressive" since it will reduce "Chinese distortions of the American and global economies." While decoupling will not create millions of new American jobs, it can save what high-quality jobs and companies America has left. Decoupling is about "avoiding losses rather than generating benefits."

Industrial policy

To Arthur Herman, a policy scholar at the Hudson Institute, industrial policy (IP) refers to "a program of economic reforms that give the government extraordinary authority, as well as fiscal and regulatory powers, to change a country's industrial structure or—less ambitiously—promote a targeted sector of the economy." IP advocates are alarmed by the relative deindustrialization of America and by a fear that the U.S. lead in technology is disappearing.

Industrial policy has a long and negative history in the U.S. primarily because it goes against so many market precepts, mythological or otherwise, that dominate American thinking. As the American economist Gary Hufbauer remarked, before "...the Trump era, industrial policy—in the sense of detailed government guidance of economic

life—was regarded as a hangover from the Soviet Union, to be embraced only by misguided developing countries." Critics of industrial policy say that it "does not work" since the government is "incapable of picking winner and losers." They also argue, with some justification, that IPs are prone to abuse by politicians and industry.

IP advocates assert that the critics present a distorted picture of IP, and that the recent American experience with markets has been a great deal less impressive than many economists and policy advocates claim. In particular they bristle at central planning comparisons and note that IP, like mercantilism, is a form of capitalism. As Herman said: "...limiting government's role to merely umpiring market mechanisms is hurting both our economic future and our national security. [Policy options] beyond market fundamentalism...exist [and] a failure to pursue these alternatives might put us on a different road to serfdom." The point is not "...to curb private enterprise but to spur it in a new direction..."

IP currently is enjoying a revival both on the left and right, and a large number of politicians such as Senators Marco Rubio, Sherrod Brown, and

Sheldon Whitehouse, and former Ambassador to the United Nation Nikki Haley are supportive of a greater government role in the economy. A national-security-oriented IP would use a coherent and narrow set of government measures to reduce specific national security vulnerabilities such as in artificial intelligence, quantum computing, semiconductors, and 5G. One of the most high-profile current IP efforts is found in legislation to increase the domestic U.S. manufacturing of semiconductors and block as much indigenous Chinese chip development as possible. A broader IP would attempt to reinvigorate an entire industry, such as the automotive sector, by renewing or creating the full supply chain in the U.S. and friendly countries.

The industrial policy debate raises a deeper U.S. conflict on American values and capitalism, and the proper relationship between the private sector and the state. Heretofore, questioning the utility of markets, free trade, and globalization has not been a winning formula in the U.S. The issue now is: Has the competition with China altered this reflexive ideological attachment? Or perhaps, has American generational change made IP more acceptable?

discussion questions

1. Is China an economic partner or strategic economic threat? Can China be brought back into an American-led international economic system?

2. Is decoupling from China in the American interest? How much reshoring is practical or advisable?

3. Should the U.S. redefine the appropriate role of government in the U.S. economy in order to help corporations compete better with China? Can the U.S. compete successfully without a more cooperative relationship between the public and private sectors?

4. Would government intervention through an industrial policy invariably result in lower economic growth and lower prosperity? Even if it did, might such a policy be justified given other security and social goals?

5. What are the dangers of an ever-intensifying technology and economic Cold War with China?

suggested readings

Atkinson, Robert. **How Nine Flawed Policy Concepts Hinder the United States From Adopting the Advanced-Industry Strategy It Needs**. ITIF. 2020. Few policymakers and even fewer pundits or economic analysts understand U.S. competitiveness problems in a way that would lead them to the logical conclusion that China is a major economic threat and that a national innovation and competitiveness strategy is the required solution.

Gertz, Geoffrey and Miles M. Evers. **Geoeconomic Competition: Will State Capitalism Win?** *Washington Quarterly*. Summer, 2020. The authors examine the unfair fight between the U.S. and China in the corporate sphere. They detail three broad ways for the U.S. government to leverage the private sector in an effort to reduce China's economic advantage.

Herman, Arthur. **America Needs an Industrial Policy.** American Affairs. Hudson Institute. 2019. There has been a recent shift in mood and attitude about the proper role of government in shaping America's economic destiny. Fear that limiting government's role to merely umpiring market mechanisms is hurting both our economic future and our national security. Policy options beyond market fundamentalism exist, and a failure to pursue these alternatives might put us on a different road to serfdom.

Mann, Katherine. **For Better or Worse Has Globalization Peaked?** Citigroup. 2019. Personal experience has led many to conclude that globalization is a failure, Mann, however, thinks that a retreat from globalization will so reduce output that everyone will be worse off. The challenge, therefore, is "to revive trade integration and find strategies to better distribute those gains. The key to this is in better domestic economic policies.

Rubio, Marco. **American Industrial Policy and the Rise of China**. American Mind. 2019. Senator Rubio makes the case for reinvigorating American manufacturing and strengthening national security through targeted, domestic economic interventions.

Scissors, Derek. **Partial decoupling from China: A brief guide.** AEI. 2020. Chinese state-capitalism has seriously damaged America's economic intersts. If it is not checked, it will continue to destroy American jobs and industries. A partial and strategic decoupling is the only way to protect American economic and security intersts.

Don't forget: Ballots start on page 98!!!!

To access web links to these readings, as well as links to additional, shorter readings and suggested web sites,
GO TO **www.fpa.org/great_decisions**
and click on the topic under Resources, on the right-hand side of the page.

The future of Persian Gulf security

by Lawrence G. Potter

Protesters hold up an image of Qasem Soleymani, commander of Iran's Quds Force and a national hero, during a demonstration following the U.S. airstrike in Iraq which killed him, in Tehran, Iran, Jan. 3, 2020. (ALI MOHAMMADI/BLOOMBERG/GETTY IMAGES)

The future of security in the Persian Gulf is high on the list of the many foreign policy challenges faced by the incoming administration of Joseph R. Biden. The aim of presidents Barack H. Obama and Donald J. Trump to reduce the U.S. footprint there and "pivot toward Asia" has been stymied, due to the strategic importance of the Gulf and the continued high state of tension there. In recent years there has been a cascade of adverse events, including the resurgence of ISIS in Iraq and Syria since their "defeat" in 2017–18, U.S. withdrawal from the Iran nuclear deal (May 2018), the Iranian attack on Saudi oil facilities (September 2019), and the assassination of Iranian general Qasem Soleymani (January 2020).

In contrast to previous U.S. presidential campaigns, foreign policy did not play a major role in the election, nor did either candidate lay out a comprehensive strategy for the Middle East. The most contentious topics were Iran and Saudi Arabia, with Trump and Biden taking very different views. This lack of interest seems to reflect public exhaustion after a long history of intervention that has been very costly in American lives and treasure (an estimated $6.4 trillion since 9/11) but has led to few lasting benefits for either the U.S. or regional states.

LAWRENCE G. POTTER *teaches in the School of International and Public Affairs at Columbia University and was deputy director of Gulf/2000, a major research and documentation project on the Persian Gulf states based there, from 1994 to 2016. He is a longtime contributor to GREAT DECISIONS and published "The Persian Gulf: Tradition and Transformation" in FPA's* Headline Series *Nos. 333–334 (Fall 2011).*

The current disorder in the Persian Gulf derives partly from changes that arose after the U.S. invasion of Iraq in 2003 and the Arab Spring uprisings of 2011. In the latter, massive anti-government and pro-democracy protests swept the Arab World, overturning governments in Tunisia, Egypt, Libya and Yemen. There were violent crackdowns in Bahrain and Oman and demonstrations in Kuwait, the UAE and Saudi Arabia. This thoroughly rattled Gulf monarchs, who responded by buying support, blaming Iran, and instituting a crackdown on human rights. Outside the Gulf, intractable civil wars continue in Syria (nine years), Libya (six years) and Yemen (5 years).

Most recently, the crash of oil prices that took place following the onset of the coronavirus pandemic in the spring of 2020 has dealt a major economic blow to the entire region, as a supply glut and reduced demand converged. For example, the Saudi budget for 2020 was based on an oil price of $80 a barrel. In May 2019, the price of oil was $67, which by May 2020 had dropped to $32. (In April, U.S. oil dropped to zero for a short time as producers ran out of storage capacity.) By November, the price was in the $40 range.

The role of U.S. policy

The U.S. may want to step back, but it is still very much involved in the Persian Gulf. Since World War II its main goal in the region has been to safeguard access to the region's oil and to prevent any other power (first the Soviet Union and later Iraq and Iran) from threatening this. The Gulf states also figure in a number of other American foreign policy concerns, including terrorism, the spread of weapons of mass destruction, radical Islam, democratization, human rights and the Arab-Israeli peace process.

After the British voluntarily withdrew from the Gulf in 1971, the U.S., tied down by war in Vietnam, was not ready to assume responsibility for Gulf security. It delegated this to Iran and Saudi Arabia, and these "Twin Pillars" kept the peace until the Iranian Revolution broke out in January 1978. In 1980 President Carter announced a new policy to guarantee security in the Gulf and exclude outside powers, namely the Soviet Union. This eventually led to a major U.S. naval intervention to protect oil tankers in 1987, and an expanding military buildup thereafter.

Formulating an effective policy to assure the security of Gulf oil exports has not been easy. Over the past four decades, the region has experienced a revolution (Iran, 1978–79) and three major wars (Iran-Iraq, 1980–88, Persian Gulf, 1990–91 and Iraq, 2003–11). Since the Iranian revolution U.S. primacy has partly depended on close cooperation with friendly Arab governments, especially the six Gulf Cooperation Council (GCC) states: Saudi Arabia, Kuwait, Qatar, Bahrain, the United Arab Emirates (U.A.E.), and Oman.

Up until the attacks of 9/11, Washington was satisfied with maintaining the status quo, even permitting Saddam Hussein to remain in power after Iraq was defeated in war. However, in a major change of approach, in 2003 President George W. Bush waged a preventive war against Iraq in a bid to overthrow Saddam and install democracy. It has not turned out that way.

Reevaluating U.S. interests

In light of the end of the Cold War and overt U.S.-Soviet rivalry in the Middle East, and decreased American reliance on Gulf oil, many feel it is time to reevaluate U.S. interests. A distinguished U.S. diplomat with deep knowledge of the region, William J. Burns, has warned that American policy in the Middle East is at a crossroads: "we need a significant shift in the terms of our engagement in the region—lowering our expectations for transformation, ending our habit of indulging the worst instincts of our partners and engaging in cosmic confrontation with state adversaries, finding a more focused and sustained approach to counterterrorism, and putting more emphasis on diplomacy backed by military leverage, instead of the other way around."

The most critical U.S. interest in the Gulf has always been safeguarding oil exports. However, by 2018 only 15% of U.S. oil imports came from there, and thanks to shale oil the U.S. has become a net exporter. Currently more than 80% of Gulf oil goes to Asia. The main customers for Persian Gulf crude are China (19%), India (16%), Japan (15%) and South Korea (13%). The Gulf states themselves are now reorienting their foreign policy to "Look Eastward."

Analysts wonder whether the U.S. should reduce its footprint there and let others, such as Russia, China or India, assume more responsibility for security. Trump himself has declared that the American decision to get involved in the Middle East "was the single biggest mistake in the history of our country." On the other hand, "to say that the Middle East matters less to the United States does not mean that decreased U.S. involvement will necessarily be good for the region," according to Mara Karlin of Johns Hopkins and Tamara Cofman Wittes of the Brookings Institution.

Gulf security historically

The security of the Persian Gulf has been a concern of outside powers for the past 500 years, and the situation today resembles that which has long prevailed: an imperial hegemon—now the United States—tries to maintain stability thanks to naval superiority and an alliance with key regional states. However, the U.S., like Britain before it, has never been able to exert complete control over these states nor prevent local rivalries.

A succession of European powers controlled the Gulf once the route around the Cape of Good Hope was discovered by Portuguese explorer Bartolomeu Dias in 1488. Based on the island of

Before you read, download the companion **Glossary** that includes definitions, a guide to acronyms and abbreviations used in the article, and other material. Go to **www.fpa.org/great_decisions** and select a topic in the Resources section. (Top right)

Hormuz at the mouth of the Gulf, the Portuguese exercised hegemony from 1505 until 1622, followed by a century of Dutch control. The British, relying on seapower, assumed control over the Gulf in the early 19th century, although they were challenged by Ottoman incursions in the 19th century. With the defeat of the Ottoman Empire in World War I, Britain remained the predominant outside power there until 1971.

During the Pax Britannica the British goal was to protect navigation and communication routes to India. They also wanted to safeguard overland routes to Europe, as well as prevent Russia from exercising undue influence on Persia. The British maintained a maritime peace in the Gulf after 1835, and took under their protection the Arabian shaikhs ruling there. In return for their fealty and British control over foreign relations, they expected a guarantee that they and their families would remain in power. Britain drew the modern state borders, starting with Iran in the late 19th century, and took the lead in exploiting the oil resources discovered in Iran (1908), Iraq (1927), Bahrain (1932), and Saudi Arabia and Kuwait (1938).

Gulf security today

Just as the Gulf constituted a distinct region geographically and historically, many analysts believe we should regard the Gulf today as a "regional security complex" rather than focus on the foreign policy of individual countries. This is because most interactions in this region are with each other rather than with outsiders, according to Professor F. Gregory Gause, III, of Texas A & M University. Above all in the Gulf there is an intertwining of internal and external security challenges, as is illustrated by the ongoing conflict in Yemen, seen by some as a proxy war between Iran and Saudi Arabia.

"Spiraling tensions in the Persian Gulf have placed unprecedented strain on a regional security structure little changed since the 1980s," according to Kristian Coates Ulrichsen, Fellow for the Middle East at Rice University. He emphasizes that the concept of what constitutes security is itself changing,

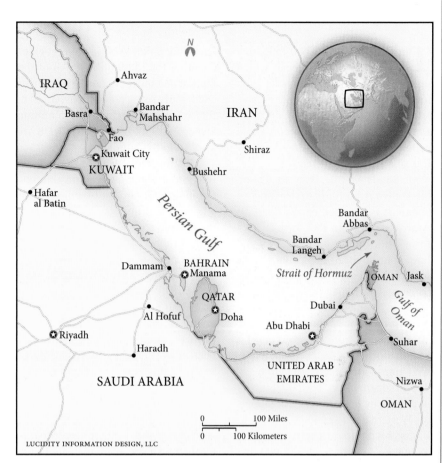

LUCIDITY INFORMATION DESIGN, LLC

Gulf History and Society

The unique identity of the Gulf has been well-defined since antiquity and it cannot be viewed as an appendage of Mesopotamia, Arabia or Iran. The Gulf world differs from the region we have come to call the Middle East in its physical, economic, and social aspects. It is set apart by physical barriers—mountains to the north and east, marshes at its head, and forbidding deserts to the south. In the past, people living on its shores had closer relations with each other than with those living in the interior, which is typical of littoral societies. For millennia it was a region characterized by the constant interchange of people, commerce, and religious movements. Before the modern era, peoples of the region shared a maritime culture based on pearling, fishing, and long-distance trade, and were part of an interlinked system that included agricultural villages and oases that sustained the caravan trade. The Gulf region was oriented outward, toward the Indian Ocean, and was part of a cosmopolitan world of mixed race, religion, and ethnicity. A historic lack of borders, a multiplicity of identities, and the considerable autonomy that Gulf ports enjoyed until recent times led to a hybrid society that was unlike other parts of the Middle East.

from "hard" military might protecting nations to the "soft" security issues—climate change, demographic increase, food and water security, environmental pollution—that are increasingly recognized as constituting the most pressing future threats to peoples' lives.

The impact of globalization and

media penetration of the region, the widespread availability of information online and the growing youth bulge, all presage a new kind of politics in which ruling elites are increasingly called to account by their citizens. The real threats to ruling dynasties come from within and are driven by policies

Profile of the Persian Gulf

The Persian Gulf is a 600-mile-long arm of the Indian Ocean which separates the Arabian peninsula from Iran. (Since the 1950s Arab states have referred to it as the Arabian Gulf, in an attempt to give it a new identity and belittle Iran.) The Gulf is bordered by Iran and seven Arab states: Iraq, Kuwait, Saudi Arabia, Bahrain, Qatar, the United Arab Emirates (UAE) and Oman. It is bounded by the Shatt al-Arab waterway in the north, which forms the frontier between Iran and Iraq, and the Strait of Hormuz in the south, which connects it to the Gulf of Oman and the Indian Ocean. The strait, which is 34 miles wide at its narrowest point, is the choke point of the Gulf: In 2018, about 21 million barrels of oil, a fifth of global petroleum consumption, were transported out of the Gulf every day on supertankers. The possibility of its closure by Iran has been a nightmare for Western defense planners since the Iranian revolution.

In mid-2020, the eight littoral states contained some 182.4 million people, representing many ethnic, religious, linguistic and political communities. In 1950, their combined population was estimated to be around 24 million people; it is projected to rise to 235.4 million by the year 2050. This population is unevenly distributed, with Iran, Iraq and Saudi Arabia together accounting for 158.9 million. All of the Gulf states must contend with young and rapidly rising populations. (In Iran, for example, a population of 35 million at the time of the revolution in 1978 has swollen to 84.2 million.)

Muslims (followers of the Islamic religion) are split into two major sects, Sunni and Shi'a. The two differ over who was legitimately entitled to lead the Islamic community after the death of the Prophet Muhammad in 632 A.D. Sunnis predominate; they believe that the community should choose its own leader. Shi'as, who are a majority in Iran, Iraq and Bahrain, believe leadership is vested in the family of the Prophet. Sunni Islam has historically been associated with bestowing legitimacy on the power of rulers; Shi'i Islam, with opposition, martyrdom and revolt. Following the success of the Iranian Revolution, radical Sunni groups such as Al Qaeda and ISIS arose to create their own version of political Islam.

The majority of Iranians were converted to Shi'ism in the 16th and 17th centuries. Although southern Iraq and the holy cities of Najaf and Karbala have always been the Shi'i heartland, Iraq only became majority Shi'a in the 19th century. A Shi'ite community existed in Bahrain and eastern Arabia (Al Hasa) from about the 10th century, but since the rise of the Wahhabi movement in Arabia in the mid-18th century, and particularly since the formation of the state of Saudi Arabia in 1932, Shi'ites in eastern Arabia have come under heavy pressure.

Since the revolution in Iran in 1978–79 and the rise of Shi'ites in Lebanon in the 1970s, Shiism has been regarded as a powerful political force that can mobilize the downtrodden (*mostazafin* in Persian) and pose a challenge to ruling regimes. By the late 20th century some Shi'i-majority countries that had Sunni governments–such as Iraq and Bahrain–witnessed the rise of resistance movements. Since the fall of Saddam Hussein in 2003 Iraq had been led by Shiites. Most outsiders associate Shiism with its Iranian version, and have underestimated the countervailing force of nationalism, as demonstrated by Iraqis during their war with Iran in the 1980s.

Another major cleavage pits Arab against Persian. Arabic, a Semitic language, is spoken in Iraq and the states of the peninsula. Iran has an Aryan heritage, and its main language, Persian (Farsi), is an Indo-European tongue. Persians regard their cultural legacy as richer than that of the Arabs, although their religion, Islam, was founded by an Arab, the Prophet Muhammad.

---

which promote social division and economic inequality. The "ruling bargain" by which Gulf rulers provide their citizens jobs, housing, education, and health care in return for political acquiescence is now breaking down. As became evident at the time of the Arab Spring, people in the Middle East, including the Gulf, are finding their voice and losing their fear of confronting rulers who exercise autocratic control.

In the wake of the failed Arab Spring revolts, rulers became increasingly authoritarian and less tolerant of any criticism, which stoked internal unrest in Shi'a-majority areas of Bahrain and Eastern Saudi Arabia. As governments now confront the Covid-19 crisis and increase their control over society, "they have been relying upon a new nationalist rhetoric and collective responsibility which they have been nurturing in recent years," according to Dr. Kristin Diwan of the Arab Gulf States Institute in Washington. Amnesty International charged last October that GCC states, specifically Bahrain, Kuwait, Oman, Saudi Arabia, and the UAE, have used the Covid-19 pandemic as a pretext to continue pre-existing patterns of suppressing the right to freedom of expression.

Destabilizing factors

Today the Gulf presents "an intractable security dilemma," according to Mehran Kamrava of Georgetown University, in which policymaking is driven by fear and the Gulf is less secure than ever before. This is a result of "the highly divergent perspectives on the sources of tensions, depending on whether you are sitting in Washington, Tehran, Riyadh, Abu Dhabi, Doha or elsewhere," says Robert Malley, president of the International Crisis Group.

What factors account for this insecurity? One is the relative size of states, in which Iran (with a population estimated at 84.2 million in mid-2020) finds it hard to take seriously a smaller state like the UAE (9.8 million), while Saudi Arabia (35 million) is dismissive toward tiny Qatar (2.8 million).

The GCC, if unified, could act as a powerful bloc to oppose Iran and Iraq. However, the inability of its members to work together because of mutual suspicion has almost made the GCC irrelevant. "Since the beginning, the [Qatar] crisis has served to refute the existence of a collective security regime among the GCC states. They share neither similar values nor common interests. Their conflict also conceals different leadership visions about the future of the region," according to Marwan Kabalan of the Arab Center for Research and Policy Studies.

Since security has long been provided by outsiders, the GCC states never developed strong armies in which citizens were required to participate. Many, especially the richest ones—Qatar, the U.A.E. and Kuwait—have a tradition of subcontracting their security needs, usually to Sunnis from the Arab World and South Asia. Those fighting in the Yemen War on the Saudi side are primarily mercenaries from Sudan, Somalia, and other places. The UAE has also hired thousands of mercenaries and private military contractors to fight in Yemen and Libya.

Another factor is the transnational nature of regional states. Most harbor within them ethnic, religious, and linguistic minorities that rulers fear may be more loyal to their brethren across borders than to the state itself. In the Gulf most states have an Arab, Sunni, citizen majority (except in Iran, Iraq and Bahrain), but also accommodate Shi'a and other minorities that are viewed with suspicion.

Ever since the Iran-Iraq War, with the unrestrained mutual disparagement of Sunni and Shi'a and Arab and Persian, the discourse in the region has served to inflame sectarian tensions. Especially since 2003, the advent of Shi'i leadership in Iraq has alarmed Sunni monarchies, fueling sectarianism and stoking fears of a malevolent "Shi'a crescent." While once regarded as an Islamic sect, today the Shi'a are seen as a security threat.

Disputes over Islam can also be divisive. The competing versions of Islam promoted by Turkey and Saudi Arabia amount to a struggle for the allegiance of all Muslims. Although Saudi Arabia and Qatar both follow

Saudi soldiers at a border post near Yemen, May 2, 2015. (TOMAS MUNITA/THE NEW YORK TIMES/REDUX)

the Wahhabi school of Sunni Islam, the version adhered to in Saudi is much more stringent. Saudi leaders "don't like bottom-up movements that threaten their control, like the Muslim Brotherhood [favored by Turkey and Qatar] or salafi jihadism, not to mention revolutionary Shiism," according to Prof. Gause. Saudi Arabia and the UAE have now declared the Brotherhood a terrorist organization.

Another issue is contested borders. Many boundary disputes in the Gulf have been settled in recent decades, including one between Qatar and Bahrain that was resolved by the World Court in 2001. However, other disputes persist, such as that over the Shatt al-Arab River which forms part of the boundary between Iran and Iraq. One of the most durable disputes has been over ownership of three tiny islands, Abu Musa and the two Tunbs, claimed by Iran and the UAE. The islands issue has poisoned amity in the Gulf for years. Other boundary disputes pit Kuwait against Iraq, Saudi Arabia against the UAE and the UAE against Oman.

There is also the specter of terrorism, employed by radical groups such as Al Qaeda and the Islamic State, which have tried to destabilize Saudi Arabia and Iraq and export their ideology to conflict zones in Syria, Yemen, and Afghanistan. In March 2019 the

U.S. announced the final destruction of the ISIS "caliphate" and that October killed its leader, Abu Bakr al-Baghdadi. However, the UN declared in August 2020 that an estimated 10,000 Islamic State fighters were currently active in Iraq and Syria. Last August, the second-highest leader of Al Qaeda was assassinated in Tehran "by Israeli operatives at the behest of the U.S.," according to the *New York Times*. Iran and Saudi Arabia each accuse the other of being the main sponsor of terrorism in the region.

The nature of rule in the Gulf monarchies, which are run by family dynasties rather than individual kings such as in Jordan and Morocco, can also be a complicating factor. Power is exercised autocratically and policy is made by a small circle of royals who are not accountable to citizens.

The confluence of destabilizing factors and fear of their neighbors has led to a pervasive sense of insecurity. Gulf rulers prioritize regime security over the security of the state. They have favored a realist approach to foreign policy that is focused on hard power (weapons) and balance of power considerations. However, it is clear that arms do not provide security: extensive Saudi purchases of top of the line military equipment could not protect its oil installations at the time of the Iranian attacks.

The Gulf today: regional dynamics

Today in the Persian Gulf, as in other parts of the Middle East, political concerns have become overshadowed by two major interconnected crises: the Covid-19 pandemic, and the crash of oil prices. The sudden arrival of the coronavirus, which was first recorded in the region in Iran on January 22, 2020, is ravaging the Gulf and putting unprecedented pressure on health systems. By last fall Iran was the worst-hit country in the Middle East. The GCC states imposed strict restrictions, and many migrant workers returned home. Saudi Arabia cancelled the annual Hajj to Mecca and announced a cease-fire (not a peace agreement) in the war in Yemen. Emirates Airlines, the flagship carrier of the UAE, cancelled all flights between March 25 and July 15. Today, many websites have appeared in Dubai giving advice on how to close down your company.

At the same time the price of oil has dropped to below break-even cost, which is leading to huge deficits in Gulf states' budgets. Only Qatar can break even at the current price of around $40 a barrel. Aside from the drop in current demand, the long-term outlook for oil revenues is not good as the world transitions away from its dependency on petroleum. British Petroleum, the world's sixth largest oil and gas company, made a controversial statement last September that the demand for oil may be close to its peak and will fall for the next 30 years as the shift away from fossil fuels speeds up. Since the Gulf states are the lowest-cost producers, they will be less affected than others, but still need to plan for lower revenues. States outside the Gulf will be hurt by a reduction in bilateral trade, fewer job opportunities and reduced remittances.

Some regional issues that bear watching and will be discussed below include domestic developments in Saudia Arabia and Iran, the ongoing blockade of Qatar, Turkey-UAE rivalry and the new normalization agreements with Israel. Also of interest is the potential role of China, Russia and Iran as security providers in case the U.S. steps back.

Iran in crisis

The multiplying calamities now afflicting Iran have been exacerbated by stringent U.S. economic sanctions that seek to halt most imports and ban international transactions. These have drastically reduced oil exports and therefore government income. In April 2018 the Iranian currency, the rial, was valued at 45,000 to the dollar; by November 2020 it had collapsed to 285,000 to the dollar. In April 2018 Iran was exporting 2.5 million barrels of oil a day (bpd). In November 2020, Iran claimed the amount exported had been 600,000 to 700,000 bpd since the previous March, but this does not include an unknown amount smuggled out. With fluctuating exchange rates, rampant corruption and lack of protection under the law, many foreign companies are not about to invest there regardless of sanctions. Iranian banks are cut off from the world financial system and suffer from mismanagement, capital shortfall, and a lack of transparency.

The unilateral U.S. withdrawal from the Iran nuclear deal in May 2018, after three years, has dashed hopes of a better future for Iranians and reinforced the role of hardliners running the state. "There is an undeniable sense of hopelessness in Iranian society, affecting everything from record high rates of those who want to emigrate to record low numbers of new marriages," according to Alan Vatanka of the Middle East Institute. The multiplying internal problems have led to widespread anti-government protests—the most recent cycle lasted from November 2019 until the outbreak of the Covid-19 crisis.

Ayatollah Khamenei, the Supreme Leader since the death of Ayatollah Khomeini in 1989, is 81 and ailing and his succession may come in the near future. The original "reign of the ayatollahs" has now morphed into rule by the security services, above all the Islamic Revolutionary Guard Corps (IRGC), who are expected to fight hard to preserve their power. The Guard has increased its role in foreign policy and has been in the forefront of exerting Iran's influence abroad, for example through Shi'i militias it has sponsored in Iraq. The IRGC seeks to preserve Iran's revolutionary legacy and has strong economic interests in a state that has rewarded them well. They will make it very difficult to select a moderate successor to President Hassan Rouhani in the next election, scheduled for June 18, 2021. Although many Iranians might prefer a different form of government, there is no viable

Saudis and foreign residents circumambulate the Kaaba in the Grand Mosque complex in the holy city of Mecca, on October 4, 2020. Authorities partially resumed the year-round Umrah (lesser pilgrimage) for a limited number of pilgrims amid extensive health precautions after a seven-month coronavirus hiatus. (AFP/GETTY IMAGES)

opposition leader or movement inside the country.

In light of the rhetoric emanating from its adversaries, Iran feels vulnerable. Mohammad bin Salman, then the Saudi Deputy Crown Prince, ominously warned in May 2017 that any future battle would be fought inside Iran, not the Gulf states. However, the Iranian attack against Saudi oil facilities was a stark reminder that Iranian missiles could easily lead to the ruin of the Gulf Arabs should they be aimed at desalination facilities or architectural icons like Burj al-Khalifa, the world's tallest building, in Dubai.

Saudi Arabia

The brash crown prince, Mohammad bin Salman (MbS), who will likely succeed his father to the throne, has shaken up domestic affairs in the kingdom. He has also pursued an aggressive and reckless foreign policy, inspired by the regional turmoil and a fear that Riyadh can no longer rely on the U.S. to protect it. Since he took control in 2015 MbS has abandoned the traditional practice of making political decisions by consensus among a small family elite, with input from the Sunni ulama. MbS has now consolidated all power and authority in himself as he tries to remake Saudi society. He reportedly is popular with the younger generation, and has imposed striking reforms, such as allowing women to drive, restraining the religious police and allowing western-style entertainment. In 2016 the crown prince introduced "Saudi Vision 2030," a major set of reforms that aim to reduce government subsidies, cut dependency on oil and empower the private sector. Due to the severe revenue shortfall many goals will have to be scaled back or deferred.

The future course of Iran-Saudi relations is critical for the region. At his UN speech last September 24, King Salman described Iran as a force for chaos. Most worrying is the vow of MbS in March 2018 that his country would obtain a nuclear weapon if Iran does. The U.A.E. opened its first nuclear power plant in August 2020, and Saudi Arabia is making plans to

Saudi Crown Prince Mohammad bin Salman. (BALKIS PRESS/ABACA/SIPA USA/NEWSCOM)

do the same, but has made clear it will not agree to the safeguards the U.S. demanded of Abu Dhabi. However, Saudi has cooperated with Iran in the past over oil prices, and may of necessity be pushed to reach a modus vivendi.

Game of thrones

The dispute that broke out in June 2017 between Qatar and a quartet of adversaries—Saudi Arabia, the UAE, Bahrain, and Egypt—has shuffled regional alliances, benefited Iran, and caused a serious policy dilemma for the U.S.

Although ostensibly about Qatari perfidy, it is a continuation of intermittent Saudi attempts over a long period of time to expand their power throughout the Arabian peninsula.

Statements attributed to the amir of Qatar on May 23, 2017 allegedly expressed support for Iran, Israel, Hamas (a Sunni Palestinian organization based in Gaza) and Hezbollah (a Shi'i militant group based in Lebanon). The Qatari government denied such remarks had been made, and claimed that hackers were spreading false rumors. Shortly thereafter Saudi, Bahrain, the UAE, and Egypt withdrew their ambassadors from Doha and expelled Qatari diplomats, closed their airspace to Qatar Airways, the national carrier, and sealed the land border between Saudi Arabia and Qatar, denying vital food imports to Qatar.

Qatar's opponents subsequently submitted an ultimatum with 13 demands which were so extreme that they clearly could not be considered the basis for a settlement, including that Qatar downgrade relations with Iran, close the Al Jazeera media network and sever relations with the Muslim Brotherhood.

The quarrel forms part of the fallout of the Arab Spring, in which each state took a different approach toward political Islam and the role of elections. It was not about sectarian issues: for

Saudi defense ministry spokesman Colonel Turki bin Saleh al-Malki displays pieces of what he said were Iranian cruise missiles and drones recovered from the attack site that targeted Saudi Aramco's facilities, during a press conference in Riyadh on September 18, 2019. (FAYEZ NURELDINE/AFP/GETTY IMAGES)

The Emirati, Israeli and U.S. flags are pictured attached to an airplane of Israel's El Al, adorned with the word "peace" in Arabic, English and Hebrew, upon its arrival at the Abu Dhabi airport in the first-ever commercial flight from Israel to the UAE, on August 31, 2020. (KARIM SAHIB/AFP/GETTY IMAGES)

example, Shi'i Iran came to the rescue of Sunni Qatar while Saudi Arabia has taken steps to reconcile with Shi'i leaders in Iraq.

This attempt to pressure Qatar has now backfired and put Saudi and the UAE on the back foot. Doha acquired new trading partners, notably Turkey and Iran, and set up alternate air routes. Despite diplomatic efforts to resolve it, the dispute continues to be stalemated. Most concerning, it has led to the virtual collapse of the GCC, supposedly a shield against external threats and a model for regional cooperation.

Rivalry between the U.A.E. and Turkey

The current power struggle between Turkey and the UAE and their respective leaders, Recep Tayyip Erdogan and Shaikh Mohammad bin Zayed, is "defining the politics of the Middle East at the moment," notes Emile Hokayem of the International Institute for Strategic Studies. They were on opposite sides during the Arab Spring, with Qatar and Turkey backing the Muslim Brotherhood government in Egypt and the UAE and Saudi Arabia working to replace it. The two powerful leaders promote different versions of Islam and in a bid to increase their

power have backed different sides in regional disputes. The UAE regards the Turkey-Qatar alliance as harmful to it, while each has intervened on a different side in Libya's civil war. The UAE is suspicious that Erdogan wants to be regarded as the leader of the Sunni world and revive Ottoman pretentions to control the Gulf.

Israel and the Gulf

Support by Gulf Arabs for the Palestinians has always been strong, at least rhetorically, which ruled out official relations with Israel. The leadership in Israel and the Gulf monarchies, however, have been on the same side on some issues. They both backed President Mubarak of Egypt against the anti-government protests in 2011, for example. The two sides have had discreet links for some time. Israel briefly opened trade offices, now closed, in Doha and Muscat, and their intelligence agencies cooperate against Iran and Islamic terrorism. Because of common hostility to the government in Iran, it has long been suggested that they could form an opposition front.

In surprise announcements in August and September 2020, the UAE and Bahrain normalized relations with Israel, joining Egypt (1979) and Jordan

(1994). Other Arab states may follow suit. This breaches the red line set in the Arab Peace Initiative proposed by Saudi Crown Prince, later King Abdullah in 2002 and endorsed by the Arab League, which specifies that an Israeli withdrawal from occupied territories and formation of a Palestinian state must precede recognition of Israel.

Under the Israel–UAE deal, Israel agreed to "suspend" annexation of territory it occupies on the West Bank. The accord was expected to lead to cooperation in investment, tourism, aviation, technology, agriculture and energy, and permit the opening of embassies and airline flights. (The first direct El Al flight from Tel Aviv to Abu Dhabi was allowed to cross Saudi airspace and arrived on August 31.) Both Israel and the Emirates expect major arms packages (perhaps including F-35 fighter jets) to be approved by the U.S. as a sweetener. The new weapons deal immediately raised concerns in the Senate that it would reduce Israel's ability to maintain military superiority in the Middle East.

The agreements were a valuable endorsement of Israel as a legitimate part of the region. A major prize would be Saudi recognition, but King Salman indicated by his silence on the topic at the UN last September that this would not be forthcoming. His son, the crown prince, is believed to be ready to do so if he accedes the throne.

The role of outside actors

Should the U.S. reduce its footprint, the countries with the most stake in Gulf oil are all in Asia, but can they provide security? The GCC economic policy is to "Look East," but that does not mean they want others to replace U.S. protection. Several candidates that have been widely discussed as possibly taking on a larger role in the Gulf are China, India and Russia. They have all been accused of being "free riders" on the security provided by the U.S.

China

China's relations with Iran and the Gulf Arabs have improved due to their need for each other. China is highly dependent on oil from Iran, which needs the revenue and Chinese help to evade U.S. sanctions. Iran and China have discussed a long-term economic cooperation and security agreement, not yet made public, which reportedly would include major investment in the Iranian economy and perhaps give the Chinese access to the Gulf, in return for an assured flow of discounted Iranian oil for many years.

The Gulf region also plays a role in China's signature foreign policy, the Belt and Road Initiative (BRI). This includes the ports of Gwadar in Pakistan (near the Strait of Hormuz) and Duqm in Oman, as well as investment in Jebel Ali port in Dubai, where in 2018 more than 230 Chinese companies were headquartered. As part of the BRI China has also opened a military facility in Djibouti.

China does not want to have to choose between Iran and the Gulf monarchies. "The Chinese want to do business, they don't want to be fighting wars," according to Ayesha Siddiqa of London's School of Oriental and African Studies. So far China has focused on development aid, not military aid, and does not criticize domestic policies of the Gulf states. Overall an increased Chinese military commitment to protect the Gulf seems unlikely. For China, ties with the U.S. trump those with Iran.

Some caution that Chinese influence in the Gulf may be overestimated. According to Karen Young of the American Enterprise Institute, the Chinese demand for oil will wane over the next 20 years due to a declining birthrate, which will cause a fiscal crisis for Gulf exporters: "What comes after China's Gulf fling is something American policymakers should be thinking about more seriously."

India

India has maintained close ties with the Gulf for millennia, and 8.5 million Indians were working there in 2018, most in Saudi Arabia and the UAE. That year India received $79 billion in remittances. Despite their numbers, these migrant workers avoid involvement in local politics and are not regarded as a political threat in Gulf states. However, ruling dynasties have not been willing to grant them citizenship and their status there is not secure. Now, millions are being sent home due to Covid-19, many without the salary they are due.

India does not appear to want a major security role in the Gulf. It has good relations with Iran and is helping to develop its port at Chabahar, a competitor to the Chinese-supported port of Gwadar nearby in Pakistan. Gulf rulers also have to carefully balance relations with India and Pakistan, which is an Islamic state and contributes soldiers to Gulf military forces.

Russia

Russia is believed to have long desired a warm-water port on the Persian Gulf. It was warned by Britain in 1903 and the U.S. in 1979 to stay out. However, under President Vladimir Putin Russia has acted opportunistically in the region and sought to revive the influence it had there during the Cold War. Since 2015 Russia has inserted itself in the civil war in Syria and become the strongest supporter, along with Iran, of the Bashar al-Assad government. In Libya, Russia, along with the U.A.E. and Egypt, is backing the rebel movement of warlord Khalifa Haftar. So far Russia has not shown much interest in providing security in the Gulf.

Russia and the Gulf Arabs have a common interest in maintaining a high price for oil, although they have differed on how to do so. In September 2016 Russia and Saudi Arabia decided to cooperate to manage oil pricing, with Saudi making large cuts in production. However in March 2020, in the face of falling demand, a Saudi-Russian price war broke out after Russia refused to cut production to maintain prices. Russia subsequently agreed to cuts.

What does all this mean for the U.S.? According to Ambassador Burns, "we ought to be mindful of external competitors such as Russia or China, but not unnerved by them. Vladimir Putin's Russia has played a weak hand well in the region in recent years, yet it remains a weak hand and Russia's successes are dependent upon other peoples' mistakes. China's risk aversion has only been reinforced by watching us lurch through the regional minefield."

The U.S. role in the Gulf: retrospect and prospect

In the wake of the Gulf War of 1990–91 the U.S. emerged as the dominant power in the region. In a throwback to the era of British imperialism, the strongest U.S. bond has been formed with the mini-states of the GCC, where Washington has established a permanent military infrastructure. The U.S. Fifth Fleet is based in Bahrain, and the U.S. has a major army base at Camp Arifjan in Kuwait and key airbase at Al-Udayd in Qatar. Military equipment is prepositioned throughout the region, including Kuwait, Oman and the UAE.

In place of the balance of power strategy the U.S. followed during the Iran-Iraq War, the Clinton administration (1993–2001) introduced a new policy in May 1993, dubbed "Dual Containment," which sought to pressure both Iran and Iraq and exclude them from regional affairs. The U.S. maintained that it accepted the Iranian revolution and harbored no hostility to Islam per se. But it accused Iran of trying to acquire weapons of mass destruction, supporting terrorism and assassinating Iranian dissidents abroad.

Missed opportunities

The U.S. responded positively, if cautiously, to the election of President Khatami in Iran in 1997. In an important policy statement on June 17, 1998, Secretary of State Madeleine Albright urged Iran to join the U.S. in drawing up "a road map leading to normal relations." In March 2000, she went as far as any American official has gone in making a qualified apology for the U.S. role in overthrowing the Mossadegh government during the oil nationalization crisis in 1953.

Although Iran was an irritant, both Presidents Clinton and George W. Bush (2001–09) regarded Iraq as the real regional menace. Ten years after the allied defeat of Iraq defused the immediate threat to Kuwait, the continued presence of Saddam Hussein was impoverishing and demoralizing Iraqi society and compromising the region's long-term security. The U.S. tried to contain Baghdad through four rounds of UN sanctions, by regular inspections and monitoring, and by enforcing no-fly zones in the north and south.

Administration policy on Iraq and Iran was influenced above all by the attacks of September 11, 2001, which highlighted the dangers of terrorism and weapons of mass destruction. Of the 19 Al Qaeda militants who carried out the attacks, 15 were from Saudi Arabia and 2 from the U.A.E. Whereas U.S. policy for a decade after the Gulf War was to maintain the status quo, President George W. Bush opted for major change by waging a preventive war to oust Saddam.

In the aftermath of 9/11, the Bush administration began laying the groundwork for wars in Afghanistan and Iraq. The U.S. worked with Iran to evict the Taliban and install the govern-ment of Hamid Karzai in Afghanistan in December 2001. Any goodwill and cooperation, however, was cut short by President Bush's designation of Iran as part of an "axis of evil" in his January 2002 State of the Union address.

Obama administration

When President Obama took office in January 2009 there was widespread opposition to the wars Bush had started, and a perceived U.S. bias against Muslims. Obama quickly moved to repair the American image abroad. In a major address in Cairo, Egypt, on June 4, 2009, he said he came to seek "a new beginning between the U.S. and Muslims around the world; one based upon mutual interest and mutual respect, and one based upon the truth that America and Islam are not exclusive and need not be in competition...." He said, "America is not—and never will be— at war with Islam. We will, however, relentlessly confront violent extremists who pose a grave threat to our security...." He continued to hold out hope of discussing issues with Iran "without preconditions and on the basis of mutual respect."

By the fall of 2009, however, things had changed, following revelations of a secret uranium enrichment plant under construction at Fordo, near Qom, Iran. In the spring of 2010 the UN imposed a fourth round of sanctions. In the most spectacular and successful project, the U.S. secretly worked with Israel to develop the Stuxnet computer worm, which infected and disabled computers in Iranian nuclear plants between June 2009 and May 2010. By seriously harming these computers, the U.S. achieved by cyberwarfare what would have been the aim of a military strike.

Arab Spring: the U.S. response

Calibrating the U.S. response to the events of the Arab Spring was one of the greatest foreign policy challenges for the Obama administration. Repeatedly, the U.S. was forced to take sides between a popular uprising demanding democracy, and the autocratic rulers it had long worked with who ensured security and "stability." In the case of Egypt, President Mubarak had been a close U.S. ally for 30 years and had kept the peace with Israel. After equivocating at first, eventually the U.S. voiced support for the demonstrators and accepted that Mubarak had to go.

In Saudi Arabia and Bahrain, the U.S. was notably silent and supportive of the ruling family. The Al Saud were greatly angered at the forced departure of Mubarak, and feared that the U.S. would abandon them next. While employing soaring rhetoric, Obama did not outline a coherent policy for the region. He was strongly criticized for ignoring a "red line" he had drawn in August 2012 to forestall Syrian chemical weapons use in the civil war. This was followed by a chemical weapons attack in Ghouta, Syria, on August 21, 2013. Although Congress passed a bill authorizing military intervention, this was not necessary as the Syrian government agreed to a U.S.-Russian proposal to turn over its chemical weapons stockpile for destruction.

In Obama's second term the administration, led by Secretary of State John F. Kerry, focused on Iran and achieved its signal foreign policy achievement. With its partners, in July 2015 the U.S. negotiated the Joint Comprehensive Plan of Action, or JCPOA, which achieved the paramount goal of preventing Iran from acquiring a nuclear

U.S. President Barack Obama during his speech at Cairo University, June 4, 2009. (PHOTOSHOT/NEWSCOM)

weapon in return for an easing of sanctions and normalization of relations. The agreement was widely praised but also had vocal critics—as a presidential candidate Trump disparaged it as "the worst deal ever."

When Obama met with King Salman in Riyadh in April 2016, the atmosphere was tense. When later asked if he regarded the Saudis as friends, he replied, "it's complicated." Obama pressed the king to "share" the neighborhood with Iran— an appeal he did not appreciate. He criticized the kingdom's harsh human rights record, and expressed dissatisfaction with the war in Yemen. Obama also reiterated his view that Saudi Arabia and the GCC states in the future needed to rely less on the U.S. for their security.

U.S. policy in the age of Trump

By the time Donald Trump took office, disillusionment with the U.S. stoked by the invasion of Iraq, U.S. equivocation during the Arab Spring, and the expansion of Iranian influence, was widespread in the Middle East. Trump came to foreign policy with a weak understanding of the region. Personal diplomacy was a hallmark of his approach, with many U.S. experts on the region sidelined. "Where his predecessor hoped to win hearts and minds, Mr. Trump... has embraced the hawks of the region, in Israel and the Persian Gulf, as his chief guides and allies," according to international correspondent David D. Kirkpatrick.

Trump made his first trip abroad to Saudi Arabia in May 2017 and formed a close bond with the Saudi royals. However, his polices were transactional and improvised, and opposed by most European allies. In interviews with Bob Woodward, legendary Washington Post journalist, Trump gloated that he saved the Saudi crown prince, Mohammad bin Salman, after widespread evidence that he had ordered the assassination of a dissident journalist, Jamal Khashoggi, in Istanbul on October 2, 2018. The administration did not retaliate for a major attack Iran car-

ried out on Saudi Arabian oil tanks and pipelines on September 14, 2019, which shocked the Gulf monarchs. It exposed their vulnerability and called into question the U.S. security guarantee that the Saudis had long relied on. The president maintained, however, "That was an attack on Saudi Arabia, that wasn't an attack on us."

The Trump administration maintained it sought to negotiate a "better deal" with Iran, but failed to do so. It reimposed UN sanctions last September 19 under "snapback" provisions of the nuclear deal. The other parties to the deal– Britain, France, Germany, Russia and China–maintained this was illegal since the U.S. had already withdrawn from the accord. Following the election loss, in the remainder of its term the administration sought to impose "a flood of sanctions" not related to the nuclear deal, such as on its ballistic missile program, assistance to terror organizations and human rights abuses. Additional sanctions were placed on Iranian banks which seek to sever Iranian ties to the outside world, and were referred to by Barbara Slavin of the Atlantic Council as "sadism masquerading as foreign policy."

"The harder the administration has pushed to kill off the deal, the more it has found itself isolated and Iran obdurate," according to Vali Nasr, a professor at Johns Hopkins. Nasr maintains that the lesson the Iranians have learned is that they must increase leverage by expanding their nuclear program before resuming negotiations. In June 2020, international nuclear inspectors accused Iran of refusing to allow inspections and sanitizing a suspected nuclear site, as the time for a nuclear "breakout" has now dropped to less than a year.

The U.S. and Iran have repeatedly arrived at the brink of conflict, often due to naval clashes in the Gulf. So far, each time they have stepped back. In the run-up to the U.S. presidential election, other than cyber warfare Iran refrained from any major actions. Iran has yet to retaliate for the U.S. assassination of military hero Qasem Soleymani on January 3, 2020, or the bombing of its

nuclear facility in Natanz (presumably by Israel) on July 2, 2020.

As soon as he assumed office, President Trump, noted for his "bromance" with Prime Minister Benjamin Netanyahu, announced he would focus on the peace process between Israel and the Palestinians. Progress however, has stalled. Designating Jerusalem the capital of Israel, recognizing the Golan Heights as part of Israel, cutting funds for the United Nations Relief and Works Agency (UNRWA), which provides aid to Palestinians in the West Bank and Gaza, and shutting the Palestine Liberation Organization office in Washington, belied a tilt toward Israel that had been avoided by previous administrations. The peace plan ("deal of the century") developed by Jared Kushner, the president's son-in-law, whose economic part was announced in June 2019 and political part in January 2020, was regarded as paving the way to annexation of Palestinian territory. It was reached without Palestinian approval, and by the end of Trump's term it was evident that the U.S. had lost all credibility as an interlocutor.

Trump did score points by brokering normalization agreements (not peace treaties) between Israel and the United Arab Emirates (August 13, 2020) and Israel and Bahrain (September 15, 2020). Dubbed the "Abraham Accords," a new anti-Iranian axis was confirmed and President Trump and Israeli Prime Minister Benjamin Netanyahu scored pre-election wins. In October, Sudan and Israel opened economic ties, although not full diplomatic relations. The Palestinians, on the other hand, felt abandoned by other Arabs. The head of the Palestinian mission to the United Kingdom, Husam Zomlot, told the New York Times that "this agreement is very damaging to the cause of peace because it takes away one of the key incentives for Israel to end its occupation–normalization with the Arab World."

Like Obama, Trump wanted to shift the American focus to Pacific Asia and avoid being hopelessly bogged down in the Middle East. With an eye on the 2020 election, he announced troop withdrawals that would only leave 2,500 U.S. soldiers in Afghanistan and 2,500 in Iraq by the end of the year, which many in the military found alarming. However, even with these cuts there are still 45,000 to 65,000 U.S. troops deployed in the area between Jordan and Oman.

There is much uneasiness about U.S. policy within its own State Department and "American policy is now in free fall," according to Daniel Brumberg, Senior Fellow at the Arab Center in Washington, D.C. By the end of Trump's term, it was clear that the expectations of both the U.S. and the Gulf Arabs have been exaggerated and unrealistic. The priorities of the Gulf states lie in regime security and in persuading the U.S. to take the lead in opposing Iran. Trump, on the other hand, has relied on the Gulf states to keep oil prices low, confront Iran and pressure the Palestinians into making peace with Israel. The U.S. has urged Saudi and the UAE to resolve their quarrel with Qatar to no avail. Like Obama, Trump has also accused the Gulf monarchies of being "free riders" that depend upon the U.S. for their security and have to "pay their way" in return for U.S. defense.

Prospects for a Biden administration

President Biden will assume office with extensive foreign policy experience and familiarity with many world leaders. According to the *New York Times*, "none [of his inner circle] are strident ideologues. Collectively they represent a relatively centrist, establishment worldview." The most pressing issue is reframing policy toward Iran. Biden has indicated that he favors restoring the nuclear ideal and would remove sanctions if Iran returns to compliance with the JCPOA. Tony Blinken, one of his top foreign policy advisers, has said that if this happens the U.S. would seek to negotiate a more comprehensive deal. Any renegotiation will not be easy, as it may take months for the administration to formulate a new policy and

probably nothing can be done before a new Iranian president is elected next summer.

Biden has been critical of Saudi Arabia, and has promised to "make sure America does not check its values at the door to sell arms or buy oil." During the Trump years Congress was repeatedly thwarted in trying to reduce weapons sales to Saudi. It passed a bipartisan resolution to end U.S. involvement in the Yemen War in April 2019, which Trump vetoed. U.S. officials are now concerned about being indicted for war crimes by selling weapons which caused civilian deaths—by late September 2020 an estimated 127,000 people had died in the war.

The GCC states are apprehensive about a Biden presidency and are afraid that once again the U.S. will devote efforts to reintegrate Iran back into the world community. In addition to "appeasing Iran," the U.S. may seek to restrict arms sales, force an end to the war in Yemen, and raise human rights concerns, according to Professor Bernard Haykel of Princeton University. A Biden administration, he concludes, "will mean that America will become a less reliable ally for GCC countries... this could spell greater instability for the region."

Policy options

The challenges to U.S. foreign policy in the Gulf would be substantial regardless of who won the presidency. What policy issues will be on the table for the new administration?

■ **Stay or go in the Gulf?** Although a U.S. withdrawal and retrenchment has been widely discussed, this would not be easy to achieve. The Gulf monarchies want the U.S. there and no other power can replace it. Ambassador Burns admits that the Middle East matters less to the U.S. now than it did 30 years ago, but he maintains that core U.S. interests still remain—access to oil, freedom of navigation, standing by allies such as Israel and some Arab states, and preventing terrorism. He suggests that we "rightsize our ambitions and realign our tools." This means assuring external protection for

the Gulf Arabs, but not supporting their meddling in places like Yemen, Libya, and Sudan.

The Quincy Institute for Responsible Statecraft, a Washington think tank, in July 2020 assessed that "a military drawdown from the Middle East does not amount to an abandonment of the region or an end to American engagement. On the contrary, the U.S. should increase its diplomatic presence and prioritize its role in reducing and/or resolving conflicts as a diplomatic peacemaker."

■ **The future of U.S. bases.** President Trump strove to end the "forever wars" in Iraq and Afghanistan, but this did not lead to a full pullout of U.S. troops. Doing so in the Gulf would reduce U.S. visibility, distancing the monarchs from close association with the Americans and their policies while pleasing Iran. Acts like closing the naval base in Bahrain would allow the U.S. to criticize human rights abuses there. Should the U.S. maintain an adequate number of troops in the region to deter terrorist activity, protect freedom of navigation and protect friendly rulers from Iran? Should bases in the Gulf be an exception to a pullout in other parts of the Middle East? Or would it be better to revert to the kind of "over the horizon" policy the U.S. employed before 1990, stationing troops outside the Gulf in the Indian Ocean area?

■ **Renew the Iran deal?** As vice-president, Biden was involved in negotiating the JCPOA, and as president he favors reactivating it. This is a policy that many foreign policy professionals, and our European allies, would agree with. However, the "obligations" Iran would have to satisfy were not specified by Biden and would be subject to dispute. A major objection raised by critics was that the agreement did not cover other issues of concern to the U.S., such as ballistic missile development, support for terrorism, human rights abuses, anti-Israeli posturing, etc. Supporters of the deal such as Ambassador Wendy Sherman, who led the team negotiating it, acknowledge that it was not perfect, but that it achieved the top U.S. goal, which was to preclude Iran from getting a bomb.

■ **A regional security organization?** Should the U.S. promote the formation of a regional security organization to include all littoral states, notably Iran and Iraq? Perhaps if the Gulf monarchs were responsible for their own security, they would be more accommodating to neighbors who will not go away. This also might facilitate the confidence-building measures that have been sorely missing in the Gulf for decades.

Following the defeat of Iraq in the Gulf War, Secretary of State James A. Baker said in February 1991 that Iran could play a role in future security arrangements in the region. But this did not happen, and no subsequent administration has been willing to recognize an Iranian a role in the Gulf. This idea, nevertheless, has persisted.

In July 2019 Russia proposed holding an international conference on security and cooperation, to be followed by the establishment of a regional security organization that would include Iran and exclude the U.S. This guaranteed its rejection by the Gulf Arabs, who regard the U.S. presence as critical to their protection. China has welcomed but not specifically backed the proposal.

In an address to the UN Security Council last October 20, Robert Malley, president of the International Crisis Group, endorsed the idea of an inclusive regional security dialogue. He warned that tensions in the Gulf could inadvertently trigger a conflict nobody wants, which could result from "miscalculation, misinterpretation or lack of timely communication" as states engage in dangerous brinksmanship.

Iranian President Rouhani floated a "Hormuz Peace Endeavor" at the UN in September 2019, which calls for the withdrawal of U.S. forces and implicitly endorses Iran as the region's hegemon. So far such a proposal has not gotten traction as Gulf Arabs fear it would be dominated by Iran. As long as the current government is in power in

U.S. President Donald Trump joins dancers with swords at a welcome ceremony ahead of a banquet at the Murabba Palace in Riyadh on May 20, 2017. (MANDEL NGAN/AFP/GETTY IMAGES)

Tehran, there is no likelihood it could be accepted by the other side.

Perhaps a formula can be found to satisfy all littoral states. UN Secretary-General Antonio Guterres said last October that he had been trying to get the Gulf states to engage in dialogue, recalling how well the Helsinki Process had worked in Europe to reconcile states after the Cold War. Guterres received strong support from all Security Council members except the U.S.

★ ★ ★

The Middle East will not be the same after the Covid-19 crisis, the crash of oil prices, and American diplomacy under the Trump administration. The sense that the U.S. will no longer protect them may have already pushed the Gulf Arabs into a less combative mode, with the Saudis and Emiratis recalibrating their actions toward Iran since the missile attack.

The future stability of the Gulf monarchies is at stake, and there are clear warning signs that the social contract that has long governed citizen-state relations must be revised. Eventually a post-oil era will arrive in the Gulf (it is already there in Bahrain, Yemen, and Oman), and the leadership must be ready for it. It is unfortunate that the

Gulf states continue to delay in trying to mitigate the "soft" security issues that are most likely to cause disruption in the future.

It appears that by default the U.S. will continue to be involved in the Gulf in a major way, as no other power is ready or able to protect the region, or would be accepted by local states to do so. The U.S. presence will likely be reduced and perhaps revert to an "over the horizon" status. Washington still has interests to protect, which do not necessarily coincide with those of Iran, Iraq, the Gulf monarchies or Israel. Many would disagree with Martin Indyk, veteran diplomat and former U.S. ambassador to Israel, who said the Middle East is simply not worth it anymore, and the U.S. has few vital interests there.

The American people, as reflected by sentiment in Congress, are now experiencing fatigue from trying to do too much in the Gulf for too long, at huge cost and without positive results. What is needed is a reevaluation of U.S. policies, no matter how long they have been in place, in consultation with our allies. The Biden administration has a major job ahead in restoring mutual trust, and formulating policies appropriate for a new era that the American public can support.

discussion questions

1. What interests does the U.S. have in the Persian Gulf? How can they best be realized?

2. If the U.S. reduces its footprint in the Gulf, is it realistic to expect other countries to step up and guarantee Gulf security?

3. What do you believe is the best policy toward U.S. bases in the Gulf? Leave them as is, bring the troops home, or move to an over-the-horizon role? What is the downside for the U.S. in continuing to maintain bases there?

4. What is the significance of the new normalization agreements between Israel and the U.A.E. and Bahrain?

5. What are the reasons that the Gulf is such an insecure region? Why are regional states so suspicious of each other?

6. Many experts believe that canceling the Iran nuclear deal and re-imposition of sanctions was a bad idea. What do you think? Should the U.S. insist on changes if the deal is renegotiated?

suggested readings

Al-Rasheed, Madawi, ed. **Salman's Legacy: The Dilemmas of a New Era in Saudi Arabia.** Oxford: Oxford University Press, 2018. Leading experts explain the transition Saudi Arabia is experiencing under King Salman and his son.

Bajoghli, Narges. **Iran Reframed: Anxieties of Power in the Islamic Republic.** Stanford, CA.: Stanford University Press, 2019. Important insights into the role of the Revolutionary Guard.

Burns, William J. "An End to Magical Thinking in the Middle East." **The Atlantic,** Dec. 8, 2019. Thoughtful overview of U.S. policy in the region and suggestions for the future by former top diplomat. https://www.theatlantic.com/ideas/archive/2019/12/end-magical-thinking-middle-east/602953/

Gause, F. Gregory, III, "Should We Stay or Should We Go? The United States and the Middle East." **Survival,** October/November 2019, pp. 7-24. Concludes the U.S. presence provides important benefits in terns of regional and global influence

Goldberg, Jeffrey. **"The Obama Doctrine."** The Atlantic, April 2016. Famous interview reveals the president's real thoughts on the Middle East.

Indyk, Martin. **"The Middle East Isn't Worth it Anymore."** Wall Street Journal, Jan. 18, 2020. Few vital U.S. interests are at stake in the Middle East.

Kamrava, Mehran. **Troubled Waters: Insecurity in the Persian Gulf.** Ithaca, NY: Cornell University Press, 2018. New study by leading scholar examines the security dilemmas of regional states and why they have led to continuing tensions.

Nasr, Vali. "Iran Among the Ruins: Tehran's Advantage in a Turbulent Middle East." **Foreign Affairs**, vol. 97 no. 2 (March/April 2018): 108-18. Iran is an indispensable component of any sustainable order in the Middle East, and the U.S. cannot roll back its influence.

Potter, Lawrence G., **"The Persian Gulf: Tradition and Transformation."** Headline Series, Nos. 333–34. New York: Foreign Policy Association, 2011. 136 pp. This provides an overview of the recent historical evolution of the Persian Gulf.

Sherman, Wendy R. **"How We Got the Iran Deal and Why We'll Miss It."** Foreign Affairs, September/October 2018. The lead negotiator of the deal explains why it was a mistake to cancel it.

Ulrichsen, Kristian Coates. **Insecure Gulf: The End of Certainty and the Transition to the Post-Oil Era**, Revised Ed. New York: Oxford University Press, 2015. An incisive discussion of the changing politics of the Gulf and the post-oil future.

Don't forget: Ballots start on page 104!!!!

To access web links to these readings, as well as links to global discussion questions, shorter readings and suggested web sites,
GO TO www.fpa.org/great_decisions
and click on the topic under Resources, on the right-hand side of the page.

Brexit: taking stock and looking ahead

by Harris LaTeef

A reveler sits atop a traffic light overlooking the crowd gathered in London's Parliament Square to count down the United Kingdom's January 31, 2020, exit from the European Union. (PHOTO BY HARRIS LATEEF)

The boisterous crowd filling London's Parliament Square overflowed past Downing Street where a countdown was being projected on the Prime Minister's residence. A sea of Union Jacks and St. George's crosses stretched from the base of Churchill's statue down to Trafalgar Square. Over three and a half years after the June 2016 referendum that convulsed British and European politics, the crowd of "Brexiteers" were led in a New Year's Eve style countdown by Brexit Party leader Nigel Farage. With speakers blaring a recording of Big Ben's iconic gongs—the famed bell silenced for maintenance—the crowd cheered as the UK's 47 years in the European project came to an end.

Before the disruption wrought by Covid-19, the outcome of the 2016 UK referendum on European Union membership was the uncontested lead story in modern Britain. Touching on issues of national identity, historic consciousness, gen-

erational divides, and social and economic inequities that have plagued the country for decades, Brexit was a political Rorschach test. Supporters hailed it as the key to reversing decades of declining influence and reclaiming past glory while opponents blamed it for many of the nation's socioeconomic ills.

Questions swirling around the future of the relationship between the UK and the European Union continue to dominate political headlines and create unprecedented uncertainty for the UK's four constituent nations (England Scotland, Northern Ireland, and Wales). Just six years after a failed independence referendum that was billed as "once in a generation," the Scottish public's support for independence

HARRIS LATEEF *is researching a book on Brexit and the European Union. He is a graduate of the University of St. Andrews and the London School of Economics.*

has reached an all-time high of 58%. Across the Irish Sea in Belfast, unresolved issues surrounding the border with the Republic of Ireland threaten to rip open old wounds and reignite sectarian violence.

Brexit has shaped the tenure of three Prime Ministers. Conservative Prime Minister David Cameron's six years in office (2010–16) are defined by his 2015 campaign promise to hold a referendum on EU membership in an effort to appease his most conservative and anti-immigration supporters and by his subsequent failure to convince the British public that staying in the EU was the right course of action. Theresa May's three years as prime minister (2016–19) saw the triggering of Article 50 of the EU Charter and the subsequent failure to achieve a permanent resolution, costing the Conservative party its majority in the House of Commons and paving the way for her onetime Foreign Secretary and longtime Brexit hardliner, Boris Johnson, to succeed her. Johnson, famously unpredictable, breached key provisions of the previously ratified divorce treaty with the EU, and prompted accusations that the UK breached international law.

In order to fully appreciate the impact of the 2016 referendum and its aftermath, it is critical to look at Brexit not only as a political phenomenon but as a reflection of the insecurities of modern British society. First and foremost among them is the nation's pervasive social and economic inequality that has only grown in recent years. Professor Philip Alston, the United Nations Special Rapporteur on Extreme Poverty, concluded in his 2019 report that "much of the glue that has held British society together since the Second World War has been deliberately removed and replaced with a harsh and uncaring ethos."

'A United States of Europe'

Since the days of the Roman Empire, the fate and fortunes of the British Isles have been tied to events and political developments on the European continent. As much as staunch British nationalists hail the independent mentality of their island nation, an outlook which they credit for securing Britain's place in the world, the UK has been inextricably linked to Europe. Think of the Norman Conquest of 1066, the cultural exchanges during the Renaissance, the Napoleonic Wars, the world wars, and the Cold War.

In the shadow of the deadliest conflict in human history, Prime Minister Winston Churchill, speaking at the University of Zürich in 1946, advocated for the creation of a political and economic framework that would prevent conflict among European powers. Churchill argued that the only way "hundreds of millions of toilers [would] be able to regain the simple joys and hopes which make life worth living" was the creation of "a kind of U.S. of Europe." This vision for deeper European political and economic integration first took the form of the European Coal and Steel Community (ECSC) established in 1951.

Although the UK was a founding member of the Council of Europe in 1949, it stood on the sidelines and declined to join the six founding members of the ECSC, as the U.S. had done with the League of Nations two decades earlier. Jean Monnet, one of the architects of the ECSC, said: "I never understood why the British did not join. I came to the conclusion that it must have been because it was the price of victory—the illusion that you could maintain what you had, without change."

Six years later, the British declined to enter into the 1957 Treaty of Rome that established the European Economic Council (EEC). Envious of the postwar French and West German economic recovery, Britain sought admission in 1961 only to have their entry into the organization vetoed by French President Charles de Gaulle (1959–69), who feared British involvement would be a conduit for American influence. After Georges Pompidou (1969–74) succeeded de Gaulle and the threat of a French veto was eliminated, Conservative Prime Minister Edward Heath led Britain into the EEC in 1973.

Further integration

The divisive 2016 Brexit referendum was not the first time the citizens of the UK were asked to decide the nature of their country's relationship with its neighbors on the European continent. Less than three years after joining the EEC, a referendum resulted in 67% of the electorate endorsing continued membership in the organization after both Labour Prime Minister Harold Wilson and Conservative opposition leader Margaret Thatcher campaigned for the "Keep Britain in Europe" movement.

Over the next several decades, political and economic integration of the European continent culminated in the establishment of the European Union in 1993. In addition to Britain, Denmark and Ireland joined the EEC in 1973. EEC membership continued to grow with the admission of Greece in 1981, and Spain and Portugal in 1986.

The 1985 Schengen Agreement eliminated most internal border checks among the original five signatory nations (Belgium, France, West Germany, Luxembourg, and the Netherlands). The Schengen Area created by the treaty would eventually grow to include 26 states with a population of over 400 million people. This marked the first of several major steps toward further integration among European nations in which the UK declined to participate. Although European citizens would enjoy the right to live and work in the UK, as British citizens were allowed to do in the other EU member states, entry immigration

! Before you read, download the companion **Glossary** that includes definitions, a guide to acronyms and abbreviations used in the article, and other material. Go to **www. fpa.org/great_decisions** and select a topic in the Resources section. (Top right)

ARCTIC OCEAN

Queen Elizabeth Islands

Ellesmere Island

GREENLAND (DENMARK)

Beaufort Sea

Victoria Island

Baffin Bay

Baffin Island

Davis Strait

Denmark Strait

Reykjav

ARCTIC CIRCLE (66°33')

ALASKA (U.S.)

Great Bear Lake

Anchorage

Gulf of Alaska

Juneau

Aleutian Islands

Great Slave Lake

Churchill

Hudson Bay

Labrador Sea

CANADA

NORTH AMERICA

Lake Winnipeg

Great Lakes

NORTH ATLANTIC OCEAN

NORTH PACIFIC OCEAN

Vancouver

Seattle

UNITED STATES

Montréal

Québec

Ottawa

Toronto

New York

AZORES (PORTUGAL)

Denver

Chicago

St. Louis

Washington, D.C.

San Francisco

Los Angeles

Dallas

Atlanta

BERMUDA (U.K.)

CANARY ISLANDS (SPAIN)

WESTERN SAH (ADMINISTE BY MOROC

Monterrey

Miami

Nassau

THE BAHAMAS

TROPIC OF CANCER (23°27')

Honolulu

HAWAII (U.S.)

Gulf of Mexico

MEXICO

Havana

CUBA

VIRGIN ISLS. (U.S.)

BRITISH VIRGIN ISLS. (U.K.)

ANGUILLA (U.K.)

Nouakchott

ATOLL

Mexico City

Veracruz

HAITI

Port-au-Prince

DOMINICAN REPUBLIC

ST. KITTS AND NEVIS

ANTIGUA AND BARBUDA

GUADELOUPE (FR.)

CAPE VERDE

Dakar

Praia

ALMYRA ATOLL (U.S.)

GUATEMALA

Belmopan

BELIZE

JAMAICA

Kingston

Santo Domingo

PUERTO RICO (U.S.)

DOMINICA

MARTINIQUE (FR.)

THE GAMBIA

Banjul

Bissau

GUINEA-BISSAU

Conak

Freeto

Guatemala City

Guatemala

HONDURAS

Caribbean Sea

MONTSERRAT (U.K.)

ST. LUCIA

BARBADOS

San Salvador

Tegucigalpa

NICARAGUA

ARUBA (NETH.)

ST. VINCENT AND THE GRENADINES

GRENADA

SIERRA M

EL SALVADOR

Managua

NETHERLANDS ANTILLES (NETH.)

Port-of-Spain

TRINIDAD AND TOBAGO

KIRITIMATI (CHRISTMAS ISLAND)

COSTA RICA

San José

Panama

PANAMA

Caracas

VENEZUELA

Georgetown

Paramaribo

Cayenne

ISLAND U.S.)

Medellín

Bogotá

GUYANA

SURINAME

FRENCH GUIANA (FR.)

EQUATOR

Cali

COLOMBIA

Quito

ECUADOR

GALAPAGOS ISLANDS (ECUADOR)

Iquitos

Manaus

Belém

MARQUESAS ISLAND (FR. POLYNESIA)

PERU

BRAZIL

Recife

FRENCH POLYNESIA (FRANCE)

Lima

SOUTH AMERICA

TUAMOTU ARCHIPELAGO (FR. POLYNESIA)

Cusco

La Paz

BOLIVIA

Brasília

SOCIETY ISLANDS (FR. POLYNESIA)

Sucre

Rio de Janeiro

TROPIC OF CAPRICORN (23°27')

TUBUAI ISLANDS (FR. POLYNESIA)

PITCAIRN ISLANDS (U.K.)

EASTER ISLAND (CHILE)

ISLA SALA Y GÓMEZ (CHILE)

Antofagasta

PARAGUAY

Asunción

São Paulo

SOUTH

ATLANTIC OCEAN

JUAN FERNÁNDEZ ISLANDS (CHILE)

CHILE

Santiago

URUGUAY

Buenos Aires

La Plata

Montevideo

ARGENTINA

SOUTH PACIFIC OCEAN

Bahía Blanca

FALKLAND ISLANDS (ADMINISTERED BY U.K. CLAIMED BY ARGENTINA)

SOUTH GEORGIA AND THE SOUTH SANDWICH ISLANDS (ADMINISTERED BY U.K. CLAIMED BY ARGENTINA)

Punta Arenas

Stanley

Scotia Sea

Drake Passage

SOUTH ORKNEY ISLANDS (B.A.T.)

SOUTHERN OCEAN

Amundsen Sea

Bellingshausen Sea

Weddell Sea

Ross Sea

Ross Ice Shelf

Ronne Ice Shelf

Legend:

VENEZUELA Independent state

GUADELOUPE (FRANCE) Dependent territory

Ottawa ✸ Capital

Bangalore ● Major city

Scale 1:35,000,000

Robinson Projection with standard parallels 38°N and 38°S
Source: CIA World Factbook

For over 100 years, the Foreign Policy Association has served as a catalyst for developing awareness, understanding and informed opinions on U.S. foreign policy and global issues. From mass media to grassroots organizations, the FPA promotes active civic participation in the U.S. foreign policy process, by engaging with the global public.

heads of state and pre-eminent experts on foreign affairs. Founded in 1954, the FPA's flagship program Great Decisions is the largest nonpartisan public education program in the world, and provides the American public with the tools to become informed members of the global community.

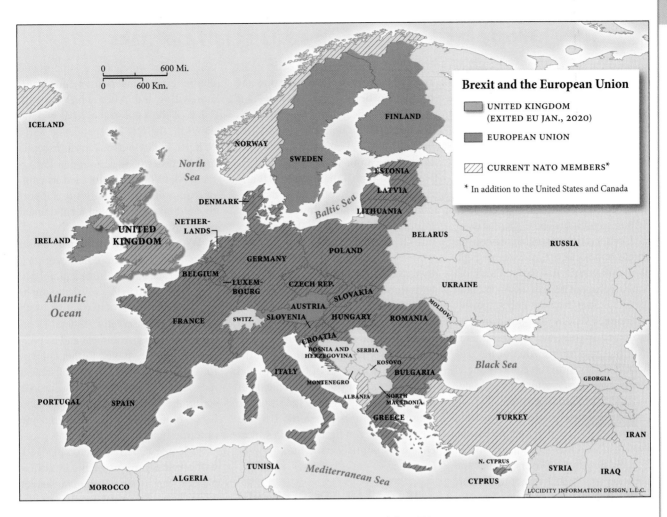

Brexit and the European Union

- UNITED KINGDOM (EXITED EU JAN., 2020)
- EUROPEAN UNION
- CURRENT NATO MEMBERS*

* In addition to the United States and Canada

LUCIDITY INFORMATION DESIGN, L.L.C.

controls were maintained throughout Britain's EU membership.

The 1987 Single European Act passed by the European Parliament would lay the groundwork for the EEC to work toward the creation of a single economic market by 1992—a goal supported by Margaret Thatcher's Conservative government. Thatcher's support for a "free-trade" vision for Europe was unequivocal. Speaking to a group of British business leaders in 1988, Thatcher laid out her vision for the common market that her party would eventually repudiate during the Brexit debate:

"Just think for a moment what a prospect that is. A single market without barriers—visible or invisible—giving you direct and unhindered access to the purchasing power of over 300 million of the world's wealthiest and most prosperous people. Bigger than Japan. Bigger than the U.S. On your doorstep. And with the Channel Tunnel to give you direct access to it.

It's not a dream. It's not a vision. It's not some bureaucrat's plan. It's for real. And it's only five years away."

In 1992, this vision became a reality with the signing of the Maastricht Treaty, which established the European Union with an economic and monetary union at its core and a new focus on greater cooperation among members in the realms of foreign policy, national security, and home affairs. With the addition of Sweden, Austria, and Finland two years later, the EU grew to cover nearly all of Western Europe.

Aside from the common economic market and the creation of the European Union, the Maastricht Treaty began the process that would result in the creation of a common European currency—the Euro. After a decade of preparation, the Euro was first launched as a non-physical currency (e.g. for bank transfers, travelers' checks, etc.) in January 1999 and then as coins and banknotes three years later, replacing the currencies of

12 countries in the largest cash change-over in history.

The introduction of the Euro was another example of where the UK chose not to continue down the path of further economic and political integration with Europe. As part of the Maastricht Treaty, the UK secured an opt-out from joining the Eurozone and, along with Denmark, became one of two EU countries that had not adopted the Euro nor were legally bound to eventually do so.

Following a landslide victory in 1997, the early premiership of Labour Prime Minister Tony Blair established a period of warm relations between the EU and the UK with Britain joining the EU's social chapter and delivering some of the social protections long coveted by the political left. The 2009 Euro crisis, the 2015 migrant crisis, and the rise of far-right parties campaigning on nativist and anti-immigration platforms, Euroscepticism began to proliferate on the fringes of British politics.

Europe at the center of British politics

Since the initial debate surrounding the UK's involvement in the ECSC, Britain's relationship with Europe has played a central role in domestic politics. The internal party debate surrounding the 1975 EEC referendum firmly established the issue of Britain's relationship with Europe as a wedge issue among the country's major political parties. Although supportive of Britain's continued EEC membership, the Conservatives encountered considerable opposition from extreme right elements within the party. The most strenuous opposition to membership in the EEC came from the Labour party's left wing. The 1983 Labour manifesto promised withdrawal from the EEC after the pro-Europe wing of the party split off to form the centrist Social Democratic Party, which would later become the Liberal Democrats.

With Europe featured as a topic of common internal debate across the British political spectrum, historian Vernon Bogdanor observed that the question of whether or not to support further political and economic integration with Europe would become the true dividing line in British politics:

"Some might argue that the fundamental conflict in post-War British politics is not so much between left and right as between those who believe that Britain's future lies with Europe and those who believe it does not. This profound political divide has cut across the parties and it unites some very odd bedfellows: if you look at the pro-European camp, you have to include Harold Macmillan, Edward Heath, Roy Jenkins, and Tony Blair; the anti-Europeans are Enoch Powell, Michael Foot, and Margaret Thatcher—very odd alignments."

In December 2011, as EU leaders tried to tackle the bloc's economic problems through a treaty setting new budget rules, Conservative Prime Minister David Cameron demanded exemptions for the UK and then vetoed the pact entirely. This controversial move set the UK adrift in the eyes of his critics and delighted the Eurosceptic elements of his party. By highlighting the strains in the relationship between the UK and the EU, Cameron thrust Britain's most poisonous political issue back on center stage.

The road to a referendum

By the time the local and European parliament elections were held in May 2014, far-right parties that capitalized on the economic and social anxieties associated with immigration and ra-

cial tensions were gaining support and challenging Conservative candidates across England. After achieving only 3.1% of the vote in the 2010 general election, the UK Independence Party (UKIP), led by outspoken Eurosceptic and Member of the European Parliament Nigel Farage, refocused its campaigning efforts on building support by fielding candidates in local council elections across the country.

With a majority of their electoral gains fueled by blue-collar workers, UKIP's focus would turn squarely to building support in this key demographic. Widespread dissatisfaction with Cameron's Conservative-Liberal Democrat coalition government and its policies of austerity fueled further support for UKIP's populist, anti-establishment message. With UKIP making inroads across the country, Cameron needed to find a solution to stop the hemorrhaging of formerly loyal Tory voters.

In January 2013, Cameron pledged, without the support of his coalition partner, the Liberal Democrat leader Nick Clegg, that a referendum on the UK's membership in the European Union would be held should the Conservatives secure a majority in the 2015 general election. Cameron laid out his plans to renegotiate the nation's relationship with the EU and then give people the "simple choice" between accepting the new terms or leaving altogether. He argued that the longer the referendum was delayed, the more likely the British people would elect to leave the pact:

"Simply asking the British people to carry on accepting a European settlement over which they have had little choice is a path to ensuring that when the question is finally put—and at some stage it will have to be—it is much more likely that the British people will reject the EU. That is why I am in favour of a referendum. I believe in confronting this issue - shaping it, leading the debate. Not simply hoping a difficult situation will go away."

Slammed by the Labour leader Ed Miliband for kowtowing to UKIP and

Anti-Euro protester holds his placard aloft outside the British Houses of Parliament June 9, 2003, (SCOTT BARBOUR/GETTY IMAGES)

the fringe elements of his own party, Cameron set his country down the path toward the 2016 referendum. The immediate effect of announcing his referendum pledge was a surge of support for Eurosceptic parties whose dream of leaving the EU, the central tenant of their political existence, was within reach for the first time in decades.

Riding a growing wave of populist resentment and anti-immigrant fervor, the 2014 local elections saw UKIP win 163 seats in local councils across the country, up from just 35. Meanwhile, the party received the greatest number of votes (27.5%) in the European Parliament elections of any British party, earning the party 24 seats. This result, the first time since 1906 that a party other than the Conservatives or Labour had won the most votes in a national election, placed UKIP and Farage firmly in the political spotlight.

As the UK approached the 2015 general election, polling data showed an increase of support for UKIP after both the Conservatives and Labour lost supporters to the Eurosceptic cause. However, the results of the election would surprise pollsters and the prime minister himself. The Conservatives not only exceeded expectations, thanks largely to a collapse in support for Scottish Labour, the rise of the Scottish National Party (SNP), and the loss of 49 Liberal Democrat seats, Cameron was able to achieve a slim majority in the House of Commons. Although UKIP able to take only one seat in the Commons, the 12.6% of the vote the party received confirmed a growing wave of populist support.

Cameron believed he was bound to deliver on the campaign promise that may very well have allowed him to retain his position, renegotiate the British relationship with the EU and then put the choice to leave or remain to the public. Confiding to European Council president Donald Tusk after his surprise election victory, Cameron admitted that he never thought he would be in a position where he had to honor his campaign promise on an EU referendum. Speaking to the BBC, Tusk recalled his conversation in the wake of the election:

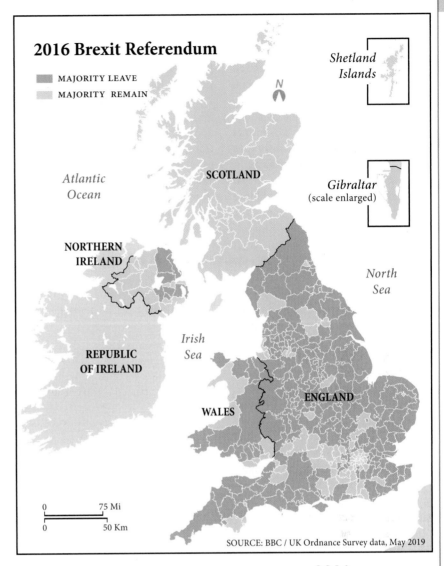

2016 Brexit Referendum

- ■ MAJORITY LEAVE
- ▨ MAJORITY REMAIN

Atlantic Ocean

SCOTLAND

NORTHERN IRELAND

REPUBLIC OF IRELAND

Irish Sea

WALES

ENGLAND

North Sea

Shetland Islands

Gibraltar (scale enlarged)

N

| 0 | 75 Mi |
| 0 | 50 Km |

SOURCE: BBC / UK Ordnance Survey data, May 2019

"I asked David Cameron, 'Why did you decide on this referendum, this—it's so dangerous, so even stupid, you know,' and, he told me—and I was really amazed and even shocked—that the only reason was his own party. [He told me] he felt really safe, because he thought at the same time that there's no risk of a referendum, because his coalition partner, the Liberal [Democrats], would block this idea of a referendum. But then, surprisingly, he won and there was no coalition partner. So paradoxically David Cameron became the real victim of his own victory."

With no coalition partner to provide Cameron the excuse to restrain the Eurosceptic elements of his party, the most poisonous subject in British politics was now unavoidable.

2016

The plans for the membership referendum were announced in the Queen's Speech three weeks after the election. The European Union Referendum Act (EURA) 2015 went before the House of Commons the next day. The bill passed 544 to 53, approving the holding of a referendum, with only the SNP voting against. Notably, the law did not contain any requirement for the British government to implement the referendum's results. After the resignation of Labour leader Ed Miliband, in the wake of his party's under performance in the election, acting leader Harriet Harman committed her party to supporting the referendum plans, eliminating any potential resistance.

What followed next was a series of missteps and miscalculations by the ostensibly pro-European prime minister. Despite objections from the Scottish, Northern Irish, and Welsh devolved governments, Cameron announced in February 2016 that the referendum would be held on June 23, launching the campaigning season with a deadline set squarely in the middle of summer holidays when many Britons would be out of the country. Unlike in the Scottish independence referendum held two years earlier, Cameron and the House of Commons did not approve enfranchising 16- and 17-year-old citizens, who would have to live the longest with the consequences of the referendum. Cameron lost the debate over the wording of the referendum question itself. Writing in his largely repentant and apologetic memoir, *For the Record*, Cameron said that his pro-European campaign had lost "the positive word 'Yes'...and 'Leave' sounded dynamic in contrast to 'Remain.'"

At the launch of the campaigns, and in a rare exception to the concept of Cabinet collective responsibility, Cameron allowed his ministers to campaign on either side of the "Leave" and "Remain" argument, diluting his own chances of success. When his chancellor of the Exchequer, George Osborne, urged Cameron to campaign aggressively against Leave leaders Boris Johnson and Michael Gove, Cameron feared such "'blue on blue' attacks

Scottish Independence

The future relationship between the UK and the European Union is not the only unanswered question posed by Brexit. The end of the UK's membership in the European Union has stirred up the age-old question of Scotland's status in the UK.

Ever since the 1707 Acts of Union, under which England and Scotland joined to create the Kingdom of Great Britain, Scottish nationalists have called for the return of Scottish sovereignty. Although linked by centuries of cultural and historical ties, Scotland's and England's national and international outlooks have often clashed. In recent years, Scotland's unique political culture has further diverged from that of the rest of the UK. With a diaspora population of over 30 million, historian Sir Tom Devine observed that Scotland's unique view of the European Union can be attributed to the Scottish people's outward-looking orientation as a nation of emigrants: "Scotland has never suffered over the past twenty to thirty years the kind of inward-looking form of nationalism that England has."

After decades of advocacy, a 1997 referendum reestablished the long dormant Scottish Parliament. Authority over Scottish domestic affairs—including the economy, education, health, justice, housing, environment, transport and taxation—was devolved to Edinburgh, giving the Scottish people direct control over many aspects of their lives and society for the first time in nearly three centuries.

The Scottish National Party (SNP)—the driving force behind the independence movement—made steady gains in both the newly formed parliament and in Scotland's delegation to the UK Parliament in Westminster. The SNP has been the majority party or in a controlling coalition in the Scottish Parliament for the past fourteen years.

After running on a platform that included pledging to hold a referendum on independence, the SNP earned the most seats in the 2007 Scottish Parliament elections and set the nation on the path toward a vote on self-determination. Although national identity and democratic ideals weighed heavily in the debate surrounding the 2014 independence referendum, the economy and Scotland's future relationships with the UK and Europe were dispositive.

A 2014 Financial Times report painted a rosy picture for Scotland's independent economic future:

"If its geographic share of UK oil and gas output is taken into account, Scotland's GDP per head is bigger than that of France. Even excluding the North Sea's hydrocarbon bounty, per capita GDP is higher than that of Italy. Oil, whisky and a broad range of manufactured goods mean an independent Scotland would be one of the world's top 35 exporters."

As for the European question, while the SNP supported an independent Scotland becoming a full member state of the European Union, debate raged over whether a newly independent Scottish state would be required to undergo the readmission process and possibly face a Spanish veto due to concern about the ramifications for Spain's own separatist movements. Although the European Commission offered to provide an official opinion on the matter, UK ministers declined to pursue it so as not to bolster the independence cause.

In a vote that received the highest turnout in over a century, Scottish voters declined to go it alone and rejected independence 55.3% to 44.7%—putatively answering the "once in a generation question." Under the leadership of First Minister Nicola Sturgeon, who took the party's reins after the referendum defeat, the SNP however has made gains in both the Scottish Parliament and in Scotland's delegation to Westminster.

Calls for a second independence referendum were heard almost immediately after the Brexit referendum, which saw 62% of Scots vote to remain in the EU. Describing the result as "democratically unacceptable," First Minister Sturgeon asserted that Scotland's support for remaining in the EU was reflective of "how we see our place in the world."

The debate over Scotland's future relationship with the EU had been turned on its head. The Unionist argument that continued membership in the UK would guarantee Scotland's future in Europe was nullified with independence being the clear option for retaining Scottish

would just make the campaign look like a Conservative spat."

Campaigning was aggressive and, as subsequent investigations would reveal, featured breaches of UK electoral law, influence from foreign governments—most notably Russia—and the illegal use of voters' personal information, subsequently exposed during the Cambridge Analytica scandal.

The "Leave.EU" campaign group, founded by businessman and UKIP donor Arron Banks, featured race-baiting and xenophobic advertisements, including faked videos of migrants attacking people in the UK and posters claiming that Turkish EU admission would result in a flood of 75 million new immigrants. The campaign faced near universal condemnation after the publication of a poster advertisement featuring German Chancellor Angela Merkel and the caption: "We didn't win two World Wars to be pushed around by a Kraut."

Although many of the main Eurosceptics operated within the bounds of the traditional British political spectrum and framed their arguments around the need for economic flexibility and deregulation, the public campaigns supporting leaving the EU focused heavily on the issue of immigration. Since the days of mass migration from Britain's former colonial dominions, immigrants have faced xenophobic discrimination in the UK

EU membership. Despite the different political circumstances generated by Brexit, Theresa May and Boris Johnson pointed to the 2014 independence referendum outcome as definitive and rejected calls to allow a second vote.

The continued refusal to permit the Scots to determine their future in the UK and Europe has bolstered support for independence. In the December 2019 general election that gave Boris Johnson a historic majority in the House of Commons, the SNP emerged as the third-largest party and won 48 of 59 of Scotland's seats in the UK Parliament—a gain of 13.

Another factor in the debate over Scottish independence is the UK government response to the Covid-19 pandemic, which saw the country suffer the highest death toll in Europe. In contrast, the Scottish government's local response—and the leadership and tone set by Sturgeon—earned praise. Sir John Curtice of Strathclyde University wrote that "there's an enormous difference in public perception of how well the Scottish and the UK government have been handling [the pandemic]: 70-75% think Nicola Sturgeon is doing brilliantly, it's almost the opposite for Boris [Johnson.]"

The Scottish public's aversion to risk—key to the Unionist cause in 2014—has been drastically affected by the Covid-19 pandemic; the UK's pandemic response has been far from a winning strategy. The University of Edinburgh's Ailsa Henderson writes that "those with a greater appetite for risk were more likely to vote yes in

Scottish National Party (SNP) leader and Scotland's First Minister Nicola Sturgeon sets out the case for a second referendum on Scottish independence during a statement at Bute House on December 19, 2019, in Edinburgh, Scotland. (NEIL HANNA/WPA POOL/GETTY IMAGES)

2014, but if the status quo doesn't seem to be much of a safe haven, that risk argument can't be run in a similar way."

On the economic front, frictionless access to the EU market is of significant benefit to Scottish exports. Thomas Sampson of the London School of Economics calculates that the economic cost to the UK of leaving the EU without a comprehensive trade deal is two or three times greater, over the long term, than the financial impact of the pandemic.

By the same token, London subsidizes Edinburgh to the tune of $13 billion per annum. Scotland's budget deficit could balloon from a current deficit of 8.6% of GDP to 19% of GDP

post pandemic according to the Office for Budget Responsibility. In the balance are such popular Scottish social subsidies as free prescriptions and free personal care for the elderly, as well as tuition-free higher education.

In October 2020, an Ipsos Mori poll found that Scottish support for independence had reached an all-time high of 58% while even more—64%—agreed that the UK government should allow another referendum to be held if the SNP again secures a majority in the Scottish Parliament. With the next elections for the Scottish Parliament set for May 2021, the Scottish people may be asked once more to make a "once in a generation decision."

and increasingly restrictive government policies.

Racism remains a problematic issue in modern British society. A June 2020 YouGov survey of black, Asian, and minority ethnic (BAME) Britons reveals the extent to which prejudice and discrimination are encountered by minorities:

"Three in four BAME respondents (75%) think it is racist to dislike people who live in the UK and speak other languages in public, compared to just 58% of Britons in general. 74% have had someone ask "where you're really from?" and 64% have had a racial slur directed at them. Some 65% have witnessed someone telling a joke featuring a racial stereotype about their own race. More than half (52%) have been on the receiving end of assumptions based on race, 44% have experienced an impact on their career and 27% say their race impeded access to services or funding."

It is therefore unsurprising that Leave campaigners would rely on racist or xenophobic political arguments in order to motivate the British public to reject EU membership, which they blamed for increased immigration. An infamous example of this was UKIP leader Nigel Farage's "breaking point" poster campaign which feature an image of immigrants at the Croatian-Slovenian border and was described as a "blatant attempt to incite racial hatred." Indeed, the number of racially motivated hate crimes has increased in the UK every year since 2013.

Many of the nuanced economic arguments for and against continued British membership in the UK were often reduced to brief and often misleading sound bites hurled by "Remainers" and "Leavers" alike. Perhaps the most infamous example was the official Leave campaign's touring bus emblazoned with: "We send the EU £350 million a week, let's fund our NHS [National Health Service] instead." This assertion, which did not factor in the 1984 rebate negotiated by Margaret Thatcher nor the disbursements that flow into the UK from the EU, was described as "misleading" by the UK Statistics Authority and "absurd" by the Institute for Fiscal Studies. However, as is the case with many misleading or false statements in modern politics, it was repeated so widely and frequently by Leave politicians that it was often the only statistic average Brexit supporters referenced when describing the economic relationship of the UK and the European Union.

Lastly, pervasive income inequality that had remained largely static since the turn of the millennium and a series of austerity cuts to the British social safety net made the claims of Leave campaigners—that money being sent to the EU could be reinvested domestically—appealing to those facing financial hardship. The UK has one of the highest Gini index income inequality scores in the western world with the gap between rich and poor drastically expanding in the late 1970s and early 1980s and remaining relatively unchanged since the early 1990s.

The results and their aftermath

Of the many eye-catching headlines published after the June 23 referendum, *The Washington Post's* stood out: "The British are frantically Googling what the EU is, hours after voting to leave it."

"The whole world is reeling after a milestone referendum in Britain to leave the European Union.... [A]lthough leaders of the campaign to exit Europe are crowing over their victory,

British Prime Minister Theresa May signs the official letter to European Council President Donald Tusk invoking Article 50 and the UK's intention to leave the EU on March 28, 2017. (PRIME MINISTRY OF THE UNITED KINGDOM / HANDOUT /ANADOLU AGENCY/ GETTY IMAGES)

it seems many Britons may not even know what they had actually voted for.

Google reported sharp upticks in searches not only related to the ballot measure but also about basic questions concerning the implications of the vote. At about 1 a.m. Eastern time, about eight hours after the polls closed, Google reported that searches for "what happens if we leave the EU" had more than tripled."

Members of the British online public were not the only ones left reeling the morning after the surprise 51.8% to 48.1% victory. After six years in 10 Downing Street, David Cameron announced his resignation.

Calls for a second referendum on Scottish independence were heard almost immediately after it became clear that every Scottish constituency had voted to retain EU membership, with 62% of Scots voting Remain. Those who support the creation of a unified Ireland were boosted by the results in Northern Ireland where 55.8% voted against leaving the European bloc and the border with the Republic remains largely invisible thanks to the common market. England and Wales, home to 98% of those who voted for UKIP in 2015, provided 92% of Leave votes.

Over the course of the next year, former Home Secretary Theresa May would become prime minister and, in March 2017, formally trigger the "Article 50" clause of the European Union's Lisbon Treaty, starting the countdown on the two-year negotiation deadline in March 2017. In early June, May lost her majority in a snap general election she herself had called but held onto power in a hung parliament by entering into a coalition with Northern Ireland's Democratic Unionist Party (DUP), the only major political group to oppose the 1998 Good Friday Agreement which ended most of the political violence in Norther Ireland that had been ongoing since the 1960s. Negotiations with Brussels sputtered on for the better part of two years, until

September 2018 when the EU rejected May's "Chequers plan" which called for the creation of a UK-EU free trade area. By March 2019, her revised plan had been voted down by the House of Commons three times in spite of her offer to resign in exchange for her deal to be approved.

Despite surviving two votes of no confidence—one internal to the Conservative party and another in the Commons proposed by Labour leader Jeremy Corbyn—by late May, it was increasingly evident that the prime minister had no clear path forward with her vision for Brexit. She announced her resignation effective June 7, triggering a six-week leadership contest. Former mayor of London, foreign secretary, and the most high-profile Leave campaigner, Boris Johnson, succeeded May as Prime Minister in July 2019.

After two extensions to the Article 50 negotiation deadline, Johnson announced a revised Brexit deal in October 2019 that included provisions for maintaining frictionless trade and travel on the island of Ireland by implementing custom checks between Northern Ireland and the rest of the UK, averting the creation of a hard border. Following a third extension to the deadline forced by a parliamentary vote, Johnson called a general election to be held in December in order to obtain a mandate to proceed with his vision of Brexit. Under the motto of "Get Brexit Done," Johnson campaigned vigorously against labor leader Jeremy Corbyn, the most unpopular opposition leader since Ipsos MORI began polling 45 years ago.

When the exit poll was announced on election night on December 12, it was clear that Johnson had successfully secured a landslide 80-seat majority against the Labour Party, which had had its worst electoral showing since 1935. The SNP had secured 48 of 59 Scottish seats in Westminster, virtually wiping Scottish Labour off the political map in their worst showing in Scotland since 1910. With a clear political mandate and no meaningful opposition to stand in his way, Johnson's Conservative majority passed the European Union (Withdrawal Agreement) Act

Britain's Prime Minister and Conservative party leader Boris Johnson speaks during a general election campaign rally in East London on December 11, 2019. (BEN STANSALL/AFP/ GETTY IMAGES)

on January 23. Nine days later, the UK left the EU and entered the 11-month transition period that keeps the county in the EU customs union and single market until the end of 2020. Unless an EU-UK trade deal is agreed upon before December 31, 2020, British trade with Europe—49% of all UK trade— will be subject to WTO standard tariffs.

The fallout

Geopolitically, the UK continues to play an important role on the world stage. In the aftermath of the Second World War, the UK laid claim to a permanent seat on the United Nations Security Council. The British Commonwealth, made up of the UK and 53 former colonies, comprises 2.4 billion people—nearly a third of the global population. Yet the UK has lost tremendous power in a relatively short period of time. In the span of one monarch's reign, albeit a long one, no fewer than 50 colonies, protectorates, and mandates gained independence from the British crown.

The UK's historic global preeminence and power can only be approximated today by exercising power with others. Margaret Thatcher set out this argument in the context of the Falklands War while expressing her reservations about further European integration, a paradoxical view held by many in British conservative politics:

"The Falklands War had demonstrated to me how valuable it would be if all Community members were prepared to commit themselves to supporting a single member in difficulties.... Foreign policy co-operation within the European Community would help strengthen the West, as long as good relations with the U.S. remained paramount.

What I did not want to do, however, was to have a new treaty grafted onto the Treaty of Rome. I believe that we could achieve both closer political co-operation—as well as make progress toward a Single Market—without such a treaty; and all my instincts warned me of what federalist fantasies might appear if we opened this Pandora's box."

Brexit—the voluntary surrender of the UK's seat in the forum that decides the future of Europe—will accelerate Britain's declining global geopolitical influence. Former UK Minister of State for Europe Denis MacShane states:

"Britain has had a seat, a vote, and a voice in all the big-ticket decisions on Europe's direction of travel,...in every world capital, at the WTO, and in other international bodies, British diplomats would meet with fellow EU colleagues and try to push an agenda close to desired British interests. All this comes to a shuddering stop with Brexit.

Overnight, Britain will become an international policy player that has

Workers package imported tomatoes from Spain at the Fruit Terminal at the Port of Southampton, UK, on Sept. 30, 2020. (LUKE MACGREGOR/BLOOMBERG/GETTY IMAGES)

to cool its heels in the waiting rooms of EU deciders, from the European Council to the European Commission to the European External Action Service. There will be no point in anyone in Washington, Beijing, New Delhi, Lagos, or Brasília asking the British ambassador what Europe is going to do or say on key global issues, because the answer can only be 'Search me!'"

Critical sectors of the UK economy will be adversely impacted by a no-deal Brexit. The UK farming sector, for example, exports about two thirds of its goods to the EU. Conversely, 73% of UK agri-food imports come from the EU. Half of UK financial assets are held by non-UK banks, with 45% of the UK's financial exports currently going to the EU.

Brexit also presents a serious challenge to London's status as an international financial center. The London Interbank Offered Rate (LIBOR) is a globally accepted key benchmark interest rate used in many financial transactions, including mortgage loans originated in the U.S.. "The City," London's equivalent to Wall Street, has been the hub for American financial institutions doing business in Europe. American banks invested heavily in their London operations as the City became the gateway

to Europe's growing capital markets as securities trading was deregulated.

In her book, *The Brussels Effect: How the European Union Rules the World*, Anu Bradford of Columbia Law School describes key policy areas that illustrate the interconnectedness of the UK and EU economies and the incentives that this creates for UK companies and the UK government to follow European regulations even after Brexit. From financial regulations to data protection to chemical safety regulation, Bradford concludes that the UK economy will be materially influenced by Brussels long after leaving the EU:

"In reality, the UK's departure from the EU will not liberate the country from the EU's regulatory leash, despite the belief and campaign rhetoric of Leave campaigners. Instead, the UK may soon find itself in the position of being bound by EU regulations without any ability to influence the content of those regulations. As a result, with Brexit, the UK will be ceding its role as a rule maker in return for becoming a voiceless rule taker in an even more tightly regulated Europe."

There are growing signs of a shift of bankers and assets from the City to Dublin, Frankfurt, and Paris. In a reshaping of a European financial sector historically dominated by UK capital,

Ernst & Young estimates that $1.5 trillion in bank assets are being offshored from London to European cities and that 7,500 financial services jobs have been shifted from the UK to the European Union since 2016. According to an industry survey, London was displaced by New York as the world's preeminent financial center in 2019.

From January 1, 2021, irrespective of the outcome of negotiations between the UK and the EU, the UK's status will change to that of a third country operating outside the European single market. For financial services, an unwelcome change will be the end to "passporting," the regime that enables financial firms regulated in the UK to sell their products and services throughout the EU. After January 1, financial institutions will be required to service EU clients from inside the 27-country bloc.

The future of the EU

While discussions of Brexit tend to focus on the UK, Brexit is also about the future of the EU. With the departure of the UK, the EU has lost a partner of enormous standing. Beyond its size (the third largest EU member by population), the UK is a nuclear power with significant diplomatic and intelligence assets. Paul Sheard, Senior Fellow at Harvard's Kennedy School, writes:

"For one thing, the UK leaving is a seismic event for the EU: the UK is the second largest economy in the EU with a 15.0% share of total nominal GDP and the UK's economy is (slightly) bigger than the total of the smallest 18 member states combined. With Brexit, the number of members of the EU will go from 28 to 27, but in terms of economic weight it is as if it is going from 28 to 10."

In *The Brussels Effect,* Bradford concedes that Brexit is an unprecedented challenge for the EU:

"Never before has a member state chosen to leave the EU, making the Brexit process distinctly uncertain and unsettling. Among its many negative implications, the UK's departure would seem to undermine the EU's relative economic might and, with that, its global regulatory clout. The UK has also supplied notable regulatory capacity...including a distinctly competent bureaucracy and technical expertise across a range of policy areas."

The remarkable solidarity exhibited by EU member states during Brexit negotiations with the UK is notable. It can be argued that the EU is no longer burdened by a member that was less than enthusiastic about completing the work in progress that is the European project.

The U.S. and Brexit

The Johnson government has relied heavily on a favorable trade deal with the U.S. to secure Britain's post-Brexit economic strategy. It comes as no surprise that the British government began sending envoys to the Biden campaign as soon as it became apparent that the American people could deny Donald Trump a second term.

President-elect Biden, who frequently reminds the public that the U.S. is the official depository of the 1998 Good Friday Agreement that brought peace to Northern Ireland, has stated that any UK-U.S. trade deal would "be contingent upon respect for the Agreement and preventing the return of a hard border." A bipartisan letter to Boris Johnson sent by the House Foreign Affairs Committee in September "reiterated that the U.S. Congress will not support any free trade agreement between the U.S. and the UK if the UK fails to preserve the gains of the Good Friday Agreement and broader peace process."

Brexit will complicate the U.S.-UK bilateral relationship known as "the special relationship." The UK has been described as America's window into Europe. Over the years, the U.S. stake in the future of Europe has been significant from the 1948 Marshall Plan's $12 billion ($130 billion in 2019) economic recovery package to the formation of NATO in 1949. In 2019, U.S. commercial investments in Europe were valued at approximately $3.57 trillion.

Multilateralism is the alliance of countries with a common mission. In a Biden administration, multilateralism will stage a comeback after four years in which the Trump administration undermined NATO, threatened an EU trade war, and tried to dismantle the European project. Nicholas Burns, a former U.S. ambassador to NATO, observes that America's NATO allies act as multipliers of American power in the world. Russell Berman at Stanford University goes further:

"American prosperity and security depend on the transatlantic relationship. The scope of the European economy is comparable to ours, and access to it remains vital....The partnership with Europe is also a central component of our national security architecture, especially through NATO. While the Cold War era danger of Russian tanks pouring westward through Germany has lost much of its plausibility, the hybrid attack on Ukraine, the cyber operations in the Baltics, and aggressive disinformation campaigns across Europe demonstrate an ongoing credible threat. Yet the Europeans, divided as they remain, lack the political will or military muscle to defend themselves on their own. American leadership is indispensable."

A recent survey conducted by the Pew Research Center indicates robust public support in the U.S. for the transatlantic alliance. During the Trump years, Europeans have had cause to question U.S. steadfastness as an ally. As a result, both French President Emmanuel Macron and German Chancellor Angela Merkel have advocated for greater European self-reliance in the security domain. A recommitment by the U.S. to the transatlantic alliance will require adjustment for the greater importance of France and Germany in a post-Brexit Europe.

Conclusion

After the Second World War, the UK attempted in historic fits and starts to become "more European." Even after the UK came to terms with the importance of joining the EEC, the "special relationship" with the U.S. weighed heavily in the UK's geopolitical calculus. The U.S., perhaps more pragmatic than the UK in its perception of the "special relationship," urged greater integration with Europe. Former U.S. Secretary of State Dean Acheson described the failure to fully avail itself of the European opportunity as Britain's "greatest mistake of the postwar period."

As Brexit negotiations teetered on a precipice in the final phase of talks, the European Union's chief Brexit negotiator Michel Barnier lamented that "it felt like we were going backwards more than forwards." The pull of history, it seemed, could not be overcome.

Politicians who told people what they wanted to hear rather than what they needed to hear failed the test of leadership. The full consequences of their failure will be felt for years to come.

The INEOS gas tanker transporting shale gas from the U.S. to the Grangemouth refinery in Scotland , past the Forth Bridge on the Firth of Forth. (IAIN MASTERTON/ALAMY)

discussion questions

1 Would Britain having success post-Brexit put pressure on the EU and other members that have threatened to leave? Would a disastrous Brexit hurt Europe as a whole?

2. Should the U.S. prioritize its "special relationship" with the UK over its relationship with the EU?

3. Should the European Union make an amendment to its founding treaties to make it more difficult for states to exit?

4. Should there come a time when the UK wants to rejoin the EU, what provisions, if any, should they make upon re-entry? Can the EU risk letting the UK rejoin only for anther Brexit to happen in the future?

5. Do you think Europe is stronger when united under the banner of the EU? Can the EU survive post-Merkel?

6. In the age of social media, how can vital public policy issues be informed by the facts rather than by emotions?

suggested readings

Bruford, Ann. **The Brussels Effect: How the European Union Rules the World.** Oxford University Press. 424 pgs. January 2020. For many observers, the European Union is mired in a deep crisis. Between sluggish growth; political turmoil following a decade of austerity politics; Brexit; and the rise of Asian influence, the EU is seen as a declining power on the world stage. Columbia Law professor Anu Bradford argues the opposite in her important new book The Brussels Effect: the EU remains an influential superpower that shapes the world in its image.

MacShane, Denis. **Brexiternity: The Uncertain Fate of Britain.** I.B. Tauris. 256pgs. November 2019. Denis MacShane explains how the Brexit process will be long and full of difficulties – arguing that a 'Brexiternity' of negotiations and internal political wrangling in Britain lies ahead.

Cameron, David. **For the Record.** Harper. 752 pgs. September 2019. In For the Record, Cameron highlights his government's achievements during his six years in power while offering a frank discussion of his rationale for holding the 2016 referendum on European Union membership.

Humphreys, Richard. **Beyond the Border: The Good Friday Agreement and Irish Unity after Brexit.** Merrion Press. 250 pgs July 2018. The Brexit vote for UK withdrawal from the EU has put the constitutional future of Northern Ireland center-stage once again. Beyond the Border is an authoritative, timely and up-to-date guide to the provisions of the Good Friday Agreement.

Kershaw, Ian. **The Global Age: Europe 1950-2017 (The Penguin History of Europe).** Viking 704 pgs. April 2019. In this remarkable book, Ian Kershaw has created a grand panorama of the world we live in and where it came from. Drawing on examples from all across Europe, The Global Age is an endlessly fascinating portrait of the recent past and present, and a cautious look into our future.

Lewis, Patrick, Parakilas, Jacob, Schneider-Petsinger, Marianne, Smart, Christopher, Rathke, Jeffrey and Ruy, Donatienne. **The Future of the U.S. and Europe: An Irreplaceable Partnership.** Chatham House. 51 pgs. April 2018. An in-depth analysis of the transatlantic relationship by experts at the UK's foremost think tank.

Don't forget: Ballots start on page 104!!!!

To access web links to these readings, as well as links to global discussion questions, shorter readings and suggested web sites, GO TO www.fpa.org/great_decisions and click on the topic under Resources, on the right-hand side of the page.

The coldest war: toward a return to Great Power competition in the Arctic?

by Stephanie Pezard

Ice floes surround the U.S. Coast Guard Cutter Healy in the Arcitc Ocean on July 29 (BONNIE JO MOUNT/THE WASHINGTON POST/GETTY IMAGES)

The major changes that the Arctic is experiencing as a result of global warming are repositioning it as a region of strategic importance, and as such it attracts increasing interest from both Arctic and non-Arctic nations. The U.S., which has sometimes been described as a "reluctant" Arctic nation, is quickly shifting toward a much more active Arctic policy. This shift finds its origins in a view of the Arctic as an arena for great power competition, where Russia and China are advancing their interests and the U.S. runs the risk of falling behind if it does not react quickly. This chapter lays out the characteristics of the Arctic's different sub-regions; recalls its role during the Cold War and

in its aftermath; identifies key U.S. priorities in relation to the Arctic; examines how Russia and China's policies in the Arctic might challenge these interests; and describes how the U.S. works with its allies to advance its interests in the region. It concludes with a discussion of how U.S. policy choices might constrain or, on the contrary, play an enabling role for U.S. ambitions in the Arctic.

STEPHANIE PEZARD *is a senior political scientist at the RAND Corporation. Her research focuses on European security and transatlantic relations; Arctic security; strategic competition; deterrence and use of force; measures short of war; and security cooperation.*

More than one 'Arctic'

The Arctic is commonly defined as the area located north of the Arctic Circle, which forms an imaginary line at latitude 66°33' North and corresponds to the southernmost point where the sun is visible for 24 hours on the June Solstice. By that definition, Arctic nations include the U.S. (by way of Alaska), Canada, Denmark (by way of Greenland), Norway, Russia, Iceland, Sweden, and Finland, with the first five being also Arctic coastal states.

In spite of the use of the singular, the Arctic is a diverse region, with different areas showing unique landscapes, populations, and economic patterns. The "European" Arctic, which goes from Greenland to Russia via Norway, is more densely populated and exploited economically than the "North American" Arctic comprising northern Canada and Alaska. This is the result of various factors, from climate—the Gulf stream keeps northern Norway and the Russian port of Murmansk ice-free all year long—to national politics, with the Soviet Union taking a proactive role in the industrial development of its Arctic region. As a result, the largest Arctic cities are in Russia, with Murmansk counting about 300,000 inhabitants, while the largest city in the North American Arctic is Greenland's capital city Nuuk, with a little above 17,000 inhabitants. Arctic populations also include numerous indigenous people. Alaska, for instance, counts 11 distinct native cultures. In some cases, these indigenous populations' historical lands cross modern boundaries. The Sami people, for instance, live in Norway, Sweden, Finland, and Russia.

The Arctic is experiencing the effects of climate change at an accelerated pace, resulting in profound trans-

formations to its physical environment as well as to the human activities that it can sustain. The 2019 "Arctic Report Card" published by the U.S. National Oceanic and Atmospheric Administration (NOAA) highlights dramatic changes to the extent and thickness of sea ice, the Greenland ice sheet, sea and land surface temperatures, and snow cover, which in turn have important consequences for the wildlife, fisheries, and the livelihoods of indigenous populations living in these regions. These changes have an impact beyond the Arctic: As it melts, the sea ice that reflects sun rays into the atmosphere is replaced by water, which instead absorbs solar energy, further contributing to global warming. A warmer climate has broad implications in the Arctic, from the opening of new sea routes for shipping to the displacement of fish species further north. These changes have contributed to bringing new attention to the Arctic, including from relative newcomers on the Arctic scene, such as China.

From monitoring threats above the horizon to Arctic Council cooperation

The Arctic received a lot of attention during the Cold War, as the North Pole represented the shortest route between the U.S. and the Soviet Union for bombers potentially carrying out a nuclear attack. In 1957, the U.S. and Canada created a binational organization, the North American Air Defense Command (NORAD)—renamed North American Aerospace Defense Command after 1981—to jointly anticipate and defend against air and space threats coming toward the North American continent. NORAD's aerospace warning missions were supported by networks of radars stretching from Alaska to eastern Canada—the Defense Early Warning (DEW) line, which was replaced in 1985 with the more exten-

sive North Warning System (NWS). The airspace above the Arctic was not the only source of concern: each side also feared the presence of submarines coming undetected under the ice cover. Yet even during the Cold War, the U.S. and the Soviet Union found opportunities to cooperate on some Arctic matters, for instance signing an Agreement on the Conservation of Polar Bears in 1973. In 1987, leader of the Soviet Union Mikhail Gorbachev launched the "Murmansk Initiative" to reduce the risk of potential confrontation in the Arctic and develop international cooperation on military and nonmilitary matters.

With the collapse of the Soviet Union and the end of the Cold War, the Arctic lost its strategic significance as a potential battleground between Washington and Moscow, and a sizable part of the military infrastructure that the Soviet Union had built in its Arctic region fell into disarray. Arctic nations turned their attention to "soft security" matters ranging from the protection of the Arctic environment to navigation safety. In 1996, the Ottawa Declaration established an Arctic Council with the eight Arctic nations as Permanent Members, as well as six organizations representing Arctic indigenous peoples as Permanent Participants. The purpose of the Council was to further Arctic cooperation on issues related to the environment and sustainable development and it has, over the years, led to the adoption of three international agreements on search and rescue (2011), marine oil pollution preparedness and response (2013), and scientific cooperation (2017). Economic issues are addressed through the Arctic Economic Forum, which was created in 2013. The high degree of international cooperation and peace in the Arctic even gave rise to the notion of "Arctic exceptionalism," which describes a situation where Arctic matters manage to remain impervious to geopolitical tensions elsewhere in the world.

! Before you read, download the companion **Glossary** that includes definitions, a guide to acronyms and abbreviations used in the article, and other material. Go to **www. fpa.org/great_decisions** and select a topic in the Resources section. (Top right)

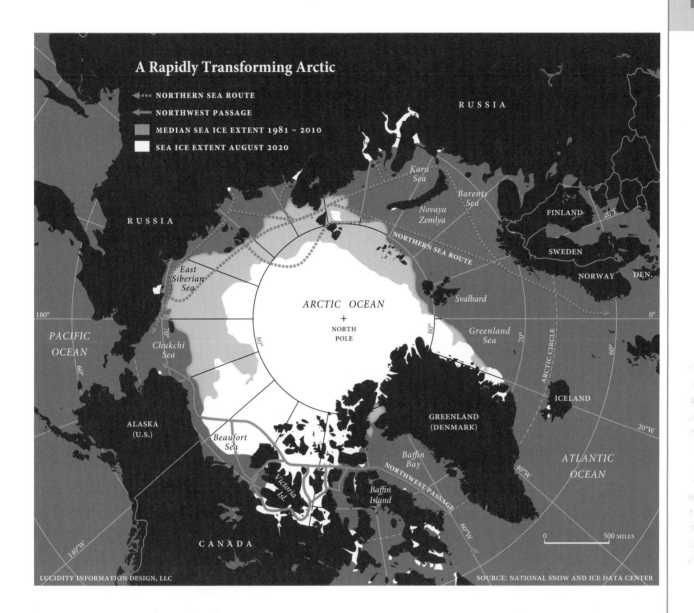

A Rapidly Transforming Arctic

- ◄---- NORTHERN SEA ROUTE
- ◄—— NORTHWEST PASSAGE
- ▨ MEDIAN SEA ICE EXTENT 1981 – 2010
- ▢ SEA ICE EXTENT AUGUST 2020

LUCIDITY INFORMATION DESIGN, LLC   SOURCE: NATIONAL SNOW AND ICE DATA CENTER

A rapidly transforming region attracts new interests

Since the mid-2000s, the Arctic has made a slow comeback as a region of strategic importance, as the result of several profound shifts. An increasingly ice-free Arctic means major transformations with regard to navigability; changed patterns in fishing; and new prospects for hydrocarbon exploitation and mining. These changes have focused increased scrutiny on the Arctic, and an interest that goes largely beyond Arctic nations. In response, the Arctic Council has progressively expanded, and as of 2020 13 non-Arctic states — China, France, Germany, India, Italy, Japan, the Netherlands, Poland, Singapore, Republic of Korea, Spain, Swit-

zerland and the UK — had observer status in the Council.

Sea ice melting results in an "opening" of the Arctic: some sea routes that were only navigable in the summer, or hardly navigable at all, can now be used for longer periods of time. In 2016, for the first time, a cruise ship with 1,700 people on board traveled along the Northwest Passage, across the Canadian Arctic archipelago. Along the northern coast of Russia, the Northern Sea Route represents a shorter route between Europe and Asia, cutting trips by several days and avoiding some potentially dangerous areas such as the Strait of Malacca. As of 2020,

this shipping route was still more of a trickle than a highway: The Northern Sea Route Information Office recorded 27 transit voyages (mostly between Europe and Asia) in 2018, down from 31 voyages in 2014. Russia imposes a fee on ships navigating through the Northern Sea Route, and makes mandatory an escort by a Russian icebreaker. Navigation, while possible, is still not particularly easy. Chunks of melting sea ice make for treacherous waters, resulting in high insurance costs and voyages whose duration is still hard to predict. Yet as sea ice continues to disappear, so will these obstacles. In 2016, China issued a lengthy navigation guide specifically for the Northwest Passage, suggesting that it intends to make more use of this route in the future. Another major prospect for Arctic navigation is the expected opening of a third route that would cross over the Pole through the Central Arctic Ocean. This so-called Transpolar Route could be navigable by mid-century or even sooner, depending on climate models.

Climate change also has an impact on fisheries, with some species moving further north in search of cold water. Combined with a global decrease in fish stocks, this increases the attractiveness of Arctic fishing, and creates tensions among nations—including groups of nations, such as the EU—with regard to fishing quotas for species like mackerel. In other cases, cooperation

prevails, as shown by the signing in 2018 of a moratorium on fishing in the Central Arctic Ocean. While there is no fishing yet in this area, which is still covered in sea ice, it is anticipated this will soon enough become a possibility due to the effect of climate change, thus requiring a "preemptive" moratorium.

An ice-free Arctic is also an Arctic where it becomes easier to drill. In 2008, a U.S. Geological Survey (USGS) assessment described the Arctic as an immense reservoir of natural resources, noting that "90 billion barrels of oil, 1,669 trillion cubic feet of natural gas, and 44 billion barrels of natural gas liquids may remain to be found in the Arctic, of which approximately 84% is expected to occur in offshore areas." Tapping into these reserves is a

long-term prospect: The technological means to drill so deep and under such harsh conditions are not available yet, and there are plenty of more accessible sites closer to the coast that can still be exploited. It will be a long time before exploiting undersea Arctic gas or oil becomes technologically feasible and economically desirable. Yet this prospect explains in part why several Arctic states have submitted claims before the United Nations Commission on the Limits of the Continental Shelf (UNCLCS) to gain recognition for a larger share of continental shelf. A state's exclusive economic zone (EEZ), where it enjoys exclusive fishing, drilling, and mining rights, extends to 200 nautical miles beyond its coast. However, if a state can gather sufficient

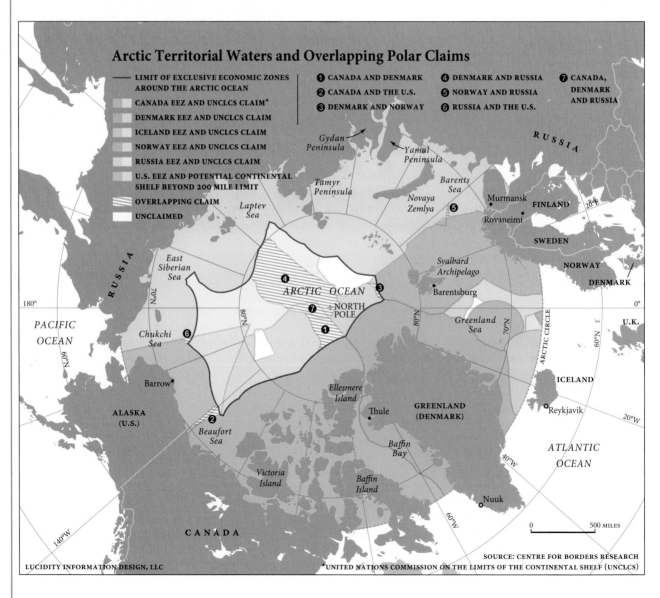

Arctic Territorial Waters and Overlapping Polar Claims

— LIMIT OF EXCLUSIVE ECONOMIC ZONES AROUND THE ARCTIC OCEAN
CANADA EEZ AND UNCLCS CLAIM*
DENMARK EEZ AND UNCLCS CLAIM
ICELAND EEZ AND UNCLCS CLAIM
NORWAY EEZ AND UNCLCS CLAIM
RUSSIA EEZ AND UNCLCS CLAIM
U.S. EEZ AND POTENTIAL CONTINENTAL SHELF BEYOND 200 MILE LIMIT
OVERLAPPING CLAIM
UNCLAIMED

❶ CANADA AND DENMARK
❷ CANADA AND THE U.S.
❸ DENMARK AND NORWAY
❹ DENMARK AND RUSSIA
❺ NORWAY AND RUSSIA
❻ RUSSIA AND THE U.S.
❼ CANADA, DENMARK AND RUSSIA

LUCIDITY INFORMATION DESIGN, LLC

SOURCE: CENTRE FOR BORDERS RESEARCH
*UNITED NATIONS COMMISSION ON THE LIMITS OF THE CONTINENTAL SHELF (UNCLCS)

scientific evidence that the continental shelf beyond that limit is a continuation of the continental shelf within the 200 nautical miles, it can file a claim before the UNCLCS. In the case of overlapping claims from two or more states, the Commission's recommendations on each claim becomes the basis for direct discussions between these states to decide on the limits of their continental shelves. When gaining such an extension of their continental shelf, states have access to the underground resources in the seabed and subsoil, such as minerals or hydrocarbons, but have no right to the column of water above it—for fishing or navigation, for instance—which remains international waters. As of 2020, there were several such claims under examination in the Arctic. Russia was the first in 2000 to submit one for an extensive area covering 1.2 million square kilometers, and comprising the North Pole. Russia revised and resubmitted its claim in 2015, after the UNCLS found the scientific evidence presented insufficient. Denmark submitted its own claim, which partially overlaps with Russia, in 2014. Canada was the last one to submit a third overlapping claim in 2019. The decision of the Commission might not be known for several years, and would in any case be only the prelude to negotiations between the three claimants.

What are U.S. interests in the Arctic?

After the Cold War ended, the Arctic largely lost its strategic significance for the U.S. Arguably, the U.S. always had a limited Arctic identity, owing solely to its purchase of Alaska from Russia in 1867. Most Alaskans live in the non-Arctic part of the state, and the notion that the U.S. is an Arctic nation does not come naturally to most Americans living in the so-called lower 48.

The Arctic started receiving more attention as the U.S. readied itself to take over the two-year rotating chairmanship of the Arctic Council in 2015. In 2013, the White House published a comprehensive Arctic Strategy, followed by an Implementation Plan in 2014. This Arctic Strategy emphasized three lines of effort: "Advance U.S. security interests;" "Pursue responsible Arctic region stewardship;" and "strengthen international cooperation." The strategy also mentioned "safeguard peace and stability" and "consult and coordinate with Alaska natives" as two of its guiding principles to implement the strategy. In August 2015, U.S. President Barack Obama undertook an extended visit to Alaska, including north of the Arctic Circle. Under the U.S. Chairmanship, the Council successfully adopted an Agreement on Enhancing International Arctic Scientific Cooperation.

This renewed interest waned as U.S. political leadership changed and the U.S. passed the baton to Finland as the new Chair of the Arctic Council in 2017. The position of Special Representative for the Arctic, created in 2014 with the idea of having an "Arctic Czar" who could coordinate across agencies and support the U.S. Arctic Council Chairmanship was left unfilled. The Arctic Steering Committee, created by a presidential Executive Order in 2015 for a similar purpose, disappeared at the same time. In 2017, the White House published a new National Security Strategy that framed U.S. security objectives in relation to the "growing political, economic, and military competition we face around the world." In that document the word "Arctic" is mentioned only once, as a "common domain" that should remain "open and free." It is not mentioned in the unclassified synopsis of the National Defense Strategy published in 2018.

Yet U.S. policy toward the Arctic experienced a significant turn in 2018–19, with the region becoming increasingly described as a theater of global strategic competition between the U.S. and its adversaries. In December 2018, Secretary of the U.S. Navy Richard Spencer suggested that the U.S. should conduct a freedom of navigation operation (FONOP) along the Northern Sea Route, to let Russia know that the U.S. considers it an international strait open to navigation, rather than internal waters that can be controlled by Russia. FONOPS are operations undertaken by the U.S. Navy according to

Russia's Foreign Minister Sergei Lavrov (2nd,L), Norway's foreign minister Ine Eriksen Soreide (L)and Sweden's foreign minister Margot Wallstrom (2nd,R)speak standing next to US secretary of state Mike Pompeo (R) while posing for a picture at the Arctic Council Ministerial Meeting in Rovaniemi, Finnish Lapland on May 7, 2019. (VESA MOILANEN/AFP/ GETTY IMAGES)

4

The Prirazlomnaya offshore ice-resistant oil-producing platform is seen at Pechora Sea, Russia, on May 8, 2016. Prirazlomnaya is the world's first operational Arctic rig that process oil drilling, production and storage, end product processing and loading. (SERGEY ANISIMOV /ANADOLU AGENCY/GETTY IMAGES)

the Freedom of Navigation Program, which was created in 1979 to counter what the U.S. calls "excessive maritime claims" that seek to deny other nations the ability to navigate freely in accordance with maritime international law. In May 2019, at the Arctic Council's Ministerial Meeting in Rovaniemi, Finland, U.S. Secretary of State Mike Pompeo reaffirmed the Arctic identity of the U.S. and stated that "the region has become an arena for power and for competition," mentioning explicitly China and Russia as sources of concern for the U.S. in the region. In August 2019, President Donald J. Trump's reported interest in buying Greenland—a self-governing territory that is part of the Kingdom of Denmark—was another indication of the U.S. perception of the strategic importance of the Arctic. Other indications of this renewed interest include the release on June 9, 2020, by the White House of a *Memorandum on Safeguarding U.S. National Interests in the Arctic and Antarctic Regions*, which reaffirmed the U.S. decision to equip itself with a new fleet of icebreakers. This effort is already underway with the Coast Guard Polar Security Cutter program, which, as the Congressional Research Service notes in its report about the program, received $100 million more in funding from Congress in fiscal year 2020 than

what had been requested. Still in June 2020, the U.S. reopened its consulate in Nuuk, Greenland, which had been closed since 1953, and in July 2020, the State Department appointed a U.S. Coordinator for the Arctic Region. The U.S. is not just signaling its interest in the Arctic; it is also doing so at an increasingly rapid pace, and through a whole-of-government approach that underlines the military, economic, and diplomatic importance of the Arctic.

Who is the U.S. competing against in the Arctic?

The U.S.' renewed interest in the Arctic is largely prompted by a concern that Russia and China are using the region to increase their political, economic, and military influence. Yet Russia and China have different stakes in the Arctic, which present different challenges for the U.S.

Russia has long seen its Arctic region as strategically important, for several reasons. The first is economic: the Russian Arctic holds important oil and gas reserves, which are essential to a Russian economy largely dependent on the exploitation of hydrocarbons. Russia is looking at its Arctic region to become a major liquified natural gas producer. The large-scale LNG plant and terminal in the Yamal Peninsula that Russia built partly with foreign invest-

ment (mostly Chinese) became operational in 2017, and another LNG project (Arctic-LNG 2) is under development on the nearby Gydan Peninsula. This makes the Northern Sea Route a major economic artery of Russia, particularly as it becomes increasingly navigable. Russia controls this route tightly for economic but also security reasons, as its northern border gradually loses the ice that used to form a natural defense. Russia's Arctic, and more specifically the Kola Peninsula, is also where an estimated two thirds of Russia's strategic deterrent is located. Russia seeks to protect this area through a "bastion" strategy that includes a dense network of air and coastal defenses.

Three issues in particular represent potential sources of tension between the U.S. and Russia. One is the progressive remilitarization, by Russia, of its Arctic region. In 2015, Russian Defense Minister Sergey Shoigu argued that preserving Russian national security required, among other things, a "constant military presence in the Arctic," and Russia has devoted substantial financial resources to reach that objective. Russia has refurbished or modernized Soviet-era bases and airfields and built new infrastructure, particularly along the Northern Sea Route. It established a dedicated northern command for the region, created two Arctic brigades—one of which is located close to the Finnish border—and is planning to increase its already large icebreaker fleet. Russia is also heavily investing in its navy, particularly submarines, with a focus on the Northern Fleet.

A second source of tensions is the increased Russian military presence in the maritime areas between Greenland and Iceland, and between Iceland and the UK (the so-called "GIUK gap"). The GIUK gap represents Russia's gateway to the North Atlantic for its Northern Fleet based out of Murmansk. The U.S., the United Kingdom, and Norway are increasing their efforts to monitor the area, particularly for submarine activity. The U.S. renovated the Keflavik airbase in Iceland, which it had left in 2006, in order to conduct maritime air patrols in the region.

Finally, the U.S. contests Russia's policy of exerting strict control over the vessels that navigate through the Northern Sea Route. Russia argues that Article 234 of the United Nations Convention on the Law of the Sea (UNCLOS) provides states with extended control over vessels navigating through ice-covered areas in order to prevent maritime pollution, which would be particularly devastating in such areas. The U.S. claims that this interpretation violates the freedom of navigation principle, and warned Russia that it might conduct freedom of navigation operations in that area, taking a first step in that direction with a joint U.S.-UK exercise in the Barents Sea in May 2020.

China, meanwhile, is expressing increasing interest in the Arctic. In its first Arctic policy published in January 2018, China describes itself as a "Near Arctic State," an unusual term that characterizes, according to the policy, "one of the continental States that are closest to the Arctic Circle." China's interest in the poles is not a new phenomenon. It has conducted scientific activity in Antarctica since the 1980s and established a first research station in the Arctic, on Svalbard, in 2004. A key motivation for this scientific activity is studying global climate change, which will have a dramatic impact on China's coastal cities and economy in particular. China's interest in the Arctic, however, goes well beyond scientific research, as its Arctic policy describes a future "Polar Silk Road" integrated to its larger Belt and Road Initiative. China is interested in investments in oil and gas exploitation, mining (particularly for uranium and rare earth minerals, which are essential to various new technologies), fisheries, and shipping. A November 2017 Center for Naval Analyses (CNA) study found that China's investments in Arctic littoral states were highest in Greenland when calculated as a percentage of the national GDP (11.6% over the time period 2012–17). China is also, after Russia, a relatively important user of the Northern Sea Route, with eight transit voyages in 2018, according to transit statistics from the Northern Sea Route Information Office, out of 19 voyages conducted under a non-Russian flag.

In his 2019 speech at the Arctic Council, U.S. Secretary of State Mike Pompeo highlighted various U.S. concerns with regard to an increased Chinese presence in the Arctic. First, he questioned China's ability to respect the rules of the game, pointing to "China's pattern of aggressive behavior elsewhere," and thus suggesting that higher economic and financial stakes in the Arctic could allow China to impose its own rules, similar to how it applies its interpretation of maritime international law in the South China Sea. A second concern is the political influence that China might gain in the Arctic thanks to its new economic weight, particularly if countries accepting Chinese investments were to find themselves unable to pay back their loans. China may thus gain a foothold in areas—such as Greenland—that the U.S. sees as important strategically. A third concern is China's potential ability to turn its economic activity into military presence, with Secretary Pompeo arguing that "This is part of a very familiar pattern. Beijing attempts to develop critical infrastructure using Chinese money, Chinese companies, and Chinese workers—in some cases, to establish a permanent Chinese security presence." According to this view, the infrastructure that China is seeking to build as part of a "Polar Silk Road" might be used not just for civilian but also military purposes. The same might be said of some of China's scientific research outposts. China's construction of an observatory for northern lights in Iceland, for instance, has raised concerns that the facility might be used for intelligence gathering purposes rather than scientific research.

Echoing some of these concerns, the response from Arctic nations to Chinese investments has so far been mixed. In 2013, Iceland signed with China a free-trade agreement—the first one ever signed by China with a European nation—yet one year earlier Iceland had also blocked the possible sale of a large plot of land to a Chinese investor, who intended to turn it into a luxury hotel and golf resort. A similar deal fell through in Svalbard, which is governed by Norway, in 2016. Still in 2016, Denmark objected to the sale of a vacant naval base in Greenland to a Chinese mining company. In 2018, after Greenland shortlisted a Chinese company to build two airports, the U.S. expressed concerns to Copenhagen, which stepped in to fund the project instead. Yet Chinese investments are also attractive to Arctic economies that are in dire need of job prospects and infrastructure.

Acting Murmansk Region Governor Andrei Chibis (R) greets oil workers at the Nanhai VIII semi-submersible drilling rig in the Kola Bay. (LEV FEDOSEYEV/TASS/GETTY IMAGES)

4

U.S. foreign policy in the Arctic

The U.S. has close allies and partners in the Arctic. Three U.S. NATO allies in particular stand out based on history and recent U.S. policy developments: Canada, Denmark, and Norway. Canada has a long history of defense cooperation with the U.S., and represents a first line of defense for the North American continent for potential threats coming from the Arctic; the U.S. is increasingly involved in Greenland, due to its strategic location between the Arctic and the Atlantic; and Norway, which borders Russia, is also strengthening its defense relationship with the U.S. and supports NATO's involvement in the region.

Canada

U.S close cooperation with Canada in the Arctic continued after the collapse of the Soviet Union, with NORAD maintaining its relevance in the post-Cold War era. In the immediate aftermath of 9/11, Operation Noble Eagle gave NORAD's commander new responsibilities regarding the protection against the threats represented by aircraft within the U.S. and Canada. In 2006, a third mission—maritime warning—was added to NORAD's aerospace warning and aerospace control missions. In 2012, the U.S. and Canada signed a Tri-Command Framework for Arctic Cooperation designed to increase their joint activities in domains such as domain awareness, exercises, information sharing, and scientific cooperation in the Arctic. The two countries regularly conduct joint exercises, such as the annual Vigilant Shield exercise, which focuses on increasing their ability to protect their homelands from incoming threats, or the biennial ICEX naval military exercise that trains Canadian and U.S. submariners to operate in the Arctic. Upcoming challenges for NORAD include the modernization of the aging North Warning System, which is due for update or replacement around 2025.

The U.S. and Canada still disagree on Canada's official definition of the Northwest Passage—the maritime route that runs along Canada's northern border— as "internal waterways." Canada closely controls the Passage through its Northern Canada Vessel Traffic Services Zone regulations, and every ship that transits the passage must register with the Canadian Coast Guard. Like Russia, Canada justifies its position on the basis of Article 234 of UNCLOS, even as the passage becomes increasingly ice-free. Canada and the U.S. have generally agreed to disagree on this issue, but this position might become less tenable as the U.S. becomes increasingly vocal against Russia's own interpretation of Article 234 as it relates to the Northern Sea Route.

Denmark/Greenland

Denmark is an Arctic nation thanks to Greenland, which is part of the Kingdom of Denmark but has the status of a self-governing territory. It thus decides on its own laws, except in the domains of foreign policy and defense, which are still decided by Copenhagen. Greenland made the headlines in August 2019 when it was made public that President Trump was considering that the U.S. purchase it. Its strategic value for the U.S. stems from its position at one end of the GIUK gap. With the rise of a more militarily assertive Russia, Thule Air Base, in Northwestern Greenland, has also regained some of the importance it had during the Cold War, and the U.S. Air Force Arctic Strategy published in July 2020 notes that "Locations like Clear, Alaska and Thule, Greenland uniquely enable missile warning and defense in addition to space domain awareness."

U.S.-Greenlandic relations have experienced several important developments. In addition to reopening its consulate in Nuuk, the U.S. announced in 2020 that it would provide Greenland with $12.1 million in development aid for various projects related to renewable energies, fisheries management, and tourism. U.S. growing interest in Greenland requires it to navigate a complex trilateral relationship with Nuuk and Copenhagen. Copenhagen still provides a block subsidy to Nuuk that is calculated annually based on different factors and covers a large share of Greenland's expenses, thus contributing to keeping Greenland within the Kingdom of Denmark.

Norway

Norway's Finnmark region borders Russia, and the two countries' bilateral relations in the Arctic have generally been cooperative. They have worked together since 1993 in the Barents Euro-Arctic Council, which supports coordination across the Barents region; they finally resolved in 2011 their 40-year old disagreement on their respective boundaries in the Barents Sea; and their Coast Guards routinely cooperate, including through joint exercises, to improve their ability to do effective search and rescue in their territorial waters and beyond.

Yet Norway is also seeing with some concern Russia's remilitarization of its Arctic region, and has advocated for a NATO presence in the Arctic. In 2017, Norway invited 300 U.S. marines to deploy a rotational presence on its territory with the purpose of training them for cold weather warfighting. The size of the rotation was increased to 700 a year later. In October and November 2018, Norway hosted Trident Juncture—a large-scale NATO exercise that gathered approximately 50,000 personnel from 31 NATO members and partner countries. In parallel, incidents with Russia have become more numerous over the years. On several instances Russia has engaged in the jamming of GPS signals and military communications to disrupt Norway's exercises. Other incidents include Russia carrying out simulated attacks against Norway's radar in Vardø, close to the Norway-Russian border, on at least two occasions in 2018 and 2019.

Norway also watches closely activity on and near the Svalbard Archipelago, located roughly halfway between the North Pole and northern Norway. Svalbard's legal status is unusual. The Svalbard Treaty (or Spitsbergen Treaty) signed in 1920 recognizes Norwegian sovereignty but also authorizes the treaty's 46 signatories to conduct commercial activities on the islands.

About a fifth of the archipelago's population lives in Barentsburg, which is a Russian settlement established around a coal mine that is still in use. Norway and Russia have regularly clashed, over the years, on the status of the waters around Svalbard. Since the treaty does not formally extend Norway's governance to the waters around Svalbard, Norway has established a Fishing Protection Zone (FPZ) around the archipelago rather than the more common Exclusive Economic Zone (EEZ), but Russia has consistently contested Norway's authority over that FPZ.

U.S. policy in the Arctic: what next?

As the U.S. becomes more committed to playing an active role in the Arctic, it faces a number of policy decisions. Two broad issues, in particular, will require the attention of decisionmakers in the years to come. One relates to the amount of resources that the U.S. is ready to devote to this region. Another relates to how the U.S. can be part of Arctic institutions' evolution, to ensure that they can meet emerging challenges.

The U.S. has long suffered from a lack of Arctic-specific capabilities, such as icebreakers. Without such assets, freedom of navigation operations along the Northern Sea Route, which is much more hazardous than the Barents Sea, will remain an empty threat, or could lead to an embarrassing situation where the U.S. attempts a failed show of force. The U.S. has long managed with a minimal float of one medium icebreaker, the Healy, and two heavy ones, the Polar Star and the Polar Sea. The only reason that the Polar Star can be at sea is because it cannibalizes the Polar Sea—which has been out of commission since 2010—for spare parts when needed. Even then, the Polar Star, which has been operational since 1976, is long past its 30-year life expectancy. Use of the Polar Star for Arctic requirements is limited by the fact that it is also needed to resupply U.S. scientific stations in Antarctica. The Polar Security Cutter program represents an important step toward remediating this situation. How the U.S. sustains this program and

Paratroopers from the Chaos Troop, 1st Squadron (Airborne), 40th Cavalry Regiment, participate in U.S. Northern Command's Exercise Arctic Edge 20 at the Donnelly drop zone at Ft. Greely, AK, Feb. 29, 2020. The exercise focuses on training, experimentation, techniques, tactics, and procedures development for Homeland Defense operations in an Arctic environment. (U.S. AIR FORCE PHOTO BY STAFF SGT DIANA COSSABOOM)

addresses other identified needs such as the creation of a deep port in northern Alaska, will play an important role in ensuring that it has the means of its ambitions in the Arctic.

A second challenge is keeping the Arctic at peace and maintaining the type of international cooperation that has benefitted all Arctic nations so far. At the 2019 Arctic Council meeting in Rovaniemi, Finland, Arctic nations for the very first time failed to agree on a common declaration at the end of the summit, because the U.S. refused to include in the text any reference to global warming. This could be the sign of a new era where bilateral relations—for instance, between the U.S. and Greenland—take precedence over multilateral institutions. Yet some of the greatest advancements in the rules-based order in the Arctic have come from effective concertation between all Arctic nations in forums such as the Arctic Council. How these institutions will evolve represents another issue. The use of the Arctic Council, by U.S. Secretary of State Pompeo, to discuss the security risks posed by Russia and China in the Arctic, is a reminder that there was no security-specific Arctic forum that might have been more appropriate. Various options have been

proposed to address this issue, including reestablishing the defunct meeting of the Arctic Chiefs of Defense Staff, which was suspended in 2014. Whether security issues can successfully be integrated in Arctic discussions will become increasingly critical as Arctic and non-Arctic states become more concerned with the return of "hard security" issues in the region. Finally, another challenge relates to the role that non-Arctic countries can expect to play in Arctic forums. For the U.S., this presents a dilemma. Broad inclusion is consistent with the U.S. view of the Arctic as a "common domain," as expressed in the 2017 National Security Strategy. Yet Secretary of State Pompeo's statement in Rovaniemi that "There are only Arctic States and Non-Arctic States. No third category exists, and claiming otherwise entitles China to exactly nothing," makes clear that the U.S. believes it has stakes in Arctic governance that China does not have. How the U.S.—and other Arctic nations—take into account the interests and concerns of non-Arctic nations will play a key role in defining Arctic institutions for years to come and ensuring that their own interests are preserved in this increasingly important strategic region.

discussion questions

1 Should countries that are part of the Arctic council prioritize policies that would attempt to limit the melting of ice? Do the economic benefits outweigh the environmental ones?

2. Why has the United States been a "reluctant" Arctic nation in the past?

3. How much should the United States government spend towards increasing the U.S' influence and capacity in the Arctic?

4. What could be some of the negative effects should the Arctic become another point of contention between the U.S. and China? Can the U.S. look to use the region as a potential source of cooperation with China?

suggested readings

Laruelle, Marlene. **Russia's Arctic Strategies and the Future of the Far North.** Routledge. 280 pgs. 2013. An expert overview of Russia's stakes in the Arctic, based on an analysis of its history, politics, demographics, and economics. It examines in detail the domestic determinants of Russia's Arctic policy, as well as its efforts to project diplomacy as well as, potentially, power. A chapter on "Climate change and its expected impact on Russia" gives a useful perspective on the upcoming challenges that Russia will face, and how they might impact its Arctic policy.

Boulegue, Mathieu. **Russia's Military Posture in the Arctic Managing Hard Power in a 'Low Tension' Environment.** Chatham House. 46 pgs. 2019. A comprehensive review of Russia's military capabilities and activities in the Arctic.

Klimenko, Ekaterina and Sorensen, Camilla T. **Emerging Chinese-Russian Cooperation in the Arctic.** Sipri 56 pgs. 2017. The paper combines expert knowledge of China's and Russia's role in the Arctic to identify the various interests that the two countries might share, as well as existing and potential points of friction. Their analysis concludes on the limits of this cooperation, providing a useful corrective to the often heard notion that Russia and China will join forces and empower each other in the Arctic.

The Arctic Yearbook is published online and gathers contributions from Arctic experts around an annual theme. The 2019 Yearbook, edited by Lassi Heininen, Heather Exner-Pirot, and Justin Barnes, focuses on "Redefining Security in the Arctic" and offers a broad view of the different meanings of "security" in the Arctic, looking at military, socio-economic, health, and sustainable development issues

Berry, Dawn Alexandrea, Bowles, Nigel and Jones, Halbert. **Governing the North American Arctic: Sovereignty, Security, and Institutions.** Palgrave Macmillan 288 pgs. 2016. This book focuses on the North American part of the Arctic that includes the United States and Canada, and extends all the way to Greenland. Contributions include, among others, an exploration of the "Arctic identity" of Canada and the United States, an analysis of Chinese mining activities in the region, and an overview of the long history of cooperation between Canada and the United States on Arctic matters.

Osthagen, Andreas, Sharp, Gregory Levi and Hilde, Pall Sigurd.. **"At Opposite Poles: Canada's and Norway's Approaches to Security in the Arctic,"** The Polar Journal, Vol.8, No. 1, 2018.

Don't forget: Ballots start on page 104!!!!

To access web links to these readings, as well as links to global discussion questions, shorter readings and suggested web sites,
GO TO www.fpa.org/great_decisions
and click on the topic under Resources, on the right-hand side of the page.

China and Africa
by Cobus van Staden

A group of performers hold Chinese and Ivorian flags during the inauguration ceremony of Ivory Coast's new 60,000-seat Olympic stadium, built with the help of China, in Ebimpe, outside Abidjan, on October 3, 2020 ahead of 2023 Africa Cup of Nations. (IISSOUF SANOGO/ AFP/GETTY IMAGES)

China's relationship with Africa can't be separated from the continent's own fraught history. While the Ming-era Chinese commander Zheng He visited the East African coast in 1413, the modern relationship dates back to Africa's anti-colonial struggle and the formation of the non-aligned movement in Bandung, Indonesia, in 1955. At that moment, China had just achieved its own communist victory, and Africa was struggling against both European colonial occupation and broader Western attempts at neo-colonial control.

China emerged as a prominent supporter of Africa's anti-colonial struggle during this era, particularly after its relations with the Soviet Union soured and then-Premier Zhou Enlai toured the African continent during the early 1960s. This phase lasted roughly until the death of Mao Zedong in 1976, and while China's subsequent relationship with Africa was very different, this early era set some parameters that have structured the relationship to this day. In the first place, Zhou articulated a set of principles that still defines Chinese foreign policy with African countries (and further

afield). These include the principle of non-interference in the domestic affairs of partner countries – still a controversial cornerstone of Chinese foreign policy, in that it opens China to criticism that it supports authoritarian governments. In the second place, while Chinese support and training of anti-colonial armies is a remnant of the cold war, South-South solidarity, and narratives of shared victimization by Western powers remain prominent tropes in China-Africa diplomacy. In the third place, one instance of China's assistance to Africa set the template for much future cooperation: The TAZARA railway.

The TAZARA railway was a response to a key problem still facing Africa: the lack of cross-border infrastructure. In the late 1960s, Zambia, a land-locked country, was desperate to get its copper exports to the global market. Its only access

COBUS VAN STADEN *is a Senior China-Africa researcher at the South African Institute of International affairs. He also is the head of research and analysis at the China-Africa Project, and co-host of the China in Africa Podcast.*

President Kenneth Kaunda (left of the two men) of Zambia and President Julius Nyerere (1922–1999, right) of Tanzania rest their feet on the sleepers of the new Great Uhuru Railway (later the TAZARA Railway), which links their two countries, during the halfway celebrations at Tunduma on the border, September 6, 1973. The railway was a joint venture between the two countries, financed by China. (KEYSTONE/ HULTON ARCHIVE/GETTY IMAGES)

to a port was controlled by two hostile entities: colonial Rhodesia (now Zimbabwe) and apartheid South Africa. China provided funding and personnel to construct an 1,860 kilometer line to Tanzania, undercutting the stranglehold of neo-colonial forces in Southern Africa, and providing a potent symbol of South-South cooperation. The railway also set the template for a key area of later China-Africa cooperation: infrastructure.

The TAZARA railway was finished in 1975, almost at the end of Mao Zedong's reign. During the early days of China's subsequent Reform and Opening Up era, engagement with Africa waned, in favor of domestic development and the courting of foreign direct investment from Japan, the U.S. and Europe. It was a very different China that returned to Africa in the 1990s.

China's return to Africa was spurred by the temporary freeze in

Before you read, download the companion **Glossary** that includes definitions, a guide to acronyms and abbreviations used in the article, and other material. Go to **www. fpa.org/great_decisions** and select a topic in the Resources section. (Top right)

its relations with Western powers following the crackdown in 1989 on pro-democracy protesters in Tiananmen Square in Beijing. The sudden diplomatic clampdown provided the impetus to look for other external partners. However, the main driver for outreach was Deng Xiaoping's Go Out strategy, which urged China's state-owned enterprises to find external markets and sources of commodities. Chinese companies initially focused on the extractives sector, trying to secure oil and other resources for the country's booming manufacturing sector. African countries, many still reeling from a series of structural adjustments imposed by the Bretton Woods institutions, were glad for the business. The result was the rapid increase in China-Africa trade and other engagement during the 1990s, which set the scene for the formalization of the relationship at the end of the decade.

Forum on China-Africa Cooperation

Arguably the most important development in the China-Africa relationship was the establishment of the Forum on China-Africa Cooperation (FOCAC). It facilitated the evolution from a rapidly growing set of ad hoc relationships, to a formal platform for cooperation. The first FOCAC meeting took place in 2000, in Beijing. Since then, it has taken place regularly every three years, alternately in Africa and in China. Initially it took place at a ministerial level, but it has been frequently elevated to the summit level (attended by heads of state.) The formalization of the relationship also allowed its expansion from a relatively narrow commercial relationship to a far more comprehensive one covering many forms of cooperation.

At the beginning of the relationship, China was already a major provider of financing to the continent. FOCAC helped to expand and centralize this role. FOCAC meetings became the occasion for the announcement of increasingly ambitious funding targets, covering several areas of cooperation, of which infrastructure was a major one. In 2006, in Beijing, the first time FOCAC took place at the summit level, the Chinese government announced $5 billion in concessional loans to Africa. In 2009, in Sharm el-Sheikh, Egypt, this was increased to $10 billion. By 2012, in Beijing, it grew to $20 billion, and then $60 billion in Johannesburg, South Africa in 2015. The same sum was again announced at the 2018 summit in Beijing. In addition, the 2006 summit also saw the establishment of the China-Africa Development Fund, with a capitalization of $1 billion, which was increased to $5 billion at the 2012 summit in Beijing.

These numbers are shorthand for complex packages of different financing instruments. For example, the allocation of $60 billion that was announced in 2015, included $5 billion in aid and interest-free loans, $35 billion in export credits and concessional lending, $5 billion of additional capital to the China-Africa Development Fund, another $5 billion as a Special Loan for the Development of African Small and Medium Enterprises, and $10 billion in capitalization for a China-Africa Production Capacity Cooperation Fund.

What this breakdown makes clear is that China differs from other development partners in that most of its development assistance comes in the form of loans, rather than grants. The division is less between loans and grants, than between different kinds of loans, with a small fraction coming in the form of interest-free loans and the majority in the form of concessional lending, which forces lenders to pay interest, albeit at lower than global market rates.

There are a few important details to keep in mind. In the first place, the condition for participating in FOCAC is that a country should have diplomatic ties with China. These ties are dependent on accepting the One China Principle, which makes it impossible to simultaneously maintain relations with Taiwan, which China sees as a separatist province. Through the decades, Taiwan had established diplomatic relations with several African countries, but the rise of China as a major development partner has also led to the erosion of these ties. Currently only one African country, eSwatini (formerly known as Swaziland), still has ties with Taiwan, and for that reason it is the only African country that doesn't participate in FOCAC.

In the second place, while FO-CAC comes across as a platform for the whole African continent to engage with China collectively, it is actually structured as a large number of bilateral relationships between various African countries and China. While China also maintains diplomatic relations with the African Union, and has pledged cooperation with this body, as well as committing itself to multilateral cooperation on issues like peacekeeping, the China-Africa relationship is more accurately described as a series of relationships. This focus on bilateral relationships means that China far outstrips its African partners in both economic and political power. This power imbalance has led to numerous calls from observers for greater collectivity in African countries' negotiation with China, which has so far not been realized.

However, African countries have managed to use FOCAC as a mechanism to address continental priorities. While China's focus in FOCAC started off relatively narrowly, with a main focus on infrastructure and resources, African pressure has ensured that several other issues have been added to the agenda. Over time, FOCAC has been expanded to include a greater focus on peacekeeping. This was especially true from 2012, after which China sent peacekeeping troops to African countries like Mali and South Sudan under the auspices of the United Nations, and participated in patrols off the coast of East Africa, which has significantly lessened the threat of piracy to international vessels. African countries also put pressure on China in the

Then-Chinese Vice-President Xi Jinping delivers a speech during the 10th anniversary of the Forum on China-Africa Cooperation (FOCAC) on November 18, 2010, in Pretoria, South Africa. (PABALLO THEKISO/AFP/GETTY IMAGES)

context of FOCAC to focus more on wildlife crime. The rapid expansion of prosperity in China has led to a growing demand for rare wildlife products like ivory and rhino horn. This fueled a poaching economy in Africa, which led to the rapid decline of wild animal populations and the eruption of illegal trade driven by criminal syndicates. Pressure from African countries arguably led to the implementation of a Chinese ban on the domestic trade in ivory in 2015, a major victory for African conservation.

Finally, African countries also managed to secure much more robust commitments to training and skills transfer. The lack of broad-based skills is one of the largest challenges facing African development. The continent's population is very young – the average African is only 19 years old. While this youth dividend holds significant promise for African development, the relative lack of training facilities is a challenge. Chinese training, boosted by high-level diplomatic facilitation at the FOCAC level, has proven a major area of cooperation. Currently, tens of thousands of Africans receive training in China. China has recently surpassed France as the most important destination for African students, and currently hosts more African students than the U.S. and the UK combined.

This training happens in many fo-

rums at once. In the first place, the Chinese government grants thousands of scholarships to African students to study at Chinese universities. In addition, many African students also self-fund their studies in China. The establishment of Confucius Institutes at African universities has facilitated this process. These bodies, akin to France's Alliance Française, provide language and cultural instruction. They have proven controversial in the U.S., where they have been characterized as state-sponsored propaganda and influence-building tools. While similar concerns exist in Africa, African universities don't have many other ways to offer their students Mandarin-language education, which is highly sought after.

In addition to university education, training also happens via Chinese companies. For example, technology companies like Huawei frequently send employees to train in China. Training also happens at the government level. Thousands of government employees are trained in China every year in a variety of disciplines, from public administration to anti-corruption. Members of some ruling parties (for example South Africa's African National Congress) also receive political training from counterparts in the Chinese Communist Party.

Finally, the police and military have emerged as major vectors for skills transfer. Training of military and police personnel in everything from weapons systems to crowd control has functioned as a basis for closer relationships between bodies like the People's Liberation Army and various African militaries, a process boosted by numerous exchange visits and joint exercises. One example of the latter is triangular naval exercises that took place between China, South Africa and Russia in 2019.

From the African side, this training helps to fill serious skills deficits. It also has the wider implication of building relations between numerous African and Chinese institutions, from the state, to the province, to the school level. These relations will have a lasting impact. In the first place, training leads to the implementation of Chinese technical standards and methodologies in Africa, which will cement mainte-

nance and upgrade relationships going forward. In the second place, Chinese universities are under much pressure to conform to current thinking within the Chinese Communist Party on a variety of issues. This thinking is also transferred to African students and trainees. In the third place, the widespread training will have the effect of building long-term relationships between African elites and China, helping to shape their worldviews and providing a shared linguistic and cultural framework linking members of various African elites through shared time in China. The long-term impact of this training will be to build longer-term Chinese influence in Africa, even as Western governments make it harder for Africans to study at institutions in the U.S., Europe and the UK.

Overall, FOCAC provided crucial impetus to the China-Africa relation-

ship. In the first place, it framed and supported the commercial China-Africa relationship. China became the continent's largest trading partner in 2009, a position it still holds today. It is now the largest bilateral lender to many of Africa's largest economies, and Chinese companies are reshaping skylines across the continent. FOCAC was a crucial factor boosting the growth of this relationship. It didn't only provide a platform for massive amounts of financing, it also provides a forum for diplomacy. The optics of crowds of African leaders arriving to greet President Xi Jinping, and the opportunity to reiterate diplomatic talking points, mean that FOCAC plays a major role in selling the China-Africa relationship to publics on both sides. In the process, it allowed the blossoming of many areas of cooperation, as outlined below.

Current issues defining the China-Africa relationship

Infrastructure

Infrastructure remains one of Africa's most pressing needs. Deliberate underdevelopment under European colonialism, and these powers' focus on extraction from the hinterland, rather than connecting domestic economic centers have proven a major reason for the continent's continued poverty. The chaotic decolonization process, which was frequently only achieved through long civil conflict, the tendency for some colonial powers to abruptly withdraw without transition plans, a debt crisis and the subsequent impact of structural adjustment programs imposed by the Bretton Woods institutions in the 1980s and 1990s, corruption, and ill-designed national development plans have all contributed to a massive lack of infrastructure. The African Development Bank has estimated that the continent needs to spend between $130 and $170 billion per year to close this gap.

The lack of cross-border infrastructure is a particularly glaring problem. The World Bank has estimated that it costs less to ship a car from Japan to Kenya, than it does to get it from Ke-

nya to Nigeria. There is currently no major roadway or railway connecting East and West Africa. This means that, in the World Bank's example, the car would have to travel highly circuitous and inefficient routes, which will take time and cost money. In addition, it will also have to clear customs several times on the way, as it moves across different borders. The customs duties paid at each border will add significantly to its price by the time it reaches the Nigerian market.

For all of these reasons, African intra-continental trade stands at 15% of its total trade – the lowest continental rate in the world. Compare this to the European, where some member states' trade with their neighbors make up to 70% of their total trade, significantly boosting the prosperity of the bloc as a whole. Africa is rapidly moving to change this, particularly through its African Continental Free Trade Agreement (AfCFTA), agreed in 2019.

The lack of cross-border infrastructure is a big challenge to the implementation of the AfCFTA. In addition, the relative scarcity of ports, ICT

networks, industrial infrastructure and stable electricity supplies all make it harder for African countries to link themselves to the global economy and to attract foreign direct investors. Amid these challenges, China has emerged as the continent's most important provider of infrastructure. The reason for this has much to do with domestic concerns within China.

First, the Chinese government (as part of its Going Out strategy) has encouraged Chinese state-owned enterprises to explore the global market. This expansion drew heavily on China's own experience of development, which was significantly infrastructure-driven. Within a few decades, China has multiplied its own infrastructure, with rail, ICT and road networks expanding across its territory at breakneck speed. This process made Chinese state-owned construction companies the repositories of massive technical resources, and the Going Out strategy increased pressure on them to apply these skills elsewhere. They were made considerably more competitive through their relatively easy access to funding from Chinese state banks, like the China Exim Bank. In addition to the FOCAC-directed funding mentioned above, these banks have funneled billions of dollars of additional funding to African infrastructure projects, in the form of loans. This aid is tied, which means that it is dependent on recipient governments employing Chinese contractors, a factor which further boosts Chinese companies' foreign expansion. This process has received significant further momentum from the Belt and Road Initiative (BRI)

These factors have contributed to Chinese actors transforming skylines in many African cities. In many cases, this infrastructure took the form of showcase standalone projects—bridges, soccer stadiums, parliament buildings, mosques and power stations. However, in some cases, these have also boosted the implementation of Chinese models of development through infrastructure, for example via so-called "Port-Park-City" projects (see the section on Development Models below).

Some of these projects have also included cross-border connectivity. Kenya's Standard Gauge Railway was a key example, revealing some of the complications involved. In its original design, the SGR was supposed to link several East and Central African countries with the Kenyan port of Mombasa. The initial section of the railway, between Nairobi and Mombasa was finalized in 2017, with a second section, between Nairobi and an inland freight center in Naivasha, completed in 2019. The third section, which was supposed to connect Naivasha to Malaba on the Ugandan border, was supposed to then extend to the Ugandan capital of Kampala, and from there to Kigali in Rwanda, and Juba in South Sudan.

The initial two phases cost $3.8 billion and $1.5 billion respectively. 90% was funded through loans from the China Exim Bank to the Kenyan government, with the remainder directly funded by Nairobi. However, when President Uhuru Kenyatta travelled to Beijing in 2019 to secure the third loan that would connect Naivasha to Uganda, Chinese authorities refused,

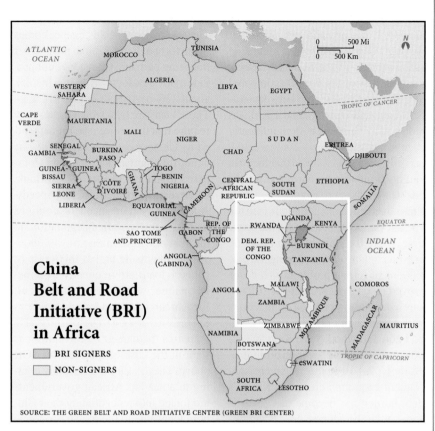

China Belt and Road Initiative (BRI) in Africa

- BRI SIGNERS
- NON-SIGNERS

SOURCE: THE GREEN BELT AND ROAD INITIATIVE CENTER (GREEN BRI CENTER)

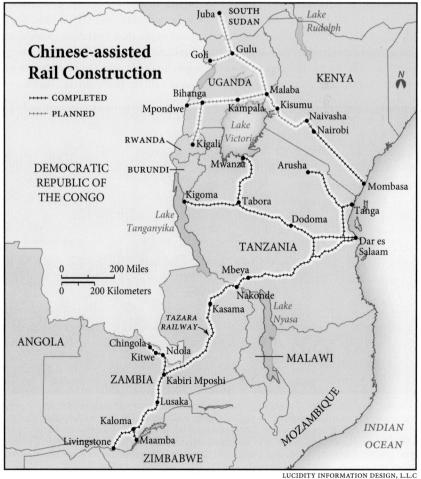

Chinese-assisted Rail Construction

- COMPLETED
- PLANNED

LUCIDITY INFORMATION DESIGN, L.L.C

and he was forced to return empty-handed. It was an early indication that Beijing was worried about the financial sustainability of the SGR. In Kenya, the high cost of the project (compared to a similar Chinese line between Addis Ababa and Djibouti, and a Turkish-built line in Tanzania, both significantly cheaper) was extremely controversial, and investigations showed that the loan had been inflated by corrupt officials, enabled by the pervasive secrecy that shrouded the loan negotiations (see the section on Debt, below.) At the same time, while the Nairobi-Mombasa line proved popular among passengers, projections of freight profits from the line proved inflated. At present it is still unsure whether the planned connections with Uganda and other countries will be built, and whether the Kenyan section of the SGR will ever be profitable. As the Covid-19 pandemic, and its subsequent economic crisis hit, Kenya's debt burden has become more worrisome, with the country now in significant danger of debt distress.

Debt

Chinese institutions like the China Export Import Bank and the China Development Bank have emerged as major financers of new African infrastructure. The vast majority of this finance comes in the form of loans. Unlike many other financing partners, China does not provide many development grants. In total, about 22% of Africa's debt is to China. These loans are tied, which means they require that the projects be implemented by Chinese contractors. On the one hand, this increases efficiency. Compared to lenders like the World Bank, Chinese projects are relatively speedy. A recent project in Ghana took only 18 months from the start of negotiations to the start of construction.

The downside is that the terms of Chinese loans are frequently extremely opaque, which makes it difficult for African courts and civil society to exercise oversight. The opacity also increases the danger of corruption, as seen in the case of the Kenyan SGR above. These issues are currently coming to a head as African governments are forced into renegotiating their Chinese loans due to the global economic impact of the Covid-19 pandemic. China has joined the G20's Debt Service Suspension Initiative (aimed at providing poor countries a temporary freeze in debt servicing to allow them to deal with the health crisis.) However,

in its debt renegotiations with African partners, Beijing has insisted on an opaque, case-by-case approach. This in turn has caused Africa's commercial and Eurobond lenders to delay their own renegotiation processes, out of fear that Chinese lenders will get better terms. As a result, African countries face the danger of running out of time and slipping into defaults on their loans while also battling an unprecedented health crisis.

The longer-term implications of this debt are still unclear. Over the last few years, American officials have warned that China is setting so-called 'debt traps' for poor countries, by enticing poor countries to lend more than they can afford. Once the country slips into debt distress, Chinese actors will then seize collateralized state assets. The main case cited as proof of this narrative is the Hambantota port in Sri Lanka, where the renegotiation of debt led to a Chinese company signing an exclusive 99-year lease on the port and surrounding areas. However, research has debunked this claim, showing that the Hambantota case wasn't a debt-for-equity swap. Rather, the deal was reached as a way for the Sri Lankan government to pay off other loans, and the Hambantota loans still have to be repaid. Up to now, there has been no evidence of Chinese actors seizing assets in Africa.

That said, it seems clear that Africa's heavy Chinese debt burden will shape its development in the future. However, this is truer for a few large African economies than for the continent as a whole. For example, during the early 2000s, the China Development Bank extended a number of oil-backed loans to Angola, a form of financing that came to be known as the Angola Model. At that time, Angola was a major oil exporter to China. The loans, to be repaid in oil, was also agreed at a moment of high oil prices. Subsequently, Angola's share of China's oil sales shrunk due to competition from Saudi Arabia, Russia, and the U.S. At the same time, global oil prices fell, which forced Angola to pay back a lot more oil than it had anticipated. In 2020 it was reported

A Kenya Railways Corp. freight train pulls shipping containers as it departs from the port station on the Mombasa-Nairobi Standard Gauge Railway (SGR) line in Mombasa, Kenya, on Sept. 1, 2018. China's modern-day adaptation of the Silk Road, known as the Belt and Road Initiative, aims to revive and extend trading routes connecting China with Central Asia, the Middle East, Africa and Europe via networks of upgraded or new railways, ports, pipelines, power grids and highways. (LUIS TATO/BLOOMBERG/GETTY IMAGES)

that these volumes made it difficult to bring sufficient oil to market. Angola was recently forced to renegotiate its loans with the China Development Bank, in the face of 2020's pandemic-related economic crisis.

While China doesn't seem interested in seizing assets in Africa, the wider implication of its loans to the continent will likely be closer political alignment between China and African countries in multilateral institutions like the UN, and the general increase of Chinese political leverage in Africa.

Technology and consumer market development

Africa is not frequently thought of as a technology hotspot, but this is changing rapidly. Africa's startup sector is growing rapidly, on the back of rapid expansion of ICT capacity in key countries. Chinese companies like Huawei, Transsion and ZTE are playing a key role in this trend. As with other forms of infrastructure, Chinese involvement in building ICT networks is aided by the close relationship between Chinese contractors and Chinese state banks like the China Exim Bank. The close relationship means that Chinese companies like Huawei are involved in almost every level of African ICT development. On the network side, Chinese contractors' experience in challenging environments mean that they are the preferred partners to state bank-funded projects including submarine network provision and the construction of 4G and 5G networks in both rural and urban environments. It is estimated that Huawei has built 70% of Africa's 4G capability.

However, the presence of these companies in Africa is more complex than their link with state banks. A company like Huawei has maintained a long presence in Africa. This includes building up close working relationships with African mobile service providers, like MTN in South Africa and Safaricom in Kenya. Huawei provides components, technical support and training to these companies. For this reason, African leaders have been loath to join pressure from the U.S. to

A staff member of Huawei introduces the latest technology of Huawei products to visitors from Benin at a forum of Northern Africa Innovation Day in Tunis, Tunisia, on Sept. 23, 2019. China's Huawei launched a forum of Northern Africa Innovation Day co-organized with the Tunisian government on Monday in Tunis. The event was attended by more than 300 Arab and African officials and specialists. (ADELE EZZINE/XINHUA/ALAMY)

stop working with these companies. Another reason for this hesitance is that these companies are also major sources of consumer electronics in Africa. The Chinese company Transsion is now the largest seller of mobile phones in Africa. Their products have been adapted to African conditions, and they sell both smartphones and old-fashioned feature phones, which frequently work better in areas with low network connectivity.

On the back of their provision of network and consumer hardware, Chinese companies are becoming more and more involved in the African tech services sector. African companies are world leaders in consumer financial technology (fintech) applications, notably in micropayment and microloan applications. Chinese venture capital investors now routinely take part in investment rounds in these sectors and joint ventures between Chinese and African tech companies are becoming more common. This is also true for media services. At the time of writing, the Chinese music streaming service Boomplay has about 65 million users in Africa (more than all the paying subscribers to Apple Music in the world.) The satellite TV company StarTimes has a similarly formidable footprint

in both East and West Africa, one that is further boosted by its provision of content in African languages, and its 10,000 Villages Project, which rolls out satellite TV access to poor communities, again with the support of Chinese state banks.

Chinese technology provers are also increasingly promoting 'Smart City' and 'Safe City' projects in Africa. These frequently have a strong public safety and policing component, powered via Chinese facial recognition, AI and surveillance capabilities. African governments promote these as responses to the problem of urban crime. However, critics are concerned that these surveillance systems could also be turned against political opponents. Chinese companies have come in for a lot of criticism from Western governments for promoting this technology in Africa, especially to authoritarian governments. However, independent research has shown that Western companies are similarly willing to provide these tools to illiberal governments.

Development models

China's engagement with Africa is strongly development-focused. This is driven by African authorities. For example, the African Union has put

In Changzhou City, Jiangsu Province, China, April 2, 2020, A worker is assembling locomotives that will be exported to Nigeria. These locomotives will serve Nigeria's Akha railway and Rai railway, which are all built in Africa with Chinese technical standards. (COSTFOTO/BARCROFT MEDIA/GETTY IMAGES)

much emphasis on its own continent-wide development plan, known as Agenda 2063, and its Programme for Infrastructure Development in Africa (PIDA). However, China's own story of rapid development carries a lot of weight in Africa. While Chinese officials frequently downplay the direct applicability of Chinese modes of development in other countries, they also promote China as a uniquely equipped development partner thanks to its own dazzlingly rapid development arc.

One of the models China promotes is infrastructure-boosted development via mass manufacturing. This doesn't only focus on individual pieces of infrastructure, like ports. It is frequently presented in a bundled form, known as the 'Port-Park-City' model. This refers to development focused on specialized industrial parks (frequently known as Special Economic Zones) which at-tract manufacturing businesses through privileged access to cheap electricity and other perks. These are linked (frequently via rail) to the 'City' – a nearby settlement supporting workers and support industries, and to the 'Port', which facilitates mass exports – a key aspect of China's development.

The Chinese-funded special economic zones of Ethiopia, linked via a rail line to the port of Djibouti, which is currently run by a Chinese company, is one of the clearest examples of this model in action. It is aimed at boosting development through low-wage manufacturing and exports. These initiatives are also frequently centrally planned by governments, rather than driven by the private sector – all hallmarks of Chinese development. Chinese investments in Ethiopian Special Economic Zones, focused on the shoe and apparel sector, helped it to establish itself as an exporter to the European market. Western brands like H&M have subsequently also started manufacturing in Ethiopia.

The Chinese model stands in contrast with Western ideas of development, which emphasize the rule of law, democracy, the building of transparent public institutions, and a strong private sector-led approach.

While the Chinese approach has been successful in Ethiopia, and several other special economic zones are being planned in other African countries, there are questions about whether they're really suited to African conditions. The rising costs of labor in China has led many to argue that offshoring some of this manufacturing to Africa could create jobs. However, many Chinese manufacturing jobs migrated to poor provinces in western China, or countries like Vietnam and Bangladesh, or were lost to automation instead. African countries' electricity supplies and support industries are frequently not well-developed enough to support the special economic zones. In addition, there are questions about whether Africa's development trajectory will include a mass manufacturing phase or whether it will leapfrog directly into a service economy, as can be seen in the rapid rise of African fintech startups.

Despite these questions, it should be acknowledged that China's record of development, and its provision of a new, non-Western development model, carry significant weight among African leaders. The history of deliberate under-development under Western colonialism is still holding Africa back today, and in that context, China is seen as a key alternative.

Future issues in the China-Africa relationship

U.S.-China tensions

The last few years have seen growing tensions between the U.S. and China, as seen in trends like the Trump administration's pressure on Chinese companies and the ongoing trade tensions between the two countries. China's lending to countries in the global south, and its Belt and Road Initiative have drawn sharp criticism from U.S. government officials. While the Trump administration has been particularly hawkish about China's growing international presence, China's rise raises concerns on both sides of the political aisle in the U.S.

China's large role as a development partner in Africa puts the continent in a difficult position in relation to these growing tensions. There are fears that

Kenyan President Uhuru Kenyatta (C) attends the launching ceremony of the 50 MW solar power farm in Garissa, Kenya, Dec. 13, 2019. The plant, designed and built by the EPC contractor China Jiangxi Corporation for International Economic and Technical Co-operation (CJIC), in conjunction with Kenya's Rural Energy Authority (REA), is one of the largest photovoltaic electricity stations in Africa. (XIE HAN XINHUA/EYEVINE/REDUX)

it will come under increased pressure to choose between its development partners, an outcome most African leaders are anxious to avoid.

As mentioned above, China's relationship with Africa is overwhelmingly structured through bilateral relationships. However, U.S.-China tensions are also increasingly playing out in multilateral arenas, like the United Nations. China's cooperation with African states in these forums date back to the Cold War, when African votes helped the People's Republic of China to displace Taiwan as China's official representative at the United Nations. More recently, African votes have helped to secure positions for Chinese officials at the head of key UN agencies. African countries also helped defeat resolutions by Western countries criticizing Chinese human rights conduct in places like Xinjiang.

The reason for this cooperation is complex. It can be partly located in the fact that China is a massive trading, investment and development partner to these countries, and African leaders see cooperation on issues like Xinjiang as a relatively low-cost way to ensure the long-term continuation of the relationship. However, this conduct can't

only be ascribed to financial factors. It also has to do with African perceptions of being largely structurally excluded from forums like the UN Security Council, the G7 and G20, and the Bretton Woods Institutions. China routinely voices support for the reform of these institutions, and supports African candidates for their leadership. For this reason, the U.S.-China tensions also play out in institutions like the World Health Organization. Any attempt at resolving these tensions will also have to include greater focus on the systemic exclusion of African countries from these institutions, and on the U.S. building wider coalitions around shared values.

Energy

China is in the unusual position of being both the world's largest implementer of coal-fired power capacity, the largest importer of foreign oil, and yet, also by far the world's largest implementer of renewable energy capacity. All these factors will have significant impacts on Africa.

In the first place, Chinese state-owned enterprises are under much pressure to find overseas markets. The expertise in these companies tend to hew more in the

direction of conventional energy (renewables are better represented in the private sector.) This means that these SOEs are actively campaigning for projects in markets like Africa. There is currently several conventional power plants being built by Chinese companies in various African countries, which lock these regions into decades of unsustainable electricity provision. At the same time, Chinese providers of renewable energy are also well-represented on the African continent. Several large-scale Chinese-funded and built solar installations have been finalized in African countries, and several more are in process.

While there is some evidence of a bias among Chinese state banks towards funding projects headed by SOEs, the choice between renewable and conventional power generation frequently lies with the African government. Chinese contractors have expertise in both sectors and Chinese banks fund both. In fact, the Chinese-led Asian Infrastructure Investment Bank recently announced that it will cease funding coal-powered electricity generation in the future.

This means that the choice between polluting or sustainable energy frequently comes down to how much

Activists march on June 5, 2018, in Nairobi carrying placards bearing messages to denounce plans by the Kenyan government to mine coal close to the pristine coastal archipelago of Lamu, on World Environment Day. (TONY KARUMBA/AFP/GETTY IMAGES)

tries have joined the initiative, including 44 African countries.

Many Chinese infrastructure projects in Africa preceded the announcement of the BRI, but they have been retroactively categorized as BRI projects. Since the coining, about 80 Chinese state-owned enterprises have launched about 3,100 BRI-related projects worldwide.

The long-term aim of the BRI is to strengthen economic and other links between China and other countries, especially those on the Indian Ocean rim, in Southeast, South and Central Asia, and in Europe, but also drawing in countries further afield. These links will aid the centrality of the Chinese economy in the world, and help to foster closer cooperation between China and partner countries in many spheres.

This push towards greater influence has drawn negative reactions from the U.S., as well as from Asian powers like India. At present, it is still unclear how much of the BRI will be built, especially in the face of a global recession due to Covid-19, and a longer-term slowing down of the Chinese economy. However, it is clear that the initiative enjoys strong political will from the Chinese Communist Party. The fact that President Xi Jinping has made it a centerpiece of his administration. The fact that the term limits on his reign were removed in 2018 makes it likely that the BRI will remain central to Chinese relations with the external world, including Africa, for the foreseeable future.

pressure local communities and civil society organizations can put on African governments, and how much power local hydrocarbon lobbies wield. There is evidence of growing resistance against coal-powered electricity from African communities. In 2018, a group of NGOs representing local communities successfully sued the Kenyan government to stop a partially Chinese-funded coal-powered plant that was going to be built in near Lamu Island, a UNESCO World Heritage site. However, in other countries like South Africa and Zimbabwe, controversial Chinese-funded coal-powered projects are still going ahead. It remains to be seen whether it will be possible to convince Chinese authorities to stop funding coal capacity.

The Belt and Road Initiative

China's Belt and Road Initiative (BRI) can probably best be described as a set of policy directives issued by the Chinese government aimed at directing a myriad of Chinese actors towards a massive global rollout of infrastructure. In a larger sense, it can be seen as a vision of a China-centric world, with infrastructure connecting China to large parts of the global south and Europe. However, it also includes numerous even bigger initiatives, including a

component focusing on space exploration, and another on health cooperation.

The BRI was announced by President Xi Jinping in 2013, and has subsequently become the centerpiece of Chinese foreign policy and international development strategies. The BRI is based on the so-called 'five connectivities.' This is shorthand for connections forged between member countries through infrastructure connectivity, free trade, financial integration, policy coordination and people-to-people exchange. Joining the BRI is open to all countries, by signing a Memorandum of Understanding with the Chinese government. As of March 2020, 138 coun-

U.S. policy recommendations

The U.S. has viewed the expansion of China's engagement with Africa with some alarm. The Trump administration has put containing Chinese influence on the continent at the heart of its Africa policy. However, African leaders have so far resisted pressure to choose sides between the major powers. Calls to stop cooperating with companies like Huawei has proven particularly unsuccessful. China's

provision of finance, its experience in building infrastructure in challenging terrain, and efficiency in project delivery outlined in this chapter explain why many African countries are unwilling to sever their relationship with China.

Rather than confronting the China-Africa relationship head-on, U.S. policymakers would be better advised to focus on rebuilding the U.S.-Africa relationship, through focusing on areas of where the U.S. has particular advantage. These include:

1) Education: While China is pouring significant resources into educational exchange with Africa, the U.S.'s university system is unparalleled in strength. Africa has a very young population and education is one of its most pressing needs. Moves by the Trump administration to make it more difficult for African students to study at American universities are extremely unhelpful, and should be reversed immediately. Rather, American universities should lead African outreach efforts. The more Africans studying in the U.S., and the more American universities collaborate with African counterparts, the more America's voice and worldview will gain influence on the continent.

2) Debt: Africa is currently suffering from unsustainable debt levels, which threaten to erase two decades of sustained economic growth. As was unpacked in this chapter, a major part of this debt is to China, and the opacity of Chinese lending practices has significantly contributed to the problem. The U.S. can do much to help its own financial sector to make it easier to provide relief of commercial debt to Africa. At the same time it would be very helpful if the U.S. spearheaded a global effort to get China to conform to global norms of transparency in lending.

3) Services: As outlined in this chapter, China has a particularly strong capacity for infrastructure provision. Few countries can compare with this ability, especially as regards project implementation in challenging terrains like one finds in Africa. Rather than facing China head-on in the sector, I would suggest that the U.S. focuses on its unparalleled strength in the service sector. Greater involvement from US legal firms, consultancies and research institutions would help a lot in making Chinese projects in African countries more sustainable, and to aid civil so-

U.S. philanthropist and Microsoft founder Bill Gates speaks during the 32nd African Union (AU) summit in Addis Ababa on February 10, 2019. While multiple crises on the continent will be on the agenda of heads of state from the 55 member nations, the two-day summit will also focus on institutional reforms, and the establishment of a continent-wide free trade zone. (SIMON MAINA/AFP/GETTY IMAGES)

ciety organizations in getting African governments to make the terms of infrastructure contracts more transparent.

4) Media diplomacy and diaspora outreach: While China has made important inroads into the African mediasphere via companies like the satellite TV provider StarTimes, American media still enjoys massive popularity on the continent. This is especially true for African American TV, music and sports. This popularity provides many opportunities to use African American media as vehicles for public diplomacy. In addition, the U.S. has a massive advantage over China due to the large communities of African expatriates living in the U.S. African countries like Nigeria and Ghana have maintained fruitful cross-Atlantic networks with diaspora populations, while also spearheading outreach to the wider African American community. These programs are extremely valuable in providing the U.S. with a voice on the continent, especially in comparison with China's frequently unhappy relationship with communities of African expatriates in cities like Guangzhou. However, the U.S.'s influence in Africa is gravely affected by well-founded perceptions that Black communities in

the U.S. face discriminatory policing and other exclusionary measures. This tarnishes the image of the U.S. among particularly middle class and wealthy populations in Africa.

5) Technology: As outlined in this chapter, China is a major internet and mobile phone provider to Africa. The U.S. has attempted to pressure African countries to stop this cooperation, to little avail. It would be more fruitful to encourage greater cooperation between the U.S. and African tech sectors. There are numerous African startups looking for venture capital, and many chances for joint ventures. Closer working relationships between the African tech sector in countries like Nigeria, South Africa and Kenya, and Silicon Valley, will be beneficial to both sides, while also offering African countries choices beyond China. Keep in mind that many African actors share some U.S. misgivings about Chinese technology, but they don't have many alternatives. Matchmaking between U.S. companies and African partners will have the effect of diversifying the African technology and startup sector, while expanding American access to the world's last major emerging market for consumer technology.

discussion questions

1. How has Africa's historical relationship with Europe shaped its relationship with China? How does the concept of South-South solidarity strengthen China's position in Africa?

2. Why have U.S. efforts to stop African cooperation with China been largely unsuccessful? Are there ways to redefine the way the U.S. approaches the issue?

3. What are the hallmarks of the Chinese development model as it relates to Africa? Do you think it is a suitable option for Africa?

4. How do you think debt will reshape the China-Africa relationship? Which options are open to Africa to make its debt burden more sustainable without giving up on its development goals?

5. What are the pros and cons of Africa collaborating with Chinese technology companies? Do you foresee other tech companies acting as competitors, and why?

6. Which role has infrastructure played in the China-Africa relationship? How do you think this affects African development?

suggested readings

Alden, Chris and Large, Daniel, **New Directions in Africa - China Studies**, 368pg: Routledge, 2019. A wide-ranging collection of writing from some of the most prominent scholars in the field on a wide range of Africa-China issues. A good introduction to the breadth of the relationship.

Shinn, David and Eisenman, Joshua, **China and Africa: A Century of Engagement**, 542pg. University of Pennsylvania Press, 2012. A comprehensive introduction to the history of China-Africa relations, providing detailed country views.

Brautigam, Deborah, **Will Africa Feed China?** 247pg. Oxford University Press, 2015, This book takes a close look at the issue of agriculture exports from Africa to China, and fact - checks allegations of Chinese land grabs in Africa. A valuable corrective to misinformation about Chinese activities in Africa

Benabdallah, Lina, **Shaping the future of power: Knowledge Production and Network-Building in China-Africa relations,** 204 pg. University of Michigan Press, 2020. This book focuses on the role of training and skills transfer in forging China - Africa relationships. A very valuable account of both civilian and military engagement

Gagliardone, Iginio, **China, Africa and the future of the Internet: New media, new politics**, 202 pg. UK: Zed Books, This book provides a detailed account of Chinese internet provision in Africa, and challenges some common perceptions of Chinese companies' impact on democracy in Africa.

Sun, Irene Yuan, T**he next factory of the world: How Chinese investment is reshaping Africa**, 224 pg. Harvard Business Review Press, An accessible account informed by field research of the impact of Chinese industrialization efforts notably in Ethiopia.

Don't forget: Ballots start on page 104!!!!

To access web links to these readings, as well as links to global discussion questions, shorter readings and suggested web sites,
GO TO www.fpa.org/great_decisions
and click on the topic under Resources, on the right-hand side of the page.

The two Koreas
by Scott A. Snyder

North Korea's leader Kim Jong Un (R) walk with South Korean President Moon Jae-in (L) during a visit to Samjiyon guesthouse in Samjiyon on September 20, 2018 in Samjiyon, North Korea. Kim and Moon meet for the Inter-Korean summit talks after the 1945 division of the peninsula, where they will discuss ways to denuclearize the Korean Peninsula. (PYEONGYANG PRESS CORPS/POOL/GETTY IMAGES)

Since the Korean War, South Korea has emerged as an economic powerhouse with growing global capabilities and influence, a knack for scientific and technological innovation, and a rapidly expanding set of cultural offerings that have captivated audiences around the world. South Korea has become a critical ally to the U.S. in Northeast Asia and serves as an example of how nations can leverage their middle power status to have an outsized impact on the global agenda. The overwhelmingly positive global assessment of South Korea's handling of the Covid-19 pandemic and cultural power of K-Pop serve as two examples of this phenomena. However, domestic economic and political woes, intensified Sino-U.S. rivalry, the continued North Korean nuclear threat, and increasing pressures on the U.S.-South Korea alliance relationship threaten to derail South Korea's aspirations for autonomy and its ability to secure its national security interests on its own. As Northeast Asia enters an era of great power conflict, South Korea may be forced to make choices between the U.S. and China that it has thus far avoided, and these choices will likely have lasting implications for the Korean Peninsula.

SCOTT A. SNYDER *is senior fellow for Korea studies and director of the program on U.S.-Korea policy at the Council on Foreign Relations (CFR). His program examines South Korea's efforts to contribute on the international stage; its potential influence and contributions as a middle power in East Asia; and the peninsular, regional, and global implications of North Korean instability.*

South Korea's Candlelight Movement President

South Korea's President Moon Jae-in is the standard bearer of the "candlelight movement," an outpouring of South Korean public demands for accountability in the wake of the allegations of corruption, extortion, and self-dealing against former President Park Geun-hye that led to her impeachment in fall 2016. Those allegations came to light when the Korean media found a lost laptop of Park's close friend and associate Choi Sun-sil containing incriminating evidence regarding Choi's efforts to use her close relationship with President Park to secure funds from the Samsung Corporation and other leading conglomerates for her daughter's equestrian career and

terests, first as a democratization movement leader and human rights lawyer in the 1980s, later as a top aide and chief of staff to progressive South Korean president and fellow human rights lawyer Roh Moo-hyun in 2003–08, and finally as the leader called to restore South Korean public faith in leadership and to bring about a less corrupt, more accountable government.

The circumstances under which Moon took office following Park's impeachment created an immediate need for inclusive and restorative leadership. Moon needed to restore the South Korean public's confidence in their president. Moon's comments at his inauguration the day after his election set the

right tone: "I will become an honest president who keeps his promises . . . Genuine political progress will be possible only when the president takes the initiative in engaging in politics that can garner trust. I will not talk big about doing something impossible. I will admit to the wrong I did. I will not cover up unfavorable public opinion with lies. I will be a fair president." Moon pledged both to restore public trust and set high expectations for his administration's performance.

In addition, Moon made striking efforts to emphasize that he was accessible and in tune with public sentiment, in contrast to the image of his cloistered and imperious predecessor. Moon had tea on the Blue House lawn with his new staff, visited Korean shop owners and factories, and fashioned an Obama-like image of accessibility and inclusion in his public appearances. Moon also established a national petition platform on the Blue House website that enabled the public to directly petition the Blue House and committed the government to respond if the public petition garnered support from 200,000 citizens within 30 days.

A second immediate challenge was the task of selecting a team of officials to build and implement Moon's policy platform without the benefit of time for a transition. In the initial weeks of his presidency, Moon was surrounded by hold-over appointees from a caretaker government largely appointed by Park. Having already assumed the office of the presidency, Moon had to appoint his own personal staff and select new cabinet ministers to lead the bureaucracy. Moon's first hundred days were more about gaining control over the levers of government than about implementing policy measures prepared in advance of his assumption of office.

Beyond those challenges, Moon inherited a daunting set of economic problems. South Korea's economy was beset with relatively low growth rates compared to prior historical performance benchmarks, overdependence on export-led growth primarily gener-

Supporters of South Korea's former president Park Geun-hye gather during a rally demanding the release of Park Geun-hye outside the Seoul Central District Court in Seoul on April 6, 2018. (JUNG YEON-JE/AFP/GETTY IMAGES)

to secure a place for her daughter at the prestigious Ewha Womans University. These revelations mobilized the largest peaceful public protests since Korea's democratization in the late 1980s, with Moon and other progressive leaders at the forefront, tanking Park's public approval ratings to four percent.

Before you read, download the companion **Glossary** that includes definitions, a guide to acronyms and abbreviations used in the article, and other material. Go to **www. fpa.org/great_decisions** and select a topic in the Resources section. (Top right)

The massive withdrawal of public support led to Park's impeachment in December 2016 and removal from office in March 2017, followed by a constitutionally-mandated snap election held within 60 days of the Constitutional Court's impeachment ruling. Moon won with 41 percent of the vote over a fellow reformist, Ahn Cheol-soo, and a conservative rival, Hong Joon-pyo. For Moon, who had narrowly lost to Park five years earlier, the victory was vindication for a career spent promoting government accountability to public inated by Korea's largest conglomerates at the expense of domestic growth, and exceptionally high youth unemployment combined with an inadequate social safety net to support South Korea's aging population.

Moon's initial economic policies focused on expansion of public sector hiring, boosting of South Korea's minimum wage, encouragement to businesses to transition workers from contract to regular work status with full benefits, and imposition of a ceiling on work hours per week. But this wage-led economic growth policy proved controversial and ineffective, especially for the small businesses that bore the brunt of mandatory wage increases and work-week limits. Under the burden of the costs imposed by new regulations, many small businesses shed workers and faced greater difficulties staying afloat.

Another of Moon's controversial policy involved real estate reforms designed to curb speculative investments, including the imposition of higher taxes on owners of more than one property, capping of rent increases, and the revamping of South Korea's traditional one hundred percent down payment rental system. The real estate taxes targeted rich South Korean landholders with multiple properties, but their impact was made more complex by the illiquidity of housing investments and the fact that Korean families have traditionally seen housing as a safer avenue for investment than the Korean stock market. The desired impact of the real estate tax reforms was to drive prices down, lowering the price of entry into the housing market for younger buyers, but instead resulted in higher prices, greater illiquidity in the real estate market, and significant public backlash.

Moon proved more successful in directing long-term government investment into areas designed to enhance provision of public goods while also stimulating economic growth. The investments mainly targeted the Digital Economy and Korea's own Green New Deal, which both involve substantial outlays of public capital but also promise to generate hundreds of thousands of

jobs in sectors that would make the Korean economy more efficient long-term.

Perhaps the most contentious of Moon's policy initiatives proved to be in the area of public sector reforms, most notably reforms of the institutional structure of the public prosecutor's office and anti-corruption agencies that generated resistance among prosecutors and public backlash. Moon's

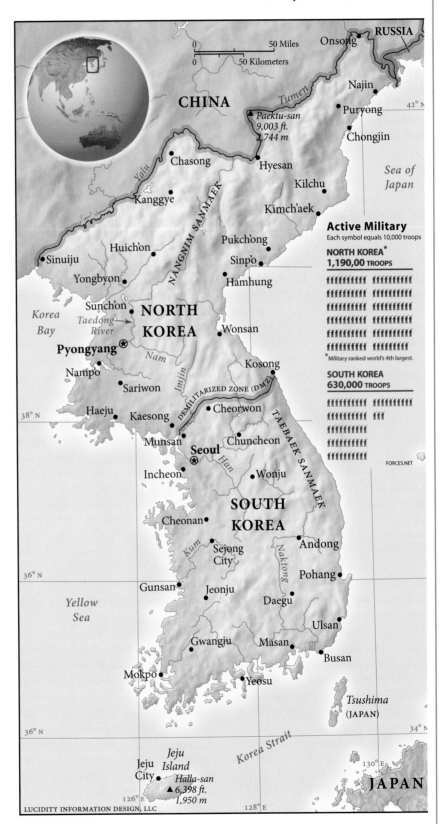

Active Military
Each symbol equals 10,000 troops

NORTH KOREA*
1,190,00 TROOPS

*Military ranked world's 4th largest.

SOUTH KOREA
630,000 TROOPS

FORCES.NET

LUCIDITY INFORMATION DESIGN, LLC

reforms touched on ingrained power-holding institutions such as the public prosecutors' office but came to be perceived among Moon critics as revenge rather than reform; i.e., designed to perpetuate progressive political power and to institutionalize a base for perpetuation of long-term political influence at the expense of conservative opposition.

Most controversial was the proposal to establish a prosecutorial office dedicated to investigation of political corruption, but without sufficient transparency as to whether the new office would truly operate independently of executive branch influence. Skeptic doubts about the new institution were inflamed by an ongoing public spat between the justice minister and the chief prosecutor over control of prosecutorial appointments within the existing apparatus. Debate continues over whether the reforms are intended to improve the system or to tilt the playing field to the benefit of the party in power.

Moon's greatest political asset as president has been the perception that he has historically operated as a "clean" leader who has avoided the political corruption scandals that have stained so many high-level Korean political leaders. On balance, Moon's steady hand, basic competency, and moderation has been rewarded with relatively high public support ratings. But Moon's caution and prudence have also resulted in political weakness to the extent that he has either been perceived as indecisive or as susceptible to manipulation by more ideologically-driven advisers.

Covid-19 and the Korean response

The world watched as the Chinese city of Wuhan reeled from the effects of a new strain of coronavirus in late January that led to a near total lockdown of the city. For South Korea, the U.S., and the rest of the world, the virus seemed a world away and the initial focus was on extricating foreign nationals from the lockdown precipitated by the contagious nature of the virus officially named Covid-19 by the World Health Organization.

South Korea and the U.S. both recorded their first cases on January 30, 2020. Within days, South Korea became the first epicenter for spread of the virus outside of China. The Korean Center for Disease Control (KCDC) nimbly applied lessons learned from the spread of previous Asian coronaviruses such as the Sudden Acute Respiratory Syndrome (SARS) in the mid-2000s and the Middle East Respiratory Syndrome (MERS) in 2014 to contain the first wave of the virus within weeks, providing a textbook example of effective contagious disease response as other countries struggled to respond.

The most important initial step in South Korea's response was the mobilization of effective public-private cooperation to produce a test for Covid-19 detection based on information about the genetic structure of the virus provided by China. This public-private coordination enabled South Korea to build out and ramp up an effective testing regime. Within days, South Korean companies were producing tests and labs were analyzing the results to diagnose Covid-19 cases. South Korea introduced drive-through testing, a technique quickly adopted around the world that made testing widely available and reduced contamination risks that would accompany patients into doctor's offices and hospital waiting rooms.

The second element of South Korea's response learned from prior experience with SARS and MERS involved the mobilization of cell phone technology to conduct contact tracing. By marrying cell phone tracking with information about the movements of those who had contracted Covid-19, the KCDC effectively traced the spread of the disease and provided text message warnings to those who had come into contact with identified Covid-19 carriers and to those visiting places that had also been visited by Covid-positive patients.

This technology-driven approach has inspired debate about balancing public health concerns and individual privacy, both through the tracing of the proximity of individuals to locations where spread occurred and through the use of information about individual whereabouts without user consent. The risks of state intrusion on individual privacy were thrown into relief by widespread reporting on Covid-19 spread. The first clash came in government use of technology to identify patrons of same sex and transgender bars where patrons sought anonymity because of the risks of social stigmatization. A second clash came through the government's use of technology to identify patrons of churches that had become conservative catalysts of political opposition to the Moon administration.

The third element of South Korea's successful initial Covid-19 response involved treatment practices, including effective triage of severe cases that reduced the burden on hospital caseloads and provision of quarantine facilities where doctors and nurses could monitor patients while reducing the risk of further spread. South Korea's quarantine protocols and offers of testing for undocumented migrants in Korea without fear of deportation also included quarantine requirements and provision of room and board for foreigners to prevent travelers from introducing the disease from outside South Korea.

South Korea's response to Covid-19 benefited from high South Korean trust in specialized expertise within South Korean government institutions. KCDC Director Jeung Eun-kyung and her colleagues led South Korea's response with twice daily briefings that emphasized the importance of a public health response to the virus and provided the South Korean public with clear guidelines on how to respond.

South Korea also benefited from the

fact that the habit of mask-wearing was already a part of the culture, as a means to prevent spread of illnesses, to show courtesy to others, and due to worsening air quality in South Korea. The benefits and utility of mask-wearing were already widely accepted in South Korea, and further strengthened by guidance from the KCDC emphasizing the importance of personal protective equipment (PPE), social distancing, and hand cleaning.

Thanks to its mobilization of public-private cooperation, technology-driven approach, effective treatment practices, culture of mask-wearing, and the relatively high compliance of the South Korean public with government instructions, South Korea avoided a China-style lockdown in its initial response. South Korean day-to-day activities in many areas were subdued, but not suppressed, by state guidelines. Many restaurants remained open, though economic activity was hindered by Korean personal choices to avoid dining choices that might heighten the risk of community spread.

South Korea quickly dropped from the country with the second largest number of detected cases at the beginning of March to ranking seventy-fifth in number of cases at almost 20,000 by the end of August. South Korea experienced around three hundred Covid-19 deaths from January to August out of a population of fifty million people, or a rate of six deaths per million people. South Korea recorded the 150th highest mortality rate per capita among over 200 countries and territories during this time period. South Korea's successful initial response has become a talking point for the Moon administration at international meetings, and South Korea's supply of Covid-19 test kits and PPE has become a diplomatic opportunity for it to enhance its positive image and engender international good will.

In contrast, North Korea's response to the pandemic remains shrouded in secrecy and characterized by disinformation. North Korea's isolation means that the international community knows little about the true impact of Covid-19 on the North Korean people. The North Korean state media emphasized public awareness of the virus early on and imposed a strict quarantine on import of goods as well as restrictions on foreign diplomats in Pyongyang, enhancing state control over both information and goods from the outside and reducing the possibility of Covid-19 spread.

While publicly denying any Covid-19 cases since the outbreak began to receive public notice in January 2020, North Korea has quietly requested Covid-19 test kits and PPE from international organizations as well as friendly states such as China and Russia and rejected offers of assistance from South Korea and the U.S.. Both the level of state media attention to Covid-19 and periodic reports from defector-based media suggest that Covid-19 deaths have occurred inside North Korea, but it is impossible to know how widespread the virus might be or to believe that North Korea would not succeed in utilizing draconian methods to quash the virus once detected. Ultimately, Covid-19's impact on North Korea will likely stem not from the spread of the virus itself, but from the enhanced state measures undertaken to quarantine imports and to contain the spread of the virus.

The revival and decline of inter-Korean summitry

Civilians from Hungnam in North Korea boarding the landing ship 'USS Jefferson County' (LST-845) of the US Navy, as they flee their city during the Korean War, 19th December 1950. The evacuation of Hungnam was code-named Christmas Cargo. A US Navy Defense Department photograph. (US NAVY DEFENSE DEPARTMENT/FPG/ARCHIVE PHOTOS/GETTY IMAGES)

South Korean President Moon Jae-in's most heartfelt policy priority has been to serve as a peacemaker with North Korea. Perhaps, because his family originated in North Korea but fled south as part of the U.S.-led Hungnam evacuation in December 1950, Moon felt destined to reunite the two Koreas. Moon sought to restore a progressive policy of inter-Korean engagement and summit dialogue following in the footsteps of his predecessors Kim Dae-jung (1998–2003) and Roh Moo-hyun (2003–08). During that time, engagement with North Korea was premised on the idea that functional cooperation through promotion of a joint industrial complex at Kaesong and a tourism project at Mount Kumgang would lead to inter-Korean economic integration, to change inside North Korea, and eventually, to the long-held dream of Korean unification.

But conservative South Korean leaders reversed and dismantled these inter-Korean cooperation projects in response to six North Korean nuclear tests between 2006 and 2017 and the

In this handout image provided by South Korean Defense Ministry, A North Korean soldier (L) shakes hands with a South Korean soldier during a mutual on-site verification of the withdrawal of guard posts along the Demilitarized Zone (DMZ) on December 12, 2018 in DMZ, North Korea. (SOUTH KOREAN DEFENSE MINISTRY/GETTY IMAGES)

passage of over ten UN Security Council sanctions resolutions condemning those tests. The U.S. and North Korea were on a trajectory toward confrontation over North Korea's nuclear and missile development. Moon sought to reverse the deterioration in relations with North Korea, but to do so, he would have to overcome North Korea's animosity and reverse its nuclear development.

In July 2017, Moon began his quest with a policy speech in Berlin, the same city where Kim Dae-jung laid out his approach to inter-Korean relations in 2000. Moon emphasized the need for a permanent peace regime on the Korean Peninsula while calling on North Korea to accept "complete, irreversible, verifiable denuclearization" as an essential condition for achieving this peace. Moon sought to institutionalize a permanent peace structure on the peninsula and to draw a "new economic map on the Korean peninsula" by reconnecting railways and promoting nonpolitical exchange and cooperation.

Moon's speech appeared to fall on deaf ears in Pyongyang as North Korea continued a break-neck pace of long-range missile testing and conducted its largest nuclear test to date in September 2017. But following a November 2017 test of its largest missile yet, the

North Koreans announced that their long-range testing was complete. Kim Jong-un pivoted toward a diplomatic charm offensive, first sending an athletic team and a high-level delegation led by his sister, Kim Yo-jong, to the 2018 Pyeongchang Olympics in South Korea. Using inter-Korean Olympic engagement as a backdrop, Kim Jong-un pledged to "work toward complete denuclearization" in a series of three summit meetings with Moon Jae-in in April, May, and September 2018.

The April 27, 2018, Panmunjom Summit, held on the South Korean side of the demilitarized zone (DMZ) dividing the two Koreas, involved a full day of negotiations, private one-on-one meetings, and photo opportunities, which culminated in the announcement of the Panmunjom Declaration. The declaration included a road map for and pledges to institutionalize inter-Korean exchanges and dialogue in a wide range of areas, reduce military tensions, and establish a permanent peace regime on a denuclearized Korean Peninsula. The Panmunjom Declaration reaffirmed and built on the commitments made in prior inter-Korean declarations, serving as a catalyst for inter-Korean exchanges and for the construction and establishment of an inter-Korean liaison office at Kaesong.

A second impromptu, then-secret inter-Korean summit between Moon and Kim occurred a month later on the North Korean side of the DMZ in a successful effort to put back on track preparations for the first U.S.-North Korea summit meeting between Donald J. Trump and Kim Jong-un to be held in Singapore on June 12, 2018. Moon played a critical intermediary role in setting up the historic Singapore Summit on the basis of the explicit recognition that inter-Korean relations and U.S.-North Korea relations must move together to achieve lasting progress toward peace-and-denuclearization on the Korean Peninsula.

By the third inter-Korean summit on September 18–20, 2018, there appeared to be real momentum for a transformation of the situation on the Korean Peninsula. The Agreement on the Implementation of the Historic Panmunjeom Declaration in the Military Domain, known as the Comprehensive Military Agreement, removed guard posts from the DMZ and guns from the Joint Security Area and committed the two Koreas to joint remains recovery efforts inside the DMZ. The Pyongyang Declaration pledged the resumption of economic cooperation, cultural and sports exchanges, humanitarian exchanges for families divided by the Korean War, and the dismantlement of North Korean missile and nuclear facilities at Dongchang-ri and Yongbyon. These measures never got off the ground, and an anticipated visit by Kim Jong-un for a fourth summit in South Korea never materialized.

The summit pledges all rested on the assumption that the partial scope of North Korean nuclear dismantlement would satisfy the Trump administration sufficiently to secure UN Security Council sanctions relief or exceptions for inter-Korean economic projects. However, the "small deal" that the Moon administration hoped for and expected as the main outcome of the second Trump-Kim summit in Hanoi never materialized. The "small deal" failed in part because the North Koreans never engaged directly with American counterparts at the working level to negotiate specifics of denuclearization and in part because Trump determined that North Korean offers were insufficient to ensure that they would ever lead to the goal of "complete denuclearization."

The Hanoi Summit failure undermined prospects for inter-Korean progress and appeared to sour the personal relationship between Moon and Kim. North Korea issued scathing criticisms of South Korea for failing to act independently of the U.S. on issues like inter-Korean cooperation and for failing to turn on the economic spigot of aid to North Korea that had flowed so generously in the early 2000s, prior to North Korea's nuclear tests. Moon went from crucial intermediary to marginalized extra, not even getting a seat in the room at a third Trump-Kim meeting on June 30, 2019, at Panmunjom, which accomplished little more than a photo op and false hopes for renewed denuclearization talks between the U.S. and North Korea.

Kim Jong-un's sister Kim Yo-jung publicly targeted Moon's failure to stop North Korean refugees from sending leaflets by balloon into North Korea, shut down almost all inter-Korean communications, and ordered the demolition of the inter-Korean liaison office at Kaesong. Although Moon continued to hold the door open for peace talks with Kim Jong-un in 2020, Kim appeared to have moved on. Kim has doubled down on nuclear deterrence, self-reliance, and isolation as a safer and more secure option than the risks of an inter-Korean engagement unaccompanied by economic subsidies and nuclear blackmail on a scale necessary to keep nuclear North Korea afloat.

The future of North Korea

When Kim Jong-un took over as North Korea's supreme leader following the death of his father, Kim Jong-il, in December 2011, questions swirled about whether his father's associates, who were 40 years his senior, would accept or subvert Kim's rule. A decade later, Kim Jong-un is the longest-serving leader in Northeast Asia. He has consolidated power by removing all potential rivals within or outside of his family – either through dismissal and demotion of military leaders or via the brutal execution of his uncle Jang Song-taek and assassination of his half-brother, Kim Jong-nam. Kim has charted a military and economic course that is making North Korea both stronger and more dangerous.

Kim Jong-un has indisputably been a more capable leader than his father Kim Jong-il both in terms of presenting a charismatic public image and in pursuing more effective economic policies. But he presides over a brutal system that demands unquestioning political loyalty from its people. Expressions of political loyalty to Kim are indoctrinated from cradle to grave through North Korea's educational system and state media, and are an unconditional prerequisite to opportunities for limited personal and economic advancement within North Korea's ideologically-based social hierarchy. Conversely, expressions of political disloyalty or defections within one's immediate family make individuals vulnerable to confiscatory bribes and punishments by North Korean security services, banishment from Pyongyang, and an effective death sentence through assignment to political gulags in the countryside.

In contrast to his father, who eschewed public speaking, ruled via the nine-person National Defense Commission, and marginalized the party and government institutions, Kim Jong-un has normalized regular party functions, presided directly over party meetings, and given regular public addresses charting the country's challenges, needs, and successes. Though he still occupies a god-like status within North Korea, Kim Jong-un has adopted a more open and direct style rather than ruling behind the curtain.

In 2013 Kim Jong-un announced his first major policy initiative, known as byungjin, or simultaneous economic and military development, which was intended to transform North Korea

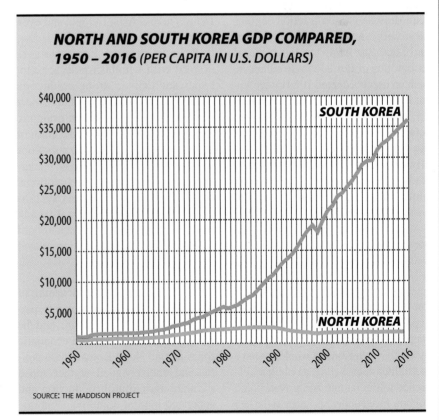

NORTH AND SOUTH KOREA GDP COMPARED, 1950 – 2016 (PER CAPITA IN U.S. DOLLARS)

SOURCE: THE MADDISON PROJECT

Behind K-Pop's Global Reach

For the world, 2020 has been a year marked by calamity, but South Korea's cultural offerings have provided a silver lining to global viewers. Bong Joon-ho's Parasite became one of the highest grossing film in South Korean cinema history and the first foreign movie ever to win best picture at the Oscars. In another first, Korean boy band BTS (Bangtan Sonyeondan, or Bangtan Boys) hit number one on Billboard's top 100 with its song "Dynamite," leading the pack of Korean artists who have begun to gain popularity internationally. The Korean drama Crash Landing On You also debuted as the third-highest rated show in South Korean cable television history, became massively popular in China, Japan, and Southeast Asia, and quickly climbed the list of most-viewed shows on American Netflix. What has accounted for the global popularity of Korean movies, music, and dramas in 2020?

The South Korean entertainment industry has spent over two decades building a global brand. Early on, Korean dramas gained traction regionally, with viewers in Japan, China, and Southeast Asia. The international recognition of Bong Joon-ho's Parasite with an unprecedented 2020 Oscar win for Best Picture, along with Best Director, Best Original Screenplay, and Best International Feature Film, represents the culmination of decades of gradually increasing international acclaim for Korean cinema. Critics praised the film's theme of class conflict, a South Korean story with global application in an era of widening social and class inequality.

South Korean directors such as Bong, Park Chan-wook, and Lee Chang-dong have built solid careers over decades and have earned international recognition from their peers for films such as Joint Security Area, Peppermint Candy, The Host, Burning, and Oldboy. Bong and Park have both directed English language films, including Okja, Snowpiercer, and Stoker, that have received positive reviews and acclaim from Western critics and audiences. Most significantly for the Korean film and drama industries, popular streaming platforms Netflix, Hulu, and Amazon Prime Video have made a wide array of titles available, ensuring that Korean cultural influence becomes even more popular and deeply-rooted in the American consciousness going forward.

Beyond the big screen, Winter Sonata was a breakout love story that experienced massive success with Japanese viewers in the mid-2000s. Winter Sonata and other Korean dramas including Jewel in the Palace, Boys Before Flowers, and Secret Garden made inroads across Asia, Europe, and even countries such as Iran.

Korean dramas keep viewers hooked with whiplash-inducing plot twists and deliver strong production values and excellent presentation. Most importantly, they focus on dramatic thematic elements such as the clash of family identity with social expectations in Korean society, the clash of modernity and urbanization with traditional cultural values, and themes such as class divides, income inequality, and social injustice that have struck a chord with overseas audiences and translated

into international success. Most recently, highly-rated dramas such as Crash Landing On You, Kingdom, and Guardian: The Lonely and Great God have experienced great success in the West, likely thanks in part to their availability on Netflix.

But the "Korean wave" of cultural products has not been confined to screens, large or small. Korean pop music acts such as BoA, Rain, Wonder Girls, Super Junior, Big Bang, 2NE1, and Girls' Generation gained popularity in the 2000s across Japan, China, and Southeast Asia. These groups brought a uniquely Korean style to their music, along with catchy beats and impeccably synchronized and choreographed dancing. These elements drew ever-wider audiences to the fanbases that flourished both across Asia and globally. But Korean pop music, or K-pop, did not catch the attention of most Americans until PSY's 2013 breakout hit "Gangnam Style" set YouTube records with over one billion views and a "pony dance" built on a satirical view of the cultural hypocrisy and excesses of Seoul's most wealthy district.

South Korea's BTS has become the most successful group in the history of K-pop both domestically and overseas. BTS is the first Korean group to hit number one on Billboard's Top 100 with its single "Dynamite," which topped the charts the first week following its release in August 2020. BTS' success has brought into the limelight the unique fanbases that bolster the popularity and success of K-pop bands and have used their power to circumvent the role of distributors within the music industry. The "BTS ARMY"

into a "strong and prosperous state." On the economic front, Kim Jong-un expressed in one of his earliest public speeches the desire to lead an economy in which North Koreans would not have to "tighten their belts," an oblique reference to the famine and privation the country faced under his father in the late

1990s. Kim authorized a loosening of North Korea's command economy, partial privatization of agriculture, and the establishment of 15 special economic zones around North Korea. These policies and relatively good weather helped stabilize agricultural production and generated modest domestic economic

growth through 2017, but the North Korean economy began to stumble in 2018 due to increasingly strict UN Security Council sanctions in response to North Korea's nuclear and missile tests. By 2019, Kim Jong-un was urging self-reliance, tightening control over the economy, and warning that North Koreans

NEW YORK, NEW YORK - DECEMBER 31: BTS performs during the Times Square New Year's Eve 2020 Celebration on December 31, 2019 in New York City. (MANNY CARABEL/FILMMAGIC/GETTY IMAGES)

fanbase has driven the viewership of BTS music videos on YouTube, elevated BTS-related terms to trending on social media, and organized campaigns that lead to BTS concert tickets selling out within seconds. When touring became impossible due to Covid-19, BTS held the world's largest virtual concert with a paying audience of 756,000 concurrent viewers in 107 countries and territories.

South Korean music labels have successfully recruited and trained Asian voices from across the world through a rigorous (and to some critics, abusive) regimen to meet high production values and develop their images as "idols" for a global audience. Blackpink, whose four members include vocalists from South Korea, New Zealand, and Thailand, has also made the Billboard Top 100 and is the first Korean girl group to produce two music videos with over a billion views on YouTube. Youth interest in K-pop has catalyzed a wave of Korean language learning among global fans, but top K-pop acts have also increasingly incorporated English lyrics into their songs and begun to partner with international stars, such as Blackpink's recent collaborations with Lady Gaga, Cardi B, and Selena Gomez, to produce English songs.

The secret to the global appeal of Korean movies, dramas, and music has been their ability to show and tell unique aspects of a Korean story in ways that have global appeal, while also translating and redesigning popular elements of global culture by adding uniquely Korean characteristics. This combination of an openness to absorption of global culture and the ability to tap into universal themes of the Korean experience has enabled Korean artists to ride the Korean cultural wave to new heights of global popularity in 2020.

---

may have to tighten their belts again to achieve a "frontal breakthrough" against hostile global forces.

Kim has doubled down on North Korea's nuclear and missile development, crediting these programs as part of the legacy of his father and grandfather and inscribing North Korea's nuclear status in the preamble of a revised constitution. Kim conducted four nuclear tests of increasing size and yield between 2013 and 2017. Simultaneously, he presided over a sprint to develop survivable missile strike capabilities that could reach the U.S., by securing mobile launch capabilities, and by developing solid fuel versions of missiles that required shorter preparation times prior to launch. By November 2017, North Korea successfully tested the Hwasong-15 missile that, according to then Defense Secretary James Mattis, could reach any point on the globe. Kim declared his effort to build a nuclear deterrent successful and pivoted to a diplomatic charm offensive in early 2018.

Kim Jong-un framed his 2018 diplomatic outreach to South Korea, China, and the U.S. as possible thanks to his missile development success, but many external observers interpreted Kim's willingness to come to talks as a sign of weakness and as evidence that Kim feared Trump's 2017 proclamations of "fire and fury" and was feeling the effects of U.S. "maximum pressure" sanctions. Although Kim paid lip-service to the objective of "complete denuclearization," at summits with Moon in Panmunjom and with Trump in Singapore, Kim's primary objective ap-

pears to have been to legitimize North Korea as a nuclear state and to secure relief from the UN sanctions standing in the way of North Korea's economic development goals.

The February 2019 Hanoi summit between Trump and Kim marked the failure of Kim's bid for sanctions relief and shaped a reversion in North Korean policy by the beginning of 2020 to a focus on economic self-strengthening and reliance on nuclear deterrence. The 2020 triple whammy of continued economic sanctions, self-imposed quarantine in response to the Covid-19 pandemic, and extensive flooding from monsoons and typhoons comprise the most severe challenges North Korea

has faced under Kim Jong-un's rule.

Kim's reportedly poor personal health and periodic extended absences from the public eye have raised questions about the future succession prospects for the Kim family regime in the absence of offspring old enough to take charge. The rise of Kim's sister, Kim Yo-jong, to ever more powerful positions within the Korean Worker's Party has fueled speculation about her future role. Kim's gambit of achieving the twin goals of nuclear-backed security and market-reform driven prosperity to foster a strong and prosperous North Korea appear to have reached a dead end, with no face-saving way of reversing course.

New challenges for the U.S.-South Korea alliance under unorthodox political leadership

At first glance, it would appear that U.S. President Donald J. Trump and South Korean President Moon Jae-in have little in common, yet the U.S.-South Korea security alliance has both created incentives for them to work together while also constraining their ability to pursue independent paths. The two leaders have steered in different directions despite the strong bureaucratic institutional alignments that keep the alliance robust, but they have also found a distinctly political basis

upon which to pursue a narrow window of cooperation based on common interest in a relationship with North Korean leader Kim Jong-un.

Trump is brash and direct. Moon is cautious but firm. Though the two have not embarked golf diplomacy like Trump and Japan's Shinzo Abe, they have met relatively often, with little of the drama that has accompanied Trump's meetings with other U.S. allies such as Germany's Angela Merkel or Canada's Justin Trudeau.

The most striking convergent political interest between Trump and Moon has been their shared focus on summit diplomacy with Kim. Without Moon's facilitation and intermediary role, the conditions for the Trump-Kim summit in Singapore in June 2018 would have never materialized. A last-ditch secret inter-Korean summit at Panmunjom certainly kept it from going off the rails.

Moon has sought primarily to ensure peace on the Korean Peninsula through diplomacy toward North Korea. He perceives U.S.-North Korean reconciliation—and a resulting peace-and-denuclearization process that facilitates North Korea's transition into the international community – as an important step toward that goal. Moon asserts that South Korea should drive such a denuclearization-embedded peace process. This policy overlaps substantially with the U.S. preferred peace-embedded denuclearization approach, but places peace as the primary goal rather than denuclearization. This approach also appealed to Trump's sense of drama and history: if only Trump's personal relationship with Kim could be leveraged to mobilize tangible steps toward a permanent peace treaty to replace the Korean Armistice Agreement, catalyze tangible North Korean steps toward de-

North Korean leader Kim Jong Un, U.S. President Donald Trump, and South Korean President Moon Jae-in inside the demilitarized zone (DMZ) separating South and North Korea on June 30, 2019, in Panmunjom, South Korea. (HANDOUT PHOTO BY DONG-A ILBO/GETTY IMAGES)

nuclearization, and put Trump's name in the history books as the author of a peace with North Korea.

Unfortunately, Moon's peace gambit derailed due to his inability to deliver sufficient concessions from either Trump or Kim to keep them moving forward during their February 2019 summit in Hanoi and Kim's continued commitment to a strategic goal of legitimizing North Korea as a nuclear weapons state. Building on the September 2018 inter-Korean Pyongyang Declaration and military agreement, Moon and his team eagerly awaited an outcome from Hanoi in which North Koreans might allow the resumption of international inspections at North Korea's main fissile material production site at Yongbyon in return for partial sanctions lifting. But the no-deal Trump-Kim summit in Hanoi marginalized Moon and resulted in a dramatic deterioration in inter-Korean relations.

A second source of stress in the U.S.-South Korea relationship has revolved around the shared challenge of how to manage China's rise. Moon has sought China's understanding, cooperation, and support for a peace process with North Korea, but the Trump administration has increasingly identified China as a potential adversary, trade cheat, and challenger to U.S. primacy in East Asia. As Sino-U.S. tensions have grown, the space for South Korea to balance between its economic dependence on China and security alliance with the U.S. has shrunk, constraining South Korea's ability to avoid making choices between Washington and Beijing. South Korean angst has risen over U.S. pressure to join the Free and Open Indo-Pacific strategy, while China has pressured South Korea to join its Belt and Road Initiative to build out infrastructure across Asia.

Despite a strong convergence of interests reinforced by North Korea's nuclear threat and a continued mutual security commitment, Trump's long-standing personal view of South Korea and other American allies as free riders has also raised tensions in the relationship. The two leaders successfully revised the Korea-U.S. Free

South Korean conservative protesters participate in a pro U.S. and anti-North Korea rally on February 23, 2019 in Seoul, South Korea. (CHUNG SUNG-JUN/GETTY IMAGES)

Trade Agreement and closed the U.S. bilateral trade deficit with South Korea following Trump's complaints that the agreement favored South Korea, but these revisions did not assuage his desire to raise South Korea's financial support for the U.S. military presence on the peninsula.

Following a tense negotiation that produced a one-year deal in 2019 that increased South Korean contributions of on-peninsula costs for Korean local labor, logistics, and bases by eight percent to $860 million, the Trump administration upped its demands the following year to $4.6 billion – a five hundred percent increase that included U.S. off-peninsula costs in support of the deployment of forces and equipment necessary to provide for South Korea's defense. South Korea stood firm in its insistence on keeping the longstanding formula for cost-sharing, seeking a multi-year deal with a thirteen percent increase that would bring South Korea's annual contribution to around $1 billion per year. But the underlying source of friction in the relationship was Trump's portrayal of the alliance as a relationship based on mercenary and mercantile incentives rather than on shared history, values, and interests.

Other sources of potential friction in the relationship revolve around Moon's political objective of demonstrating South Korea's freedom of action and ability to independently pursue its national security interests. Moon sought to implement a transition in Operational Control arrangements by the end of his term that would underscore South Korea's full military partnership in executing war-time operations in the event of a Korean conflict. But Moon's political deadline generated frictions over agreed-upon capabilities and circumstances that had to be achieved as a prerequisite for the transition, including a joint assessment that North Korea's nuclear program was under control.

But the most dangerous source of political friction between Trump and Moon has remained the risk that Trump's vision of "America first" would combine with a progressive "North Korea first" policy advocated by some Moon supporters to undermine decades of alliance-based cooperation aimed at deterring a common North Korean threat. The outcome of the fall 2020 U.S. presidential election will influence the magnitude and proximity of those risks, but they will not completely subside unless both the U.S. and South Korea can to stay in lockstep on how to most effectively deal with Kim Jong-un.

discussion questions

1. Can the U.S. hope to reach a deal with North Korea regarding denuclearization without the support of China? How can the U.S. bring China to the table?

2. If South Korea is forced to choose which relationship to maintain between the U.S. and China, which nation would be better for South Korean interests?

3. Should the U.S. shift focus toward dealing with a nuclear North Korea, or do you think denuclearization is still possible?

4. Do you believe that Kim-Jong-un would launch an unprovoked nuclear attack on either the U.S. or Japan? Does the U.S. risk provoking China

5. Do you think that South Korea can leverage their growing influence over pop culture (Kpop, Korean Dramas etc.) to a more prominent role in global politics? What has helped the U.S. maintain such a hold over global entertainment, and could these same mechanisms benefit the ROK?

suggested readings

Snyder, Scott A. **South Korea at the Crossroads: Autonomy and Alliance in an Era of Rival Powers.** 376 pg: Columbia University Press, 2018. In South Korea at the Crossroads, Scott A. Snyder examines the trajectory of fifty years of South Korean foreign policy and offers predictions and a prescription for the future. Pairing a historical perspective with a shrewd understanding of today's political landscape, Snyder contends that South Korea's best strategy remains investing in a robust alliance with the U.S...

Oberdorfer, Don. **The Two Koreas: A Contemporary History**, 560 pg. Basic Books, 2013. In this landmark history, veteran journalist Don Oberdorfer and Korea expert Robert Carlin grippingly describe how a historically homogenous people became locked in a perpetual struggle for supremacy -- and how other nations including the U.S. have tried, and failed, to broker a lasting peace.

Cha, Victor. **South Korea Offers a Lesson in Best Practices** Foreign Affairs Magazine, April 2020.

Cumings, Bruce. **Korea's Place in the Sun: A Modern History.** 544 pg. W.W. Norton, 2005. Korea has endured a "fractured, shattered twentieth century," and this updated edition brings Bruce Cumings's leading history of the modern era into the present.

Demick, Barbara. **Nothing to Envy: Ordinary Lives in North Korea,** 336 pg. Random House, 2009. In this landmark addition to the literature of totalitarianism, award-winning journalist Barbara Demick follows the lives of six North Korean citizens over fifteen years—a chaotic period that saw the death of Kim Il-sung, the rise to power of his son Kim Jong-il (the father of Kim Jong-un), and a devastating famine that killed one-fifth of the population.

Kim, Suki. **Without You, There Is No Us: Undercover Among the Sons of North Korea's Elite** 320 pg. Crown, 2015. Without You, There Is No Us offers a moving and incalculably rare glimpse of life in the world's most unknowable country, and at the privileged young men she calls "soldiers and slaves.".

Don't forget: Ballots start on page 104!!!!

To access web links to these readings, as well as links to global discussion questions, shorter readings and suggested web sites, GO TO www.fpa.org/great_decisions and click on the topic under Resources, on the right-hand side of the page.

The World Health Organization's response to Covid-19

by Mara Pillinger

A passenger looks on from a vehicle containing French citizens after their evacuation from the Chinese city of Wuhan, as it arrives in southern France on January 31, 2020, following their repatriation from the coronavirus zone. A plane carrying around 200 French citizens evacuated from the Chinese city of Wuhan, epicentre of the coronavirus outbreak, landed near Marseille, None of the passengers showed symptoms of the virus that prompted the World Health Organization to declare a global emergency. (GERARD JULIEN/AFP/GETTY IMAGES)

On July 7, 2020, President Donald Trump notified the United Nations of his intent to withdraw the U.S. from the World Health Organization (WHO). With the Covid-19 pandemic raging in the U.S. and around the world, the President asserted that WHO had failed in its duty to warn the world early on about the dangers posed by the new coronavirus because the agency and its Director-General, Dr. Tedros Adhanom Ghebreyesus, are too "China-centric". Administration allies, like Senator Rick Scott (R-FL), accused WHO of "helping Communist China cover up a global pandemic"Leading global health experts have overwhelmingly decried the U.S. decision to withdraw from membership and to withhold financial support from WHO. Pointing to numerous factual inaccuracies in the Trump administration's account of events, they argue that Trump's attacks on WHO are a blatant attempt to deflect blame from the administration's own failures to check the spread of the virus within the U.S. They point out that WHO declared a "public health emergency of international concern" (PHEIC) on January 30, one month after the first reported cases, and at a time when

MARA PILLINGER *is an Associate at the O'Neill Institute for National and Global Health Law, Global Health Policy & Politics Initiative. Her work focuses on HIV policy and global health governance, including the COVID-19 response and the politics of reform at WHO and other global health organizations*

there were only 83 reported cases and no deaths outside China. And they remind critics that Tedros and WHO consistently warned governments to "act now" to urgently escalate social distancing, testing, contact tracing, and isolation in the face of "this very grave threat"—warnings that many governments chose to ignore until it was too late.

Experts also caution that abandoning WHO will undermine U.S. health security and diplomatic goals far beyond Covid-19, damaging long-standing priorities like polio eradication, access to flu vaccines, and the ability to detect and respond to the next pandemic. As Bill Gates put it, "halting funding for [WHO] during a world health crisis is as dangerous as it sounds." In short, the consensus is that if the U.S. withdraws from WHO, it would be cutting off its nose to spite its face.

But even as global health thought leaders criticize the U.S.'s planned course of action, many also acknowledge that WHO's early response to Covid-19 was not what it should have been. For example, David Fidler, a leading international lawyer and fellow in global health at the Council on Foreign Relations, told The Guardian that "[y]ou've got a situation where it looks like WHO doesn't want to exercise its authority." Richard Horton, editor of the prestigious medical journal *The Lancet,* said that WHO "has been drained of power and resources.... Its coordinating authority and capacity are weak. Its ability to direct an international response to a life-threatening epidemic is non-existent." These and other experts paint a picture of an agency that was timid when it needed to be bold, unable to compel the Chinese government to share information or rally other governments to act early to stop the coronavirus outbreak before it became a pandemic.

Amid all this back-and-forth, readers looking to understand WHO's response to Covid-19 should be asking three sets of questions. First, how did we get here? How does WHO work, and what role is it supposed to play in pandemic responses? Second, what is happening now, during Covid-19? What is WHO doing well, and what could/should it do differently, bearing in mind its existing capacities and limitations? Third, where do we go from here? What needs to change in order for WHO to do better in the future? Because for all the uncertainty around the current pandemic, perhaps the only certain thing is that it will not be the last pandemic. Placing blame is a political exercise, but understanding what went right, what went wrong, and how we do better is a necessity for policymakers.

How Did We Get Here? WHO, SARS, and the IHR

Created in 1948, WHO is the specialized agency of the United Nations responsible for global public health. WHO is a Member State organization, comprised of 194 countries. To understand WHO's response to Covid-19, we first need to familiarize ourselves with its structure and mandate, as well as how the organization is funded and what kinds of limitations it faces.

Structure & governance

WHO has four main structures. First is the World Health Assembly (WHA), a parliamentary body in which Member States come together to conduct health diplomacy, reach policy and international legal agreements, and establish WHO's programmatic agenda and budget. On paper, WHA operates on a one-state, one-vote principle; in practice, by ironclad tradition, decisions are taken by consensus or not at all. The need to reach consensus among Member States can be a formidable barrier to action, particularly on issues like WHO reform—but at the same time, it works to keep Member States at the table through disagreements, which is essential to WHO's legitimacy as a long-term diplomatic project and a globally representative body. At the same time, because WHO is an intergovernmental organization in which only states have a vote, the agency has struggled to provide substantive and equal-access opportunities for participation by non-Member States (e.g. Taiwan) and civil society. Second, in addition to the WHA, WHO is governed by an Executive Board comprised of 34 technical experts nominated by their governments. The Executive Board sets the agenda for the WHA and then oversees implementation of WHA decisions.

Third, the Secretariat, led by the Director-General, is WHO's administrative and executing arm, responsible for carrying out the programmatic agenda set by Member States. Among its other roles, it coordinates the response to global health emergencies, like Covid-19. But importantly, with a few exceptions (like emergencies), the Secretariat is not an implementing agency that oversees or carries out activities on the ground. Instead, it works closely with national Ministries of Health of to provide technical guidance and support through WHO's regional and country offices.

Fourth, to a degree unique among UN agencies, WHO is a highly decentralized organization, with six regional offices overseeing 150 country offices. These regional offices are highly autonomous, each led by a Regional Director elected by the region's Member States, governed by its own Regional Assembly, and with command over its own budget. Together, the regional and country offices oversee as much as three quarters of WHO's staff and more than half its total expenditure. Consequently, there is very little accountability to WHO's headquarters in Geneva, Switzerland, and, at times, a great deal of tension and competition across lev-

Before you read, download the companion **Glossary** that includes definitions, a guide to acronyms and abbreviations used in the article, and other material. Go to **www.fpa.org/great_decisions** and select a topic in the Resources section. (Top right)

els. On the one hand, this decentralized structure can help foster closer relationships and better coordination with governments. But it can also lead to "pathological fragmentation," creating inefficiencies, overlaps, and breakdowns in coordination between Geneva and the regional and country leves, which undermines Geneva's ability to coordinate global action.

Mandate

WHO's constitution sets out a vast mandate—promoting "the attainment by all peoples of the highest possible level of health"—that essentially covers all health issues, everywhere in the world. The constitution goes on to lay out 22 specific functions for the agency, ranging from the very general ("proposing conventions, agreements, and regulations with respect to international health matters") to the specific (e.g. "standardizing diagnostic procedures"). Initially, the agency's focus was very much on infectious diseases. But over time, as the global burden of disease has shifted, our awareness of the need to address various health challenges has evolved, and Member States' priorities have varied, WHO's focus has continually expanded to include things like non-communicable diseases, road traffic accidents, addiction, mental health, universal health care, and strengthening of health systems.

More concretely, WHO's mandate can be broken down into four roles. First, it is a global hub of scientific and technical expertise, gathering and analyzing information, issuing guidelines, providing technical advice and assistance to governments, regulating things like the quality of medicines, and so on. Second, it is a normative agency, setting goals and agendas (e.g. advocating for universal health care as a human right), and drafting and steering the diplomatic negotiations around international health treaties and regulations. Importantly, WHO's normative activities can be proposed and executed by the Secretariat, but they must be approved by the WHA. Third, WHO is the chief convening and coordinating authority in global health, bringing together the constellation of

A picture taken on January 12, 2020, shows the World Health Organization (WHO) headquarters prior to a combined news conference following a two-day international conference on Covid-19 coronavirus vaccine research and a meeting to decide whether Ebola in DR Congo still constitutes health emergency of international concern in Geneva.(FABRICE COFFRINI/AFP/GETTY IMAGES)

global health actors—including governments, other multilateral global health institutions, civil society, philanthropic donors, and scientists—to shape policy agendas and technical guidelines. Finally, it is a political venue in which Member States seek to advance their interests. Taken together, WHO's vast mandate essentially leaves the agency in the position of trying to be all things to all people on all health issues everywhere in the world.

Financial woes and other limitations

Fulfilling such a mandate would be a challenge even for a powerful and well-resourced organization. WHO is neither. WHO's budget for 2020–21 is $2.4 billion dollars per year—roughly the budget of a large hospital in a wealthy country and a quarter of the budget for the U.S. CDC. This budget is funded in two ways: mandatory assessed contributions from Member State governments and voluntary contributions from governments and non-governmental donors (e.g. the Bill and Melinda Gates Foundation). The latter are usually earmarked for specific purposes. Since assessed contributions were frozen two decades ago—and since Member States frequently fail to pay those dues

on time—WHO has had to increasingly rely on voluntary contributions, which now comprise up to 80% of its budget. Moreover, almost 65% of WHO funding comes from just 15 donors. Consequently, WHO's funding flow is unstable, subject to the whims of donors, and constrained, leaving the agency unable to make long-term plans or address critical global health issues if they are not donor priorities (e.g. Ebola, prior to 2014). And because most of its funding is not flexible, WHO must launch emergency appeals to be able act in the face of each new crisis, as with Covid-19. Member States recognize that these financial problems hamstring WHO and have taken partial steps to address them—yet prior to Covid-19 they have consistently rejected efforts to implement the basic necessary fix of increasing assessed contributions.

Second, WHO is primarily an advisory and coordinating organization. It does not supply governments with funding, nor, crucially, does it have any enforcement authority to force governments to abide by their agreements or follow its recommendations. It can coordinate global action but—like a conductor in front of an orchestra—its effectiveness depends entirely on Member States' willingness to play along.

Thus, as Steven Hoffman & John-Arne Røttingen describe, WHO staff are forced "to walk uncomfortably along many fine lines: analyzing but never auditing; advising but never directing; participating but never interfering; guiding but never governing; leading but never advocating; evaluating but never judging... [all the while working] under the excessively limiting conditions that Member States impose." The upshot of this constant tightrope walking, as well as combined with the agency's governance structure, organizational culture, and precarious financing, is that, as a rule, WHO is highly deferential to its Member States sovereignty—all its Member States, not just the powerful ones. The Secretariat can pursue its mission and agenda in a variety of ways, but its tactics very seldom include criticizing, challenging, or circumventing governments (especially not in public).

SARS: a coming out moment

The pivotal exception to this rule of deference was WHO's response to SARS in 2003. Faced with China's attempts to hide an outbreak of a new and lethal virus, Director-General Gro Harlem Brundtland broke out of WHO's traditional mold and took unorthadox (and partially unmandated) actions in order to compel the Chinese government's cooperation and coordinate global efforts to contain the virus.

In November 2003, WHO began hearing warnings from colleagues and credible internet sources of "a strange contagious disease" that was killing people in Guandong Province, which the authorities were trying to keep from the public. WHO formally requested more information from the Chinese government, but the government responded with a series of improbable denials and deflections. The Chinese government also refused to allow a WHO investigative team to visit the site of the outbreak or to share epidemiological data or viral samples with WHO.

WHO's authority to respond to infectious disease outbreaks is laid out in an international treaty called the International Health Regulations (IHR). The version of the treaty that was in effect at the time only required governments to report to WHO cases of three specific diseases (cholera, plague, and yellow fever; not SARS), and only allowed WHO to notify the world about an outbreak based on information officially reported to it by Member State governments.

Brundtland determined that WHO's response could not be limited by the IHR. As she later told the Guardian, "[i]f the job is to direct and coordinate global health, it's not a question of what one or several governments ask you to do. We are working for humanity." So the agency launched a "naming-and-shaming" campaign, going public with the information it received from unofficial (i.e. nongovernmental) sources and bringing international pressure to bear upon the Chinese government. WHO chided the Chinese government for withholding information, warning that it was putting the world at risk by delaying efforts to contain the virus. The agency also issued emergency travel advisories warning against travel to affected areas, doing so over the objections of those governments and even though issuing such warnings had previously been left up to individual countries.

As WHO spoke, governments and people listened. The Chinese government began to share information on the outbreak, as did other affected governments. Countries followed WHO's guidance on how to contain outbreaks. These control efforts were a huge success. Although SARS spread to 26 countries, fewer than 1,000 people died, and the virus essentially disappeared.

The International Health Regulations 2005: new authority and old limitations

When the SARS outbreak occurred, Member State were in the process of revising the IHR. WHO was operating in a liminal space, and Brundtland and Heymann seized the opportunity to "test drive some very radical changes" in how the agency operated. In the end, in the new version of the treaty, Member States granted WHO many of the authorities and capacities that it had appropriated for itself during SARS, but also established strong, sovereignty-protecting guardrails limiting how WHO can exercise those authorities. In short, Member States' feedback to

A man passes by a poster warning of the danger and prevention of SARS on a street in the southern Chinese cities of Guangzhou, 12 June 2003. (PETER PARKS/AFP/GETTY IMAGES)

A sand sculpture of a mask-wearing pig by artist Sudersan Pattnaik decorates the beach Puri, about 65 km from the eastern Indian temple city of Bhubaneswar, on June 18, 2009. The swine flu virus, which was first detected in Mexico in April, has so far infected almost 30,000 people in 74 countries, killing about 150, according to the latest World Health Organisation figures. (AFP/GETTY IMAGES)

WHO regarding the initiative shown during the SARS response was "good job; don't do it again".

The IHR 2005 empowers WHO to declare a PHEIC to warn the world when there is a "serious, unusual or unexpected" health crisis "that poses a public health risk to other countries through international spread," and also establishes WHO's leadership role in coordinating the international response to such emergencies. Member States are required to notify WHO when there is a potential health emergency within their borders. Upon receiving such a report, the Director-General may summon an Emergency Committee of independent scientific experts to advise them on whether the reported outbreak constitutes a PHEIC. And in case a government once again tries to cover up an outbreak, the IHR authorize WHO to do what it did during SARS and take action based upon unofficial sources of information, like information obtained through WHO's expert networks or credible media or social media reports. Since the IHR 2005 took effect, the agency has declared six PHEICs—for

H1N1 in 2009; polio in 2014; Ebola in 2014 and 2018; Zika in 2015; and Covid-19 in 2020.

Once a PHEIC is declared, the Director-General, in consultation with the Emergency Committee, also issues recommendations about what measures should be taken to control the outbreak, including whether other countries should restrict trade or travel with outbreak-affected countries. The purpose of these recommendations is to ensure that the international response is based on science and data rather than panic and fear. In particular, one of the underlying principles of the IHR—as agreed upon by Member States—is that PHEIC response measures should "avoid unnecessary interference with international traffic and trade." This is because trade and travel restrictions are usually imposed in such a way that they are ineffective at actually containing the spread of disease- but are economically damaging and can interfere with the public health responses. For example, travel restrictions imposed during SARS are estimated to have cost the Chinese and

Canadian economies approximately $3 billion in lost tourism revenue. And during the spring of 2009, after H1N1 cases were first reported in Mexico, the Mexican economy lost $2.3 billion in trade revenue, even though WHO recommended against such restrictions. One danger is that if governments fear that reporting outbreaks will wreak havoc on their economies, they will be disincentivized from reporting in a timely manner.

However, although Member States were satisfied with WHO's aggressive action to pressure the Chinese government during SARS, they were not so comfortable with the idea that they themselves might be subject to similar pressure in the future. Thus, even as governments granted WHO new powers, they also limited those powers to preserve their own sovereign prerogatives. For example, the experts who advise the Director-General on when to declare a PHEIC are nominated by governments And when the Emergency Committee meets, outbreak-affected governements have the opportunity to present (and presumably make a case

Medical staff clean their protection suits as part of the fight against the Ebola virus on March 8, 2015 at the Donka hospital in Conakry. More than 9,700 people have died of the disease since the west African epidemic emerged in southern Guinea in December 2013, with nearly 24,000 people infected, according to the World Health Organization.(CELLOU BINANI/AFP/GETTY IMAGES)

for why a PHEIC should not be declared). Accounts reveal that one of the factors influencing Director-General Margaret Chan's long delay in declaring the West African Ebola outbreak a PHEIC was resistance from the governments of Guinea, Liberia, and Sierra Leone.

In addition, while WHO is authorized to take action and warn the world of outbreaks based on information from non-governmental sources, it must first seek to verify those reports with gov-

ernments and offer to collaborate with them to control the outbreak. Only if affected governments refuse to share information and collaborate with WHO is the agency authorized to go public with information received from non-governmental sources. In other words, WHO can go around governments, but only after it has tried to go through them and been stonewalled.

Finally, the IHR 2005 has no teeth—the treaty itself offers Member States no incentives to comply, no disincen-

tives for non-compliance, and gives WHO no enforcement mechanisms that can compel Member States to cooperate. For example, WHO consistently recommends against imposing trade and travel restrictions against affected countries, and governments consistently impose them regardless. Without any vinegar to hand, WHO has no choice but to secure governments' cooperation through diplomatic honey. This limitation would critically hinder its response to Covid-19.

What has WHO done well and what could it have done differently? The Covid-19 response

On December 31, 2019, WHO picked up reports through non-governmental channels of cases of "viral pneumonia of unknown cause" in Wuhan, China. Following the process laid out in the IHR, the agency requested more information from the Chinese government and activated its

emergency response team and global partner network. On January 3, 2020, Chinese officials formally notified WHO of the first outbreak of the disease that would be called Covid-19. Over the next two days, WHO publicly announced the outbreak on Twitter and through official channels and shared

the first scientific report with governments. On January 9, WHO reported that Chinese scientists had determined that the illness was caused by a novel coronavirus (first called 2019-nCov, later named SARS-CoV-2). And on Jan 10, after convening the first of many international scientific expert consultations, WHO issued the first set of technical guidance for countries on how to prepare for and respond to the outbreak.

They were also trying to obtain an invitation from the Chinese government to send an international team of experts to assess the situation on the ground. Behind the scenes, the Secretariat was furiously pressing the Chinese government to share more information—including more detailed epidemiological data on cases (needed to assess the virus' lethality and potential for human-to-human transmission), the virus' genome (needed to develop diagnostic tests),

The Chinese government was communicative but also cagey, putting WHO in a difficult situation. On January 12, China shared the virus' genome with WHO—on the same day that Chinese scientists published that genome in a scientific journal. The world later learned that China had delayed sharing the genome and also had known that the outbreak was caused by a coronavirus weeks before it shared this information with WHO. These delays were driven by a combination of authoritarian opacity, internal political pressures and bureaucratic dysfunction within China.

China's delayed and non-transparent information sharing also complicated WHO's attempts to communicate risk to the public. In a January 14 press conference, Dr. Maria Van Kerkhove, WHO's technical lead for the Covid-19 response, raised the prospect of human-to-human transmission, saying that "it is possible, we need to prepare ourselves." On the same day, Chinese health officials apprised the government that human-to-human transmission was likely occurring. But publicly, China was still denying that possibility, forcing WHO to backtrack. Attempting to clarify, the agency tweeted that "preliminary investigations conducted by the Chinese authorities have found no clear evidence of human-to-human transmission." (The key word missing from the end of that that tweet was "yet.") This tweet would later come back to haunt the agency, with critics

using it as evidence that WHO was assisting the Chinese government to cover up the severity of the epidemic. It wasn't until January 19/20, when the WHO Representative in China visited Wuhan, that the Chinese government publicly confirmed that human-to-human transmission was occurring and asked for WHO's assistance "in communicating this to the public, without causing panic."

By the third week of January, 575 cases had been reported in China, and 9 cases outside China (in Hong Kong, Taiwan, Thailand, Japan, Singapore, South Korea, Vietnam, and the U.S.). On January 22, WHO convened an Emergency Committee to advise Tedros on whether to declare a PHEIC. The Committee deliberated for two days but was split. Members agreed that the situation was urgent, but some felt that the available information was too limited and the number of cases outside China too few to warrant a PHEIC declaration, which is the highest level of alarm that WHO can ring. (Critics have questioned why WHO did not label Covid-19 a "pandemic" until March 11; however, the term pandemic is a colloquial one, with no set definition and no formal legal or policy significance.) In the end, the Committee recommended

against declaring a PHEIC for the moment, awaiting more information, and agreed to reconvene in ten days' time (or earlier, if necessary). Meanwhile, on the same day, China imposed a cordon sanitaire around the city of Wuhan, population 11 million; eventually, the cordon would encompass some 60 million people, the largest in history.

On January 28, Tedros took the "highly unusual" step of flying to China to meet with President Xi and plead with China to share information more quickly and transparently. Xi also agreed to allow an international team to visit China and assess the situation-though his government later stalled and did not allow the team's visit until the middle of February. On January 29, in response to the rapidly growing number of cases inside China and evidence of sustained human-to-human transmission outside China, Tedros decided to reconvene the Emergency Committee. On January 30, based on their recommendation, he declared a PHEIC.

Public praise, private frustration

Months later, it is clear that, in the words of one Emergency Committee member, China "misled" WHO

World Health Organization (WHO) Director-General Tedros Adhanom Ghebreyesus attends a press conference organised by the Geneva Association of United Nations Correspondents (ACANU) amid the COVID-19 outbreak, caused by the novel coronavirus, on July 3, 2020 at the WHO headquarters in Geneva. (FABRICE COFFRINI/AFP/GETTY IMAGES)

and the world about the extent of the Wuhan outbreak. Had Chinese officials at every level of government shared information more quickly and transparently, there is a chance that the Covid-19 could have been contained before it became a global pandemic. (Though it is equally true that if other governments, including the U.S., had acted with greater urgency in February and March, Covid-19 might not have exploded into a pandemic.)

Critically, WHO sensed it was being stonewalled. Internal communications obtained by the AP reveal top officials' frustration with China. At one point, Maria Van Kerkhove wrote "We're going on very minimal information…It's clearly not enough [] to do proper planning." Dr. Gauden Galea, the WHO Representative in China, complained that "We have informally and formally been requesting more epidemiological information….But when asked for specifics, we could get nothing" and "We're currently at the stage where yes, they're giving [information] to us 15 minutes before it appears on [Chinese state television]." And in early January, Dr. Mike Ryan, the Executive Director of the Health Emergencies Program, warned colleagues that "it was time to 'shift gears' and apply more pressure on China…'This is exactly the same

scenario, endlessly trying to get updates from China about what was going on.'" Unfortunately though, there was no way for WHO to ascertain the extent to which it was being misled. Unlike the IAEA, for example, it has no independent investigative authority to send teams into a country absent an invitation from the government.

And yet, all the while, WHO was publicly praising the Chinese government for its response to Covid-19, including its information sharing. For example, on January 30, Tedros said "The speed with which China detected the outbreak, isolated the virus, sequenced the genome and shared it with WHO and the world are very impressive, and beyond words. So is China's commitment to transparency and to supporting other countries." Simultaneously, WHO was also warning of the urgency of the situation—which is, after all, the point of issuing a PHEIC declaration—and pressing governments to "act now" to prepare. But is it probably fair to say that WHO's praise for China's response contributed to a false sense of reassurance that things were under control (or, at least, heading in that direction).

Why did WHO, through its lavish praise, paint a misleading picture of China's cooperation and transparency? Critics, including the Trump adminis-

tration, assert that it is because WHO's leadership is beholden to and under the thumb of the powerful Chinese government. In Trump's words, WHO therefore "willingly took China's assurances at face value and defended the actions of the Chinese government." But this explanation doesn't quite stand up to scrutiny. China's influence at WHO is growing, but it is still far less influential than the U.S. In a moment of unexpected candor, Tedros essentially admitted as much, saying "It is wrong to be any 'country-centric.' I am sure we are not China-centric. The truth is, if we are going to be blamed, it is right to blame us for being U.S.-centric." The U.S. is WHO's single largest donor. In 2018–19, it contributed 15% of WHO's budget; in contrast, China contributed 1.5%—and only 0.2% came in the form of voluntary contributions, which China could withdraw should it so choose. It is also inaccurate to suggest that WHO simply bowed to pressure from the Chinese government. For example, at one point, China wanted to sign off before WHO passed information received from the Chinese government on to other countries; WHO refused.

Rather, WHO's gratuitous praise of China was a strategic gambit to coax the Chinese government into cooperating with WHO, sharing information, and allowing international expert investigators into the country. In short, WHO was trying to win China over with honey and they slathered it on too thickly. The strategy was dicey—ultimately, it clearly undermined WHO's credibility and cost it the support of its largest donor (if temporarily).

But, apart from toning down the laudatory rhetoric, it's not entirely clear what Tedros could have done differently. Anthony Costello, the director of the UCL Institute for Global Health and a former director at WHO, told the Guardian, "I don't think Tedros did anything previous director generals would not have done. He needed a good relationship with China in order to get in."

Why didn't Tedros attempt to name-and-shame China, as Brundtland had during SARS? Apart from their differ-

Tedros Adhanom, Director General of the World Health Organization, (L) shakes hands with Chinese President Xi Jinping before a meeting at the Great Hall of the People, on January 28, 2020 in Beijing, China. (NAOHIKO HATTA/POOL/GETTY IMAGES)

ent leadership styles, such a maneuver would have been far more difficult to manage now than it was in 2003. For one thing, WHO felt that it was in a legal grey area. China was not sharing information fully and transparently, but it neither was it denying the outbreak or refusing to cooperate with WHO. Under the latter circumstances, the IHR empower WHO to publicize countries' non-compliance. But in this case, WHO officials felt that "since China was providing the minimal information required by international law, there was little WHO could do." Second, if the Secretariat antagonized China, they ran the risk of losing access complete. The Chinese government could stop sharing information altogether and then WHO would have no choice but to name-and-shame and hope to generate enough international pressure to induce the Chinese government to reverse course. At worst, this strategy might have been unsuccessful—China has far more international clout than it did 2003. And even if it did work, it would have taken time—time that the world did not have if it wanted to contain the virus.

In short, as one European diplomat put it, WHO's praise for China "was a tactical decision, and it was probably the only way to get access. But the optics are uncomfortable." The New York Times editorial board offered a more pointed analysis: "[The IHR] are effectively unenforceable. Individual countries routinely violate the edicts that don't suit them, and the WHO has almost no recourse when that happens. If the organization had more sticks to wield—if there were penalties for defying its previously agreed-upon rules—it might not have to meet the duplicity and delay it sometimes encounters with so much patient praise."

What else is WHO doing?

Since the earliest days of the pandemic, WHO has been frenetically active in its efforts to stimulate country preparedness and coordinate a global response to the pandemic. These efforts can be broken down into four streams: information sharing and technical guidance; capacity strengthening, par-

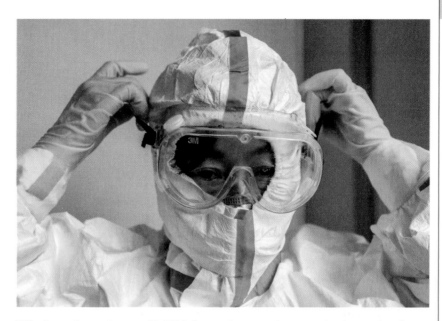

This photo taken on January 30, 2020 shows a doctor putting on a pair of protective glasses before entering the isolation ward at a hospital in Wuhan in China's central Hubei province, during the virus outbreak in the city. (AFP/GETTY IMAGES)

ticularly for low and middle income countries (LMICs); fundraising to support the global response; and high-quality research and development, and equitable distribution, for diagnostics, therapeutics and vaccines. On many fronts, WHO's efforts have been success and innovative. But there are also areas in which the agency has struggled, revealing both the internal challenges and external obstacles that limit its effectiveness.

Information Sharing and Technical Guidance

First and foremost, WHO's role in a pandemic is to share information—to gather, analyze, and publish epidemiological data; disseminate scientific finds and public health best practices/lessons learned; issue technical guidance, and combat the spread of misinformation. WHO's information sharing efforts and output are unprecedented in volume. From the outset, WHO has urged governments to transparently share data on cases and deaths, rather than try to hide the extent of the epidemic in their countries. On the whole (after China's early delays), they have been remarkably successful WHO's data dashboard publicly displays daily case-counts for nearly all WHO Member States, in-

cluding from countries in the Middle East, Africa, and Latin America that are often reluctant to publicize data.

WHO holds near-daily press briefings and #AskWHO public Q&A sessions on social media. They host weekly meetings in which governments share their experiences and best practices/lessons learned. In the first seven months of the pandemic, WHO issued 125 technical guidance documents, informed over 60 expert consultations and webinars with over 13,5000 participants from more than 120 countries. This guidance covers everything from virus transmission, social distancing, testing, contract tracing, quarantine and isolation, personal protective equipment for community members and health workers, and much more. WHO is also working with major social tech companies like Facebook, Google, and WhatsApp to combat the spread of Covid-19 misinformation.

For the most part, this guidance has been well-received by governments, scientists, and the public. That said, WHO's communications efforts have not been without mishaps. The reversals around human-to-human transmission is one example. Another is the kerfuffle over "asymptomatic" transmission, a miscommunication

Women wearing protective face masks, used as a preventive measure against the spread of the coronavirus disease (Covid-19), walk along the street in Ashgabat, Turkmenistan July 13, 2020. (VYACHESLAV SARKISYAN/REUTERS/NEWSCOM)

that boiled down to differences in the technical vs. colloquial meaning of the term. WHO quickly clarified these comments, but they nonetheless contributed to public confusion at a time when we can ill-afford it. Communicating complex scientific information to the public and maintaining an authoritative voice in an environment of high uncertainty and rapidly evolving knowledge is no easy task. Miscommunications happen, but the important thing is that WHO has moved quickly to correct those mistakes.

The more troubling criticism of WHO's technical response to Covid-19 is that the agency's internal experts, and the independent external experts who sit on its scientific advisory committees, have been too slow to integrate new findings about how Covid-19 may be spread—i.e. the possibility of transmission through small, aerosolized particles rather than large respiratory droplets—and too conservative in updating their guidance. The possibility of aerosol transmission has significant, urgent implications for the protective measures we take, particularly indoors (e.g. ventilation standards). Critics argue that WHO is stuck in old orthodoxies, keeps moving the goal posts on

what type of data would be needed to accept aerosol transmission, and has been unwilling to embrace the precautionary principle and encourage governments, businesses, and individuals to act as if aerosol transmission might be happening and take the necessary precautions. In July, a group of over 200 scientists published a commentary in *Clinical Infectious Diseases* urging WHO to reconsider the evidence. WHO did so and half-heartedly conceded that the possibility "cannot be ruled out," but emphasized other modes of transmission (droplets, fomites) and did not issue proactive new guidance. The guidance has since been updated, but critics continue to argue that WHO is not giving aerosol transmission the urgent emphasis and clear public messaging needed.

WHO was similarly slow to act in advising the public to wear masks. For many months, WHO advised against mask-wearing by non-symptomatic individuals, even in the face of growing evidence about pre-symptomatic/asymptomatic transmission. WHO officials were concerned that masks would give people a false sense of security and lead them to neglect other prevention measures like social dis-

tancing and hand washing. They also worried that mask-wearing by the general public would further strain the already-limited supply of masks for healthcare workers and about affordability for low-income individuals and countries. By the time WHO finally did recommend mask wearing in early June, around 100 countries—including many low-income countries—had already adopted some form of mask mandate.

Capacity Building and Fundraising

The second and third streams of WHO's work focuses on marshalling capacity and resources for the global Covid response, and in particular, supporting LMICs. As of mid-August, WHO had shipped over 100 million masks and tens of millions of other pieces of personal protective equipment to 148 countries. They distributed crucial medical equipment and diagnostics, including over 18.2 million respirators and over 11,700 oxygen concentrators, and over 6 million test kits and swabs. The agency also provides free digital resources for over 70,000 health care workers in over 200 countries and has deployed 180 Emergency Medical Teams to assist with countries' responses on the ground.

Unfortunately, but perhaps not surprisingly, the perennially-underfunded agency has had to struggle to secure financial support for its work. In February, the agency appealed to donors for $675 million to finance its preparedness and response work through April. According to the Guardian, by the first week in March, they had received only $1.2m. The funding target wasn't reached until early April, at which time there were already one million cases worldwide. The agency then had to issue a second funding request for $1.7 billion to carry it through December 2020; as of mid-August, the agency had received 52% of this money, with another 29% pledged, and a funding gap of $330 million.

But necessity has also served as the mother of invention. In March, WHO launched the Covid-19 Solidarity Response Fund which, for the first time, enables WHO to raise money directly from the general public. At time of writing, the Fund had raised over $233 million from more than 566,000 individuals, companies, and philanthropies worldwide, including $55 million raised from a benefit concert hosted by Lady Gaga.

Research, Development, and Distribution

WHO's fourth stream of work focuses on advancing research and development for Covid-19 diagnostics, treatments, and vaccines, and on ensuring that these vaccines are allocated equitably across all countries. For example, WHO coordinated the Solidarity Trial, an international clinic trial to identify effective Covid-19 treatments.

In addition, WHO is coordinating the Access to Covid-19 Tools (ACT) Accelerator, a massive collaboration among governments, global health organizations (like Gavi, the Global Fund to Fight AIDS Tuberculosis and Malaria, and the Coalition for Epidemic Preparedness (CEPI)), researchers, civil society, and philanthropists (like the Gates Foundation and the Wellcome Trust). Its goal is to speed up research, production and equitable distribution of vaccines, treatments, and diagnostics and to prepare health systems to roll out these tools.

One of the most critical components of this framework is the COVAX Facility, Countries can sign up to purchase vaccines through this pooled procurement mechanism, which will works with manufacturers of various vaccine to negotiate prices, expand vaccines production, use funding from high-income countries to subsidize vaccine purchases for LMICs, and ensure that vaccines doses are distributed equitably to high-risk populations and essential workers across all countries. Equitable distribution is essential both from an ethical perspective, and because countries will not be able to fully reopen their economies to trade and travel until the virus is controlled globally. The pandemic will not be over anywhere until it is over everywhere. The alternative to global coordination through COVAX is "vaccine nationalism"—an "every country for itself" approach in which countries must purchase their own vaccine supplies, negotiate their own prices, gamble on which vaccine candidates are likely to be most effective, and run the risk of being shut out due to supply shortages and geopolitical competition. This approach would have devastating consequences for people in countries that cannot afford to make massive advance purchases of multiple vaccines. If wealthy countries choose to hoard vaccine doses, as occurred during the 2009 H1N1 pandemic, the rest of the world would effectively be sent to the back of the line, and even those at highest risk would have to wait until the entire population of wealthy countries is vaccinated before they could get their shot.

WHO, Gavi, and CEPI established the COVAX Facility to prevent this scenario. But although a number of wealthy governments—including much of Europe and the UK—initially signed on to the idea and contributed funding, they proceeded to hedge on their commitment and have struck separate deals with vaccine companies to secure their own supplies. For instance, the UK pre-ordered five vaccine doses per person (of different vaccines). And like WHO as a whole, the ACT Accelerator has struggled to secure funding: as of late June, it had raised only $3.4 billion of its $31.3 billion ask, and $13.7 billion of this shortfall was considered urgent.

This situation typifies one of WHO's chief limitations. The agency is expected to act as the leading and coordinating authority in global health. But as in any orchestra, the conductor can only be as effective as the orchestra members allow them to be. If the orchestra members—the Member States—are willing to be coordinated to play along together, the result is beautiful music. If not, there is only discord, and WHO stands alone waving a baton to no avail. The decision rests with the Member States.

Where do we go from here? WHO reform

So where does WHO go from here? Member States have already initiated a review process to evaluate WHO's Covid-19 response and are discussing how to reform the agency to address some of the internal challenges and external limitations it laid bare. This is not the first time a PHEIC has triggered this kind of performance review and reform process—H1N1 and the West African Ebola epidemic did too. But this is the first time that such a review has occurred while the PHEIC was ongoing. And it is the first time since SARS that Member States have opened the door to revising the IHR—and their own commitments and obligations under it—rather than focusing purely on the Secretariat's performance.

Countries, including Australia, France, Germany, and the U.S, have begun to put forward concrete proposals for what reforms might look like. For example, a non-paper (informal discussion paper) circulated by the German and French governments, states "The international community's expectations regarding WHO's capacities outweigh by far its given financial, structural and legal abilities.... Covid-19 has to be used as an opportunity to strengthen WHO's abilities to fully act as the leading and coordinating authority in global health. Long-term strengthening of WHO overall is key in order to strengthen its role and responsibilities in pandemic preparedness and response." A Western diplomat based in Geneva told Reuters that "The [non-paper's] key point is the mismatch between WHO's mandate and financing. It's very much pro-WHO, it should have more money and [they are] asking for an increase in assessed contributions."

Margaret Chan (right), Director-General of the World Health Organization with Bill Gates, Co-Chair of the Bill & Melinda Gates Foundation, at a press conference during the 64th World Health Assemlby in Geneva, Switzerland, May 17, 2011. Bill Gates challenged health ministers and global health leaders to make vaccines their top priority to save millions of lives. (JEAN-MARC FERRÉ/UN PHOTO)

Problems to be solved

The Franco-German and Australian reform proposals—as well as proposals from independent global health experts—identify two overarching sets of problems that need to be addressed in order to have meaningful WHO reform. First are the institutional problems. Chronic underfunding and unsustainable funding leaves WHO without capacity to get the job done and makes it dependent on and subject to undue influence by donors (or, at least, creates the appearance that it is subject to undue influence). This precarious funding—coupled with the deference to sovereignty that Member States demand—mean that WHO lacks the political independence to respond proactively and decisively to health emergencies or otherwise safeguard global health as a global public good. As a group of leading experts write in the *Lancet*, "WHO must evolve to become more results-oriented and responsive. Such an evolution requires more than a functional review: it calls for a thorough transformation that overcomes political divisions and empowers WHO with the ability to question and constructively criticize national health strategies. We call for a WHO whose technical authority is fully recognized by Member States and is free of political considerations."

Second are the design weaknesses within the IHR themselves. For one thing, the PHEIC designation is a binary construct—the Director-General can either not declare an emergency or declare the highest level of emergency. This all-or-nothing approach does not lend itself to the kind of early warning system we need. When Director-General Margaret Chan acted swiftly to declare a PHEIC for H1N1 and the crisis turned out not to be as severe as expected, she was accused of "crying wolf" and undermining WHO's credibility. Tedros, on the advice of the Emergency Committee, held off declaring a PHEIC for a week in order to gather more information, and has been criticized for not acting swiftly enough.

Another issue is the lack of investigative and enforcement authority granted to WHO under the IHR. When the Chinese government spent weeks stringing the agency along, WHO officials had no authority to compel their cooperation and no ability to assess the situation independently. When governments fail in the obligation to inform WHO of possible PHEICs in a timely and transparent manner, or when they implement response measures in contravention of the IHR, WHO and other Member States have no mechanism to enforce the terms of the treaty or hold governments accountable for non-compliance.

WHO doesn't just lack sticks, it also lacks carrots. After the West African Ebola outbreak, Member States created the Contingency Fund for Emergency, a pot of money that WHO could dispense to help countries immediately respond to potential health emergencies. This was supposed to incentivize countries to report outbreaks in timely manner in order to receive funding. But the fund has been chronically underfunded and, in addition, is of no help when the outbreak occurs in a country like China that does not need financial or technical support from WHO.

Possible solutions

The reform proposals on the table go some way toward addressing these problems. For example, the Franco-German non-paper calls on Member States to consider increasing assessed contributions, or at least to shift to non-earmarked voluntary contributions that give WHO the budgetary flexibility to meet pressing needs. It also suggests shifting from a binary PHEIC declaration to a stoplight-type warning system. The Australian government proposed independent investigative authority (along the lines of IAEA weapons inspectors), which the German and French governments also support.

But in other respects, the proposed reforms may not go far enough, or may ever veer off in the opposite direction. While the non-paper mentions the need to strengthen Member States' accountability under the IHR, it stops short of proposing concrete enforcement mechanisms (along the lines of the WTO enforcement mechanism), which might infringe on countries' sovereign prerogatives. (In fact, it does not even use the term "enforcement.") Nor do we know whether Member States will ultimately be willing to lift other sovereignty-preserving guardrails in the IHR, such as allowing WHO to issue public warnings about potential emergencies based on information from unofficial sources without verification by governments.

The Australian, German, and French governments also discuss creating new oversight mechanisms to monitor WHO's handling of emergency responses. But it is not clear how these new mechanisms would fit the with existing mechanisms, such as the WHO Health Emergencies Program's Independent Oversight and Advisory Committee or the independent Global Preparedness Monitoring Board. Thus, this particular proposal risks stumbling into familiar dangers: the creation of new committees substitutes for meaningful action, and duplication and fragmentation of accountability mechanisms distracts from, rather than enhances, real accountability. In addition, the Franco-German non-paper emphasizes the need for Member States themselves to "provide adequate oversight and guidance to WHO's work in health emergencies" and suggest the creation of a sub-committee of the Executive Board for this purpose. However, one of the biggest criticisms of WHO's response to Covid-19 is that the Secretariat is too deferential to Member States and lacks the political independence it needs to do its job. It hard to see how more-intensive oversight by governments would enhance WHO's political independence.

Finally, the reform proposals advanced by Member States thus far do not address one of the most important internal limitations apparent in WHO's Covid-19 response: the non-transparency of the PHEIC decision-making process and the lack of diverse expertise informing the agency's decision-making. WHO's experts — both the Secretariat staff and external experts it consults, such as EC members — are primarily doctors and bio-medical scientists (epidemiologists, virologists, etc.) However, the decisions that these experts take when ad-

vising on whether to declare a PHEIC or formulating recommendations and technical guidance, are inherently political decisions with far-reaching economic, social, diplomatic, and legal implications. Although the Emergency Committee's deliberations take place behind closed doors, Committee members have revealed that these implications do influence their decisions. Rather than expecting epidemiologists to assess economic and political impacts, the PHEIC process could be improved by including more diverse expertise. Consulting a wider range of expert voices might also help address criticisms that the agency is too slow and orthodox in updating its technical guidance.

Conclusion

WHO's response to Covid-19 is the most robust response to a public health emergency that the agency has launched since SARS. But it has also engendered much criticism of the Director-General and the Secretariat. Some of this criticism is fair. Some is less fair, because it effectively blames the agency for not doing things that it is not empowered to do. The fundamental dilemma of WHO's performance during Covid-19 and across the board is this: Member States get what they pay for and they get what they order, but they do not magically

get what they need. Governments demand deference from WHO, and for decades, they have not provided it with adequate funding to do its job. Except when an emergency arises, they want an agency that provides behind-the-scenes technical advice and support, but that does not step on their sovereignty or publicly challenge their actions. This is the agency they have built. But when an emergency arises, governments' desires shift — they suddenly want an agency that is strong and independent, capable of compelling recalcitrant governments and stopping outbreaks in their tracks. Unfortunately, we do not live in a comic book world where mild-mannered scientist Bruce Banner is capable of transforming into the Incredible Hulk in the face of danger.

The prospects for meaningful WHO reform hinge entirely on whether Member States are willing to change what they order and what they pay for. It is easy and convenient for governments to depict WHO as a dysfunctional bureaucracy trying to execute a political two-step on the head of a pin. But as the New York Times editorial board writes, "Instead, [governments] should try seeing WHO for what it is: a reflection of the countries that created it and that wrote its bylaws. If they don't like what they see, they should work to improve that reflection."

Coronavirus model is seen with World Health Organization (WHO) logo in the background in this illustration photo taken in Poland on June 5, 2020. (JAKUB PORZYCKI/NURPHOTO/GETTY IMAGES)

discussion questions

1. Should the U.S. continue their plan to exit the WHO by July 2021? If the U.S. does shift course and stay in the WHO, what changes would be most important to implement first?

2. Do you agree with the proposals promoted in the "non-white paper" on how to improve the WHO? What are some changes you would add or take out of the proposal?

3. How much control should international organizations have over their member countries? Should organizations like the UN and WHO have authority to overstep local governments?

4. Should the main function of the WHO be to prevent any future global outbreaks like covid-19, or is it better for the organization to have multiple different interests?

5. What would be some of the drawbacks, if any, to increasing the role and authority of most international organizations?

suggested readings

Mandavilli, Apoorva. **239 Experts with One Big Claim: The Coronavirus is Airborne,** New York Time, July 4, 2020.

Chorev, Nitsan. **The World Health Organization between North and South**, 288 pg. Cornell University Press, 2012. Chorev assesses the response of the WHO bureaucracy to member-state pressure in two particularly contentious moments: when during the 1970s and early 1980s developing countries forcefully called for a more equal international economic order, and when in the 1990s the United States and other wealthy countries demanded international organizations adopt neoliberal economic reforms.

Government of France & Government of Germany. 2020. **"Non-Paper on Strengthening WHO's Leading and Coordinating Role in Global Health."** August 2020.

Cueto, Marcos, Brown, Theodore M. and Fee, Elizabeth. **The World Health Organization: A History** 388 pg. Cambridge University Press, 2019. The authors re-evaluate the relative success and failure of critical WHO campaigns, from early malaria and smallpox eradication programs to struggles with Ebola today.

Kamradt-Scott, Adam. **Managing Global Health Security: The World Health Organization and Disease Outbreak Control** 244 pg. Palgrave Macmillan, 2015. Drawing on insights from international organization and securitization theory, the author investigates the World Health Organization and how its approach to global health security has changed and adapted since its creation in 1948. He also examines the organization's prospects for managing global health security now and into the future.

O 'Neill Institute for National & Global Health Law, **"The WHO Explained".** Georgetown Law. https://oneill.law.georgetown.edu/the-who-explained/Ger

Don't forget: Ballots start on page 104!!!!

To access web links to these readings, as well as links to
global discussion questions, shorter readings and suggested web sites,
GO TO www.fpa.org/great_decisions
and click on the topic under Resources, on the right-hand side of the page.

The end of Globalization?
by Anne O. Krueger

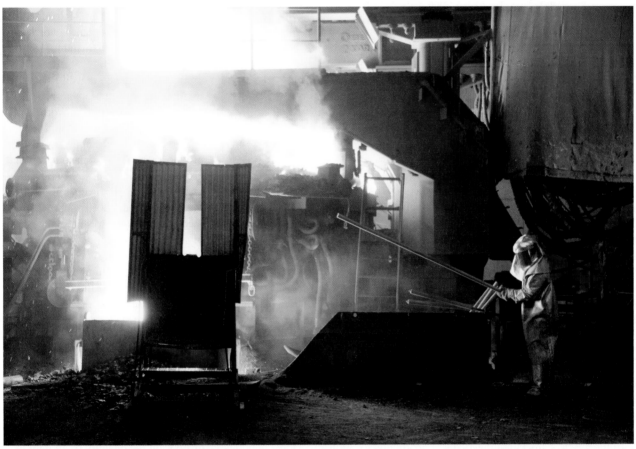

A steelworker in a protective suit checks the temperature of molten metal in a furnace at the TMK Ipsco Koppel plant in Koppel, Pennsylvania, on March 9, 2018. (MICHAEL MATHES/AFP/GETTY IMAGES)

The transformation of life in the Western world from "nasty, brutish, and short" to today's longer life expectancies, better health and nutrition, and vast increases in knowledge and living standards has certainly been among mankind's greatest achievements. Countries in the developing world are now following the western world and have embarked on the transition to modern lifestyles. Globalization has been both an important factor leading to the sea change and a result of it.

Globalization has been ongoing throughout recorded history. Migrations from Asia to the North American continent and from Africa to Europe were perhaps the earliest globalizing activities. But soon movement of goods became equally important. The Roman Empire depended on imports of African wheat. Seaborne trade among Asian countries was well established by 1000. All school children learn of Marco Polo's travels to and from India and China and the "exotic"

silks and other goods that were sought by Europeans. By the beginning of the 17th century, the East India Company and other national companies were sailing to and from South and Southeast Asia with high-value low-volume goods sought halfway around the world.

Once the industrial revolution started, trade and other economic relations between countries intensified even more rapidly. As trade volumes increased, so did living standards in the Western world. A turning point in economic history

ANNE O. KRUEGER *is the Senior Research Professor of International Economics at the School for Advanced International Studies, Johns Hopkins University. She is also a Senior Fellow of Center for International Development (of which she was the founding Director) and the Herald L. and Caroline Ritch Emeritus Professor of Sciences and Humanities in the Economics Department at Stanford University.*

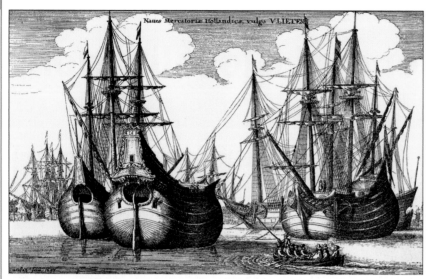

A ship of an East Indiaman, a ship of the Dutch East India Company, 17th century. (FALKEN-STEINFOTO/ALAMY)

is the beginning of the "Great Divergence," as most aspects of life in the West grew better for most people. It is impossible to reimagine a world history in which economic growth since around 1800 could have been anywhere close to what it has been if people, goods, and services, could not have been able to move outside their own country.

In many regards, the economic history—if not all history—is a story of the increasing interconnectedness and integration of people throughout the world, i.e. of globalization. To be sure, a few nations (for example Myanmar until the 1990s, China until the 1980s, and North Korea to the present day) have attempted to isolate themselves to the maximum extent possible, but they have paid the price by becoming increasingly irrelevant and a diminishing part of the international economy. Nations with open trading policies have been among the most successful. Economic history suggests that over the longer term, markets have almost always won out over the efforts of sovereigns to thwart them with controls,

as richer nations (with open trade) became more powerful and grew more than the restricting ones.

For this essay, globalization is taken to mean the process of increasing interconnectedness of the world economy. It thus covers faster and cheaper communications and transportation. It includes the increased speed of travel and the rapidity with which ideas, information, and news spreads. International trade in goods and services is a major part of it.

Globalization increases when a commodity produced in a particular place in the world is sold over a wider geographic area and when events in a particular location affect those at points further and further distant. It grows when the change in price of a commodity produced in a particular place starts affecting producers of that same commodity at points further away. For example, a poor wheat crop in India in the 21st century can affect the prices wheat farmers in North Dakota receive even if there is no trade in wheat between the two places: the wheat market is now global, and anything that affects world supply or demand has an impact on every other producer and consumer of wheat and its close substitutes.

By the late 20th century, transport and communications costs had fallen so much that trade in services (such as tourism, including such new phenomena as "medical tourism") became

increasingly important. Moreover, the volume of international trade increased rapidly and was an "engine of world economic growth." Businesses everywhere can now purchase more of their needed inputs of parts and components from low-cost producers in other countries and can sell their products worldwide. These phenomena have resulted from, and added to, the growth of real incomes, which further stimulated the demand for foreign goods and services.

Interdependence is well illustrated by the effects of the Japanese tsunami of 2011. Researchers at the World Trade Organization (WTO) estimated that the tsunami led to large supply shocks for producers in many Asian countries and elsewhere. For example, they estimated that Thailand's producers of industrial machinery experienced a supply shock, meaning a downward shift in their supply of inputs, of about 7.5%. For the U.S., supply-driven shocks were smaller, but still averaged about 0.5%. For some critical inputs, the situation was much more serious..

Integration of the world economy has resulted not only from improvements in transportation and communications, but also because government-imposed barriers to trade have been greatly reduced. Policy-induced barriers to trade include measures such as tariffs, import and export licensing (i.e., putting a ceiling or floor on the quantity of an item that can be exported or imported), holding imports to higher safety standards than domestic goods, requirements that inputs be sourced domestically, and more. In 1900, it is estimated that many tariffs on imported goods were still over 50%, while transport and communications costs were equally expensive. That meant that a commodity shipped from the U.S. to, say, Italy could cost the importer more than twice as much as the exporter received.

In the second half of the 20th century, countries agreed on and established an international organization to set rules for trade that would prevent discrimination against imports from abroad. Rules governing international transactions are essential for a well-

Before you read, download the companion **Glossary** that includes definitions, a guide to acronyms and abbreviations used in the article, and other material. Go to **www.fpa.org/great_decisions** and select a topic in the Resources section. (Top right)

functioning global economy and have underpinned the increased role of trade in goods and services. With transport and communications costs falling to less than 15%, on average, and tariffs falling to an average of 4%–5% on many industrial goods, the prices of many imports had fallen by more than half since the late 1940s for those reasons alone.

Not only have communications, transport, and goods exchanges between countries become relatively more important as costs fell, but that increase has been accompanied by a rapid growth in the flows of international finance: financing of exports and imports, short-term lending and borrowing across borders, private foreign direct investment, and equities have all increased in absolute and relative importance.

The British locomotive-building industry expanded rapidly in the 19th century and cultivated a thriving export market. Locomotive No 690, built in 1883 by Neilson & Co of Glasgow for the Chemin de Fer de l'Ouest, is seen here being loaded on board ship en route to France. (SSPL/GETTY IMAGES)

Globalization over the centuries

Despite Alexander, Marco Polo, and Chinese shipping, trade was usually confined to high-value, low-volume goods such as spices, gold, and silver until the middle of the 17th century. Around that time, trade and other contacts began increasing more rapidly: the East India Company was founded in 1600, and other European countries followed with their own trading companies. Each company received a royal charter giving it monopoly rights to trade goods in South Asia. The intended purpose was to engage in profitable trade, generate a surplus of revenues over expenditures, and thus enrich the sovereign by earning gold and silver.* Initially, the trade was highly profitable, despite dangers associated with shipwrecks, pirate assaults, and uprisings in the partner trading company.

Over time, each of these companies

It was believed that a country's wealth was determined by its gold and silver holdings. For Western European countries at that time, that meant a country had to earn more foreign exchange through exports than it spent on normal imports so that gold and silver could be purchased and accumulated.

experienced rising expenses and falling profits. By the 19th century, they were no longer dominant traders. In 1776, Adam Smith wrote his *Wealth of Nations,* challenging the ideas underlying the monopolistic trading companies. On one hand, he contradicted the notion that the objective of trade was to accumulate money to finance royal wars. Instead, he insisted that its purpose was to have private companies compete and let each country devote its resources to the most profitable lines of production. Productive capacity was the true wealth of nations. He also destroyed the idea that monopoly trading companies were desirable, explaining how competition forced companies to be efficient (or go out of business).

The industrial revolution began at about the same time as the *Wealth of Nations* was gaining influence. It is no coincidence that Smith's precepts were adopted first in Great Britain and that that country was the fastest growing country in the world in the 19th century. Before briefly sketching what happened and the effects, it is worth recalling how different life was in the

18th century, even in northern Europe, from what it is today.

Rising Standards of Living, Health, and Well-being. As trade volumes increased, so did living standards in the western world. That was a major turning point in modern economic history, known as the beginning of the Great Divergence (between living standards in the west and in other countries), as already noted.

To those living in advanced countries today, the living standards at the turn of the 18th century are almost inconceivable. Average life expectancy was a fraction of what it now is: it is estimated to have averaged 38 years in Britain in the second half of the 18th century and only 28 years in France. Of those born, 56% died before they were 15 years of age. Life expectancy in ancient Egypt and China is estimated to have been about the same (29 and 26 years respectively) as in northern Europe at the beginning of the Great Divergence.

Economic historians estimate that there had been virtually no change in standards of living worldwide in the four millennia prior to 1800. In 1800, about 75% of an English laborer's wage was spent on food and drink, 10% on clothing, 6% on housing, 5% on heating, and 4% on light and soap. Most of that consumption was produced within a short distance of where consumers lived.

Living standards in the western world rose sharply until World War 1. The U.S. was a leader. Gordon describes American living standards in 1870 contrasted with 2010: life expectancy at birth was 45.2 years, compared to 77.9 years in 2010; infant mortality was 175.5 per thousand births whereas in 2010 it was 6.8; "most Americans lived on farms and produced much of their food and clothing at home"; central heating and plumbing were virtually nonexistent; most rural households remained largely isolated even from nearby towns by poor or nonexistent roads. These low living standards were in large part the reason for low life expectancies and high infant mortality—reflecting poor nutrition (recall there were no refrigerators), lack of access to health care, and absence of the medical knowl-

Adam Smith (1723–90) Scottish philosopher and economist. Author of Inquiry into the Nature and Causes of the Wealth of Nations *1776. Etching by John Kay, Edinburgh 1790.* (UNIVERSAL HISTORY ARCHIVE/ GETTY IMAGES)

edge accrued over later years. But by around 1870 they were beginning to rise rapidly.

The divergence in living standards between the advanced countries and the developing countries began increasing. Even by 2019, when many developing countries had already grown rapidly for two decades, divergence was wide. Estimated annual income per person in 2020 in developing countries was only a little higher than it had been two millennia earlier. Between them and the advanced countries, the gap was huge. Per capita incomes in the U.S., UK, Japan and Germany were $65,118, $42,305, $40,247 and $46,258 respectively. By contrast they were $10,261 in China (where per capita incomes had more than doubled since 2000), $3,552 in Bolivia, $8,717 in Brazil, $1,643 in Cambodia, $2,104 in India, $554 in Niger, $776 in Uganda, and $1,464 in Zimbabwe. To be sure, a number of countries that were poor in the period after WW II changed their economic policies in later years. Among the most prominent were South Korea, which undertook far-reaching reforms in economic policies in the 1960s and 1970s, Chile in the late 1970s, China in the 1970s and 1980s, and India in the 1990s. In those and a number of other instances, growth rates rose markedly, and by 2020, per capita incomes were much higher than in developing countries such as Niger and Zimbabwe.

By any measure, life had improved enormously in the advanced countries, although not all in those countries had benefitted equally and a few had lost out along the way. The advanced countries enjoyed higher living standards and also longer life expectancies, health improvements, increased literacy and more. That is evident in the data, but also in the popular demands for accelerated development and higher living standards in the poor countries.

What accounts for the phenomenal transformation?

It is difficult to exaggerate the difference in lifestyles in the west in the two

centuries after 1820. The divergence in per capita incomes between the advanced and the developing countries is almost equally incomprehensible. A key question is what made this enormous leap forward possible? Much of the answer lies in globalization.

As late as 1800 the world was still a fairly insular place. Travel and communications were time-consuming and costly. Only about 2% of world GDP was traded between countries at that time. Although we read about pilgrims reaching the New World and other travel adventures, it is a reasonable guess that a very high proportion of the world's population never went more than 25 miles from place of birth in 1800, and about 90% of the world's population was engaged in agriculture.

Travel times were, however, starting to fall. It took about 90 hours to make the trip between Manchester and London in 1700 and 33 hours in 1800. Clark estimates that in Roman times news traveled from Rome to Egypt in 56 days, or at about 1 mile per hour. News of the signing of the Treaty of Nanking in 1842 reached London in 84 days (1.1 miles per hour), and of Lincoln's assassination in 1865 in 13 days (1.2 miles per hour).

Not only was travel slow until the 19th century: it was also costly. Then, the steamship began to replace sailing ships. Travel times and costs were cut because steamships were faster and because they were not wind-dependent. By the 1850s, piracy was virtually eliminated so that ships no longer had to carry heavy cannons on their decks, which greatly increased cargo capacity. Of course, the advent of canals and the railroad reduced travel time and cost for land routes (including the cost of transporting goods between inland points and coastal ports).

These and other innovations greatly reduced transport costs. The cost of shipping a ton of cotton goods from Liverpool to Bombay, for example, fell from £31 in 1872 to £1.9 in 1907.

The invention of the telegraph greatly speeded communications by several hundred percent. The first transatlantic underwater cable was laid in 1858. Later, of course, came the telephone. By standards of the 21st century, intercontinental (and even intercity) calls remained expensive. It is estimated that even in 1930, a three-minute transatlantic call between London and New York cost $290 in prices of 2000. Today, of course, the cost is less than 1% of that, and email is instantaneous and virtually free.

While transport and communications costs were falling, the leading countries in the industrial revolution were reducing and removing their tariffs on imports. The UK was the first to abandon its tariff policies and adopt virtually free trade.* Other northern European countries followed the UK's lead. Tariffs had averaged 50% or more while transport and communications costs had been very high. The cost of importing a commodity was two or more times the price in the exporting country. But by the mid-1800s, Adam Smith's message was influencing policy and the relative prices of imports (including tariffs, shipping costs, and ex-factory price in the exporting country) had probably fallen almost by half, if not more.

With transport and communications costs (and times) dropping dramatically and tariffs and other barriers to trade reduced or eliminated, the volume of international trade mushroomed.** The U.S. did not adopt free trade as rapidly as did the northern Europeans. But falling costs of shipments combined with the rapid growth in European demand for wheat and other American products nonetheless led to rapid growth of American exports. It is

estimated that by 1913, the volume of world trade was about 22% of world GDP. The move to greater reliance on private markets resulting from Smith's seminal ideas also resulted in a sharp increase in the rate of innovations and technical change. During the 19th century, the steam engine (Scotland), the telegraph, the telephone, electricity (and electric lighting in 1870), refrigeration (Persia), railroads (England), internal combustion engines (Germany), the reaper, the cotton gin, the radio (Italy) and many more new products and techniques appeared. Their development proceeded in both Europe and North America: ideas quickly spread between countries as part of the globalization process. It took little time for inventions to be adopted and improved upon by citizens of other countries.

Lowered costs of transport and communication, and hence increased trade and information exchanges, reduced artificial barriers to trade. The shift toward more reliance on private enterprise and a level playing field and innovation also each contributed to the quantum leap in living standards in the west that marked the past two centuries.

These phenomena interacted and a virtuous circle resulted. Increasing trade flows meant that countries such as England could import grains more cheaply than they could be produced at home, freeing workers to move to more productive occupations and raising their real wage (and those of the poor) as food products became cheaper. Innovations in refrigeration combined with shorter sailing times combined to provide more nutrients in food in northern climes.

These and many other changes contributed to a healthier and longer-lived population, which in turn led to a more productive labor force. Whereas the printing press with movable type was invented in China around 1040, communications were so sparse that it had to be invented all over again in Europe around 1600. By contrast, it took less than 5% of that time for personal computers to emerge in many countries at the end of last century.

(L-R) U.S. Treasury Secretary Henry Morgenthau Jr. and British economist John Maynard Keynes conferring during international monetary conference to plan for postwar reconstruction. (ALFRED EISENSTAEDT/TIME/GETTY IMAGES)

The lost years

Life as those in the west knew it by 1914 was already a very different experience from life 200, or even 100, years earlier. There was a stark difference between lifestyles in the West and those in the "underdeveloped," as they were then called, countries

WWI and the Great Depression resulted in a sharp slowdown, if not a retrogression, in globalization. Many trading ties were loosened, if not lost, in WWI. The European countries then struggled to restore prewar international financial arrangements in the 1920s, while the reparations payments required of Germany led to further international dislocation. By the end of the 1920s, the Great Depression had started. Country after country began raising barriers to international trade in the hope that higher-priced imports would lead consumers to buy domestic substitutes, thus raising domestic production levels. Instead, other countries retaliated and shrinkage of the volume of international trade intensified. The period from the beginning of WWI until the end of WWII is generally regarded as one in which globalization dramatically slowed down if it did not reverse.

---

* The UK also was the first to follow the precepts of Smith, David Ricardo, and other economists of the time and to rely on market economies with competition and level playing fields to deliver goods and services.

** The U.S. was a laggard in reducing its tariffs. The U.S. nonetheless benefited from lower costs of shipping and communication and increasing demand in Europe for imports, especially of agricultural commodities, from America.

The economic situation at the end of the war

At the end of the war in 1945, wartime destruction and the disruption of shipping routes and trading patterns had left much of the world economy in dire straits. Europe and Japan were near starvation and capital was needed to enable investment to convert to peacetime production and restore critical infrastructure. The leaders of the devastated economies had little immediate choice but to impose stringent controls on foreign trade as there were few items available for export. Those controls themselves exacerbated the plight of war-torn economies, and the first several years after the war witnessed political and social disruption.

The U.S. emerged stronger than ever. The American leadership recognized the perilous situation. Instead of demanding reparations and seeking vengeance as victorious countries had done after past wars, the U.S. administration adopted the Marshall Plan and other measures, extending aid to the war-afflicted countries.* Under the Marshall Plan European countries received funds that could finance needed investments. But the Americans insisted that the pattern of bilateral trade balancing between countries should be dropped and trade opened up quickly.

Building a better global economic architecture.

Analysis of what went wrong in the interwar period pinpointed two key culprits: the collapse of the international financial system in the 1930s with competitive devaluations, and the sharp increase in tariffs in the early 1930s after the American Smoot-Hawley tariff and the "beggar thy neighbor" retaliatory tariffs across countries.

During and after the Second World War, the U.S. took leadership in planning an "international economic architecture" intended to prevent any recurrence of the disasters of the interwar

period. That architecture has evolved over time, but its essential characteristics remain until today, and have underpinned much of the success of globalization since 1945.

The U.S. emerged from WWII as the unquestioned preeminent leader of the advanced countries. Instead of using its power bilaterally (as had happened with demands for reparations payments from Germany after WWI and in other conflicts), the U.S. chose to build a multilateral geopolitical and economic system. In coordination with other countries, plans for multilateral institutions were developed: the United Nations for political purposes, three "specialized agencies" for economic purposes (although they were and are part of the UN system). That architecture has remained the essential backbone of the international economy ever since.

The three major global economic agencies are the International Monetary Fund (IMF), the World Bank, and the World Trade Organization (WTO). Although a few countries still have not joined, membership in each has grown over the years: to 190 countries in both the IMF and the World Bank, and 164 in the WTO.

The IMF, as its name suggests, was tasked with providing the stability and smooth functioning of the international monetary system. That, in turn, was intended to underpin an open multilateral trading system. The World Bank is the agency that supports economic development, especially of developing countries, primarily through loans, with very low interest rates (concessional loans) to the least developed countries to finance development projects.

The proposed International Trade Organization (ITO) was not ratified by the U.S. Congress and never came into being, but some of its articles were taken and used to inaugurate the General Agreement on Tariffs and Trade (GATT) in 1947. The GATT was an "agreement" joined by the U.S. by executive order, whereas the World Bank

and IMF are international organizations whose members have signed their Articles of Agreement as a treaty. In 1994 the GATT transformed into an international organization, the WTO. The GATT/WTO provided the legal framework for the international economy. It collected and disseminated data from members about their trade and trade policies. It also reduced trading costs by agreeing on arrangements for such things as customs forms, permissible of phytosanitary and other standards (which could otherwise be used as protective devices), and much more. In addition, the GATT/WTO Secretariat served as the body to service members in multilateral trade negotiations (MTNs) for negotiating reciprocal reduction of trade barriers.

Three core principles underlie the WTO. Members are to extend national treatment to foreign traders, which means they have the same rights as nationals in domestic courts. Protection against imports should be provided only through tariffs (so that trade policies are transparent) and there should be no export subsidies. There should be most favored nation treatment (MFN) by each country of goods and services transactions with other countries, which assures nondiscrimination among trading partners (so that the same tariff protection is applied to all countries).

The WTO has done much for the international trading system. It has served as a secretariat for eight successful rounds of negotiations for reciprocal tariff reductions. The outcome was that, as of the implementation of the last (Uruguay) round, tariffs on manufactured goods averaged between 3% and 5% in advanced countries (compared to 45%--50% after World War II), and the WTO classified any tariff above 15% as being a "tariff peak." The WTO's Articles also provided for a dispute settlement mechanism (DSM), under which countries could bring their complaints if a trading partner were deemed to violate its obligations under

---

There was other important American assistance, including Point IV (aid to Greece and Turkey), loans to Great Britain, and much more.

the Articles or the agreed-upon tariff reductions agreed in successive MTNs. Disputes such as the Boeing-Airbus dispute between the U.S. and the European Union might well have resulted in a trade war without the DSM.

Accelerating globalization and growth after WWII

Despite much pessimism at the end of the war about global economic prospects, by 1953 the war-devastated advanced countries had rapidly attained prewar levels of output while the other advanced economies also prospered. Spurred on by the trade liberalization in Europe under the Marshall Plan and the first round of MTNs under GATT, international trading volumes grew at unprecedented rates.

Transport and communications costs and times resumed their fall after 1945. In the late 1940s, transport costs of exports added about 20% of their cost to the importers and have fallen to around 5% in this century. From rates of 40% and more in the late 1940s, average tariff rates on manufactured goods by the advanced economies fell in successive rounds of MTs to less than 5% by early in this century.

In the first years after WWII, the "international economy" essentially consisted of two groups: the rich advanced countries (most of Europe, the U.S. and Canada, Japan, Australia and New Zealand) and the poor countries of the developing world. China, the USSR, and other centrally planned economies endeavored to reduce trading and other ties with the advanced countries to the maximum feasible extent.

For the advanced countries, the quarter century after WWII was a "golden" period, with rates of growth of trade, real incomes, and real GNP never before witnessed over such a long period. From the end of WWII for more than 60 years, international trade in goods rose at twice the rate of growth of world GDP both because of falling real costs of international transactions and because of the reduction and removal of tariffs and other trade barriers.

A shop selling black and white televisions. The clients wear traditional Mao Zedong style jackets. (ERIC PRÉAU/SYGMA/GETTY IMAGES)

The WTO estimates that world merchandise trade was 7% of world GDP in 1947 and rose to 17% by 1998; in 2019, it was just over 60%. Globalization certainly contributed significantly to the accelerated growth rate of world GDP.

The emergence of developing countries

It was already seen that prior to WWII living standards in areas outside the west rose at a much slower rate, if at all, than they did in the west. The Great Divergence was taking place. The countries left behind this rapid growth became known as "developing countries" and that is the terminology that will be used here.

In the immediate postwar period, most developing countries were still governed by colonial powers, and even those that were independent, such as Brazil, Turkey, and Thailand, had strikingly lower living standards and productivity than the advanced countries. By the 1970s, almost all developing countries had become independent.

The new governments aspired to achieve economic growth and attain lifestyles similar to those of the advanced countries, including health and life expectancy, for their people. They tried to do so by putting up high tariffs and other trade barriers and refused to join in the liberalization of trade under GATT/WTO. They hoped to use

protection to encourage domestic production of many items that had been imported from advanced countries. They were exporters of raw materials (agricultural products, oil, and minerals). Their share of international trade fell over the 1950–70 period and trade linkages to the advanced countries weakened. Because of the rapid growth in the advanced countries, demand for raw materials was rising, and developing countries were able to grow modestly, although the advanced countries grew even faster.

Worse yet, over time economic growth in most developing countries was slowing. A few in East Asia (Hong Kong, Singapore, South Korea, and Taiwan), known as the "East Asian tigers," already had undertaken economic policy reforms in the 1950s and 1960s and began growing rapidly but they were exceptions at that time. Indeed, they were so successful that they are regarded as "advanced economies" today.

By the 1980s and 1990s, however, other developing countries began following the examples of the East Asian tigers and unilaterally reforming economic policy. Tariffs and other trade barriers were lowered and developing countries' economies were increasingly integrated with those of the rest of the world. China, by virtue of her size and earlier poverty, was the most spectacular reformer, but many others also ex-

Trade ministers of 11 countries of the Comprehensive and Progressive Trans-Pacific Partnership attend the Commission meeting on January 19, 2019, in Tokyo, Japan. (THE ASAHI SHIMBUN/GETTY IMAGES)

perienced greatly improved economic performance. Their rates of economic growth accelerated and, by the turn of the century, they were growing more rapidly than the advanced countries.

Economic growth rates accelerated in the 1990s for the entire world economy. The developing countries that had abandoned their import substitution policies generally began growing more rapidly and by the turn of the century, many had begun further integration in the world economy. As well, Russia negotiated to join the WTO and finally became a member in 2012. China's accession was in 2001. As is well known, by 2010, the People's Republic of China's economy had been transformed. Other countries including India experienced accelerated growth following the dismantling of their highly protectionist trade regimes and inner orientation. Globalization had accelerated for the developing countries.

Preferential Trading Arrangements (PTAs)

The GATT/WTO articles called for nondiscrimination among trading partners, but provided for an exception in cases of preferential trading arrangements under which two or more countries would mutually agree to lower all of their tariff barriers among themselves and form a free trade area

(FTA) or customs union (CU).* In the late 1940s, six European countries – Belgium, France, Germany, Italy, Luxembourg and the Netherlands – agreed to form a customs union. The reduction of tariff barriers between the countries was taking place at the same time as external tariffs against the rest of the world were falling after WTO MTNs and as those countries were reaching their prewar production levels.

It was anticipated that the collective growth of the six would slow down, but it instead accelerated. In the rest of the world, many observers attributed the successful growth of the six to the customs union, which certainly contributed. But the fact that external tariffs were falling was also important.

Over time, many other countries joined the original six. Now there are 27 members of the European Union (there were 28 until the UK withdrew). While some developing countries formed FTAs or CUs, they did so with very high external tariffs and did not greatly affect economic growth. The U.S. policy was to maintain open multilateral trade, and with exceptions

* *A free trade area is one in which there are zero tariffs between the members, but each country retains its own tariff schedule against the rest of the world. A customs union is an arrangement for countries to lower their tariffs to zero among themselves and have a common external tariff.*

of politically motivated instances (primarily Israel), remained nondiscriminatory until the late 1980s when first Canada and the U.S. agreed to an FTA and then Mexico also joined to create NAFTA. Also in the early 1990s, the USSR broke up, and many of the newly independent countries negotiated FTAs with trading partners initially while they waited to align their policies with those that were WTO-compatible and join the WTO. PTAs have become increasingly important in the international economy. Late in 2020, the Chinese and 14 other Asian countries agreed to form the Regional Comprehensive Economic Partnership (RCEP), which is to be an FTA among those countries, covering 30% of world trade.

Globalization as of the 2010s

By 2010, the process of globalization had been proceeding for more than 60 years after WWII. As already seen, life expectancies, real per capita incomes, educational attainments, and most other indicators of living standards and well-being had greatly improved throughout almost the entire world.

Whereas international trade in the 19th and early 20th century had been almost entirely in finished commodities, trade in services and in parts and components began increasing rapidly after WWII. From small beginnings, both grew enormously in size and importance. Companies located production facilities where costs were lowest: simple assembly processes using unskilled labor were shifted to countries with an abundance of unskilled labor and low wages. That enabled labor in advanced countries to be employed in higher productivity industries requiring more skilled and highly educated workers and fewer unskilled. As such, "value chains" expanded globalization and interdependence in yet another important way.

By 2018, global trade in services was about 30% of the total for goods and services and equal to about 7% of world GDP. As transport and communications costs fell, international trade in tourism, financial services, health care, transport, and much more had grown even more rapidly than trade in goods.

Other aspects of globalization had also intensified. A high and increasing fraction of university students studied abroad. International conferences and rapid communications enabled ideas and research findings to disseminate at an ever-increasing pace. The rate of innovations, as measured by the number of patents granted, had accelerated.

Last, but certainly far from least, international financial markets have become increasingly globalized. Companies from around the world listed their equities in New York, London, Frankfurt and elsewhere. International banks conducted business throughout the world, and even small exchange rate movements had international repercussions. Just as international finance has grown and facilitated trade, the growth of trade has necessarily spurred international finance. After the Great Recession, questions arose as to the adequacy of the governance of the international financial system. Doubtless more can be done, but the benefits of a well-functioning international finance system are unquestionable.

The successes of globalization

By 2015, global poverty had been greatly reduced and was still falling. Living standards, life expectancy, and other measures of well-being were all rising worldwide, in many cases dramatically in developing countries. International trade had increased from about a fifth of global output in the early postwar years to almost half 70 years later. Globalization had accelerated and played a major part in these successes.

For the world as a whole, real living standards had never been higher (although some within countries and some countries were left behind. For example, Argentina is an example of a country whose per capita income was among the highest in the world in 1900 and is now a developing country). The electronics revolution had not only enabled cell phones, internet, and much more in advanced economies, but also huge advances in developing countries.

(L. to R.) Ron Kirk, U.S. trade representative, Representative Dave Camp, a Republican from Michigan, and Thomas Conway, vice president of the United Steelworkers union, watch as U.S. President Barack Obama signs the Korea, Panama, Colombia Free Trade Agreements and the renewal of Trade Adjustment Assistance for workers in the Oval Office of the White House in Washington, DC, Oct. 21, 2011. (BRENDAN SMIALOWSKI/BLOOMBERG/GETTY IMAGES)

Fishermen in countries such as India, when beginning to return to land, were able to learn in which ports their catch commanded the highest price. Health care workers with little training in rural areas were able to obtain advice by phone and internet from clinics and hospitals in rich countries. Online courses gave access to more education and training to many.

The IMF, WTO and World Bank were continuing to work to support countries in financial difficulties, oversee international finance, lend to poor countries for development projects, provide data and forums for trade issues and more. The ninth round of MTNs had failed to reach a conclusion, however, and new issues such as ecommerce and cybersecurity called for attention in the WTO. Overall, however, the international economy had never been so important, and never delivered so much, as it did by 2016.

Skepticism about trade and globalization

By the second decade of the 21st century, there was virtually universal agreement that increased trading and other ties between nations had benefited the entire world enormously. The rate of poverty globally had fallen sharply. Other indicators of well-being were continuing to rise in most developing countries, and real incomes in advanced economies had risen, albeit more slowly than in earlier postwar periods. To be sure there were some who had been harmed along the way, and although social policies had been designed to buffer or offset them, problems remained.

Several phenomena had led to mounting skepticism about the value of globalization. In hindsight, the 9/11 attack on New York and Washington was a jolt to the U.S. and led to weaker support for internationalism. Doubts about open trade and finance were then intensified by the financial crisis of 2007–08.

Except for the years of the global financial crisis, however, trade values and volumes continued to grow, albeit at a slower rate than they had in earlier years. Until 2017, the WTO and other international institutions functioned much as they had. Some observers noted that recessions normally induce increased protection and that the global

A worker checks the quality of steel plate in Handan, Hebei province, China, July 16, 2020.
(COSTFOTO/BARCROFT MEDIA/GETTY IMAGES)

crisis had generated a smaller increase than might have been expected.

Several criticisms intensified during the decade after the Great Recession. A major concern was expressed in many advanced economies about a loss of jobs, with the losses attributed to international trade. In macroeconomic perspective, that complaint collided with the facts that employment had expanded very rapidly and the unemployment rate had fallen. Research indicated that even in those cases where jobs had been lost, a major part of the blame fell on technical change (not trade). Hardship was largely concentrated in towns and rural areas in which a key factory or other activity had been unable to survive.

Despite strong pressure from areas in which jobs had been lost, a majority of Americans still supported free trade and a leadership role for the U.S. in the world. There were skeptics in European and Asian countries, too, but the skepticism was generally more muted as most of those economies were highly dependent on trade.

American economists, especially, noted that adjustment assistance for workers was and is relatively spartan. Adjustment assistance had been added to unemployment compensation for those losing jobs because of the impact of trade. However, it was difficult

for the authorities to determine that trade was the major factor in leading to unemployment, as technical change and other factors were usually more important.

A better solution to the problems of job loss and hardship that arise should cover all causes of job loss, without differential treatment of workers because of the cause of their job loss. Until measures such as that are taken, however, it is likely that those harmed by plant closures will tend to blame foreign trade out of all proportion to its importance.

Rejection of multilateralism in trade

Until the election of President Donald Trump in the U.S. in 2016, however, interdependence continued to increase, although at a slower pace than before the Great Recession. There was widespread agreement that globalization had resulted in large positive benefits for almost all.

The Trump administration, however, chose to attack the open multilateral trading system on many fronts. An FTA (the Trans-Pacific Partnership, TPP) had already been negotiated between the U.S., Japan, and ten other Pacific-Rim countries. President Trump withdrew the U.S. from it in one of his first moves in office. He attacked Chinese trade policies, and declared a "trade war"

with China, imposing tariffs on Chinese exports to the U.S. He considered, wrongly, that the U.S. trade deficit could be cured by raising tariffs on Chinese goods, but China retaliated, and from there tensions and protectionist measures between the two largest trading countries in the world rose. There was little or no impact on the trade balance, as economists had predicted.

In addition to the "trade war" between the U.S. and China, the Trump administration imposed tariffs of 25% on steel imports (and 10% on aluminum imports) on "national security" grounds. The president denounced the WTO as inimical to the U.S.; among other actions, the U.S. refused to approve any new judges for the DSM to the point where the entire DSM was inoperative. He attempted to have companies bring their production facilities back to the U.S. and condemned Chinese companies. And much more.

These and other actions took place even before Covid-19 began. The pandemic and its economic consequences both put still further pressure on the open multilateral trading system as some countries have sought to impose measures to protect their supplies of products needed in the health care system, and other protectionist pressures arose. Although many other countries have sought to maintain economic efficiency by having health care products originate from the lowest-cost sources, it is not clear how the issue will resolve over time.

The advent of e-commerce, cybersecurity concerns, and other new issues calls for a coordinated and negotiated international response. Environmental concerns raise the need for international cooperation but in its absence, politicians experience pressure to resort to protection to address environmental issues.

With the WTO partially paralyzed and the leading country rejecting the system, the needed multilateral negotiations to resolve these problems are apparently lacking. Simultaneously, the recession-induced impacts of lockdowns and other measures designed to fight covid-19 have also led to increased calls for additional protection.

Whither globalization?

The confluence of doubts and challenges to the international economic system raises serious questions as to the future of globalization. The loss of U.S. leadership has only served to underline how important it was in the years prior to 2017. The antagonism of the U.S. administration to an open multilateral system has already damaged it. The fact that the U.S. had abandoned its support for the system has strengthened protectionist pressures in many other countries.

Given all the benefits still to be had from further global integration, the timing of the new issues with the pandemic and the withdrawal of American support are particularly unfortunate.

The question, therefore, is what the future holds for the open multilateral trading system and further globalization. Clearly, increasing protectionist measures will further stress the system and other trading nations may seek shelter from that with measures of their own. Offsetting that, over time observers will note that, by and large, countries that remain open will experience more satisfactory economic performance than those that shut their doors.

There are several possible outcomes. In the most optimistic scenario, countries would meet to negotiate and address some of their issues and restore the WTO and the open multilateral system. In some cases, such as concerns about Chinese theft of intellectual property, a multilateral approach would in any event be more likely to yield results than a single country's efforts. But in the most pessimistic alternative, countries turn inward with increasingly stiff walls of protection and insulation from international shocks.

In between these two extremes — restoration of the open multilateral system and reversion throughout the world to Smoot-Hawley-like tariffs — some observers have suggested that there may be a middle path: separation of the global economy into PTAs. One possibility would be an Asian bloc, a bloc in the Western Hemisphere, and an Afro-European bloc. There are many other possibilities (such as a Sino-East Asian African bloc, and a Russian bloc

Construction workers are seen as they work with steel rebar during the construction of a building on May 17, 2019, in Miami, Florida. The Trump administration had just announced that it would be lifting tariffs on Canadian and Mexican steel imports, nearly a year after imposing the duties. (JOE RAEDLE/GETTY IMAGES)

with some surrounding countries and North Africa joining).

It is very doubtful that most countries will revert to high-tariff regimes, à la the Smoot-Hawley tariffs and retaliation in the 1930s. Most countries are simply too dependent on trade. The members of the EU are closely intertwined, and likely to stay that way. They could raise tariffs against the rest of the world, but the EU imports a high fraction of its energy, raw materials, and items intensive in the use of unskilled labor. The economic losses from high tariffs would be great.

The situation for Asia is similar. The region has a significant share of its trade with the EU and with the western hemisphere. Likewise, the countries of the western hemisphere have a large fraction of their trade outside the region.

Moreover, it is hard to imagine the continuation of scientific and educational exchanges, collaboration on innovation, value chains for factory inputs, and much more if protectionist measures were high and applied country by country. Disruption costs would be sizeable as companies relocated their production units, but the losses would be great even after those transitory costs were absorbed.

The world may learn more about the costs of disentanglement with Brexit once the UK leaves the EU customs union at the end of 2020. Analyses anticipating trade disruption suggest the costs will be sizeable. While the costs may fall over the longer run, the prospective disruption appears to be huge.

The likelier alternative to a move toward protectionist regimes in individual countries is probably regional trading blocs. Even these would be very costly. An African PTA with Europe would perhaps result in relatively smaller losses than the EU and USMCA would incur. However, the EU trades more with Asia and the U.S. than it does with Africa. Disruption would appear substantial.

However, some countries will surely opt for maintaining open trading ties with the rest of the world. Over time, they are likely to prosper and grow more rapidly than countries or regions that have turned inward. As citizens of countries with heavier protection observe the difference, political pressures would likely again arise to lower tariff barriers, just as they did in developing countries observing the success of the East Asian tigers.

There are still many potential benefits from further globalization, including greater efficiency in services trades of many kinds, ecommerce, efficient means of addressing environmental issues, and much more. It is to be hoped that the great benefits from globalization that have already taken place will serve as a lesson and persuade countries to continue its progress.

discussion questions

1. Can any country afford to ignore the growing trends of globalization in favor of isolationist policies?

2. How can globalization be improved so that it can benefit more and more of the global populace? What has prevented this in the past?

3. What does the "next stage" of globalization look like? Would we see more power ceded to international organizations? Does globalization have a future 20 years from now?

4. What are the biggest drawbacks to globalization? What are some ways governments can better combat the disadvantages of globalization?

5. Which nation in your opinion is the "leader" of the globalization movement? Why is it and can they find a way to make it more appealing to the global masses?

suggested readings

Krueger, Anne O. **International Trade: What Everyone Needs to Know,** 268 pg, Oxford University Press 2020. With evidence-based analysis and an even-handed approach, *International Trade: What Everyone Needs to Know* lays the foundation to understand what trade does and does not do. Focusing on the importance of trade in both goods and services, Krueger explores the effects of various trade policies step-by-step and demonstrates why economists generally support free trade.

Raboy, Marc. **Marconi**, 872 pg. Oxford University Press, 2018. As Marc Raboy shows us in this enthralling and comprehensive biography, Marconi was the first truly global figure in modern communications

Clark, Gregory. **A Farewell to Alms: A Brief Economic History of the World,** 432 pg, Princeton University Press, 2009.

Findlay, Ronald and O'Rourke, Kevin. **Power and Plenty: Trade, War, and the World Economy in the Second Millennium** 648 pg. Princeton University Press, 2009. Ronald Findlay and Kevin O'Rourke examine the successive waves of globalization and "deglobalization" that have occurred during the past thousand years, looking closely at the technological and political causes behind these long-term trends.

Gordon, Robert J. **The Rise and Fall of American Growth: The U.S. Standard of Living since the Civil War** 784 pg. Princeton University Press, 2017. Weaving together a vivid narrative, historical anecdotes, and economic analysis, *The Rise and Fall of American Growth* challenges the view that economic growth will continue unabated, and argues that the life-altering scale of innovations between 1870 and 1970 cannot be repeated.

Stiglitz, Joseph E. **Globalization and Its Discontents Revisited: Anti-Globalization in the Era of Trump,** 515 pg, W.W.Norton & Company, 2017. In this crucial expansion and update of his landmark bestseller, renowned economist and Nobel Prize winner Joseph E. Stiglitz addresses globalization's new discontents in the United States and Europe.

Don't forget: Ballots start on page 104!!!!

To access web links to these readings, as well as links to global discussion questions, shorter readings and suggested web sites,
GO TO www.fpa.org/great_decisions
and click on the topic under Resources, on the right-hand side of the page.

About the balloting process...

Dear Great Decisions Participants,

As you may already know, my name is Dr. Lauren Prather and I have been working with the Foreign Policy Association (FPA) for the last five years on the National Opinion Ballot (NOB). A version of this letter has appeared in previous briefing books, so I'm only writing a quick hello this year.

My research is primarily focused on international relations. I am a faculty member at the School of Global Policy and Strategy at the University of California, San Diego (UCSD) and have research projects on a range of public opinion topics, from foreign aid to climate change to national security issues. I also teach a class on public opinion and foreign policy for my university.

One of the key difficulties in my research is that the public is often uniformed or misinformed about the topics. This is where you come in! The Great Decisions participants continue to be some of the most informed Americans about foreign policy issues, and the NOB is the perfect opportunity to voice those opinions.

The NOB is also one of the only public opinion surveys in the United States that attempts to gather the opinions of the educated public. Thus, it has great value to researchers and policymakers alike. Some of the questions in which researchers are interested include the following:

- Are the opinions of the educated public significantly different from those of the average American?
- How does public opinion about foreign policy change over time?
- How does public opinion on one foreign policy issue relate to public opinion on other foreign policy issues? For example, are people who support U.S. government policies to mitigate climate change more or less willing to support drilling in the Arctic?
- How do different segments of the population, men or women, liberals or conservatives, view foreign policy choices?

In order to answer the types of questions researchers are interested in, such as how do people's opinions change over time, the NOB needs to have certain attributes. We need to have a way to organize the ballots by participant across all topics. That way, we know, for example, how participant #47 responded to the question about climate change mitigation and how he or she responded to the question about drilling, even if those were in different topics in the NOB. Your random ID number is the **only thing** connected to your responses and **never** your e-mail address. In fact, as a researcher, I must receive the approval of my Institutional Review Board by demonstrating that your data will be protected at all times, and that your responses will be both confidential and anonymous.

If you have any questions or comments, I am always happy to respond via e-mail at LPrather@ucsd. edu. To learn more about my research and teaching, you can visit my website at www.laurenprather.org.

Thank you again to everyone who has participated in the NOB over the years. I have learned a tremendous amount about your foreign policy views and it has greatly informed my own research. In the future, I hope to communicate to the scholarly world and policy communities how the educated American public thinks about foreign policy.

Sincerely,

Lauren Prather

2021 National Opinion Ballot

First, we'd like to ask you for some information about your participation in the Great Decisions program. If you are not currently a Great Decisions program member, please skip to the "background" section.

How long have you participated in the Great Decisions program (i.e., attended one or more discussion sessions)?

- ❏ This is the first year I have participated
- ❏ I participated in one previous year
- ❏ I participated in more than one previous year

How did you learn about the Great Decisions Program?

- ❏ Word of mouth
- ❏ Local library
- ❏ Foreign Policy Association website
- ❏ Promotional brochure
- ❏ Other organization _____

Where does your Great Decisions group meet?

- ❏ Private home
- ❏ Library
- ❏ Community center
- ❏ Learning in retirement
- ❏ Online/Zoom
- ❏ Other _____

How many hours, on average, do you spend reading one *Great Decisions* chapter?

- ❏ Less than 1 hour
- ❏ 1–2 hours
- ❏ 3–4 hours
- ❏ More than 4 hours

Would you say you have or have not changed your opinion in a fairly significant way as a result of taking part in the Great Decisions program?

- ❏ Have
- ❏ Have not

Background Section: Next, we'd like to ask you som information about your background.

How strongly do you agree or disagree with the following statement? Although the media often reports about national and international events and developments, this news is seldom as interesting as the things that happen directly in our own community and neighborhood.

- ❏ Agree strongly
- ❏ Agree somewhat
- ❏ Neither agree nor disagree
- ❏ Disagree somewhat
- ❏ Disagree strongly

Generally speaking, how interested are you in politics?

- ❏ Very much interested
- ❏ Somewhat interested
- ❏ Not too interested
- ❏ Not interested at all

Do you think it is best for the future of the United States if the U.S. takes an active role in world affairs or stays out of world affairs?

- ❏ Takes an active role in world affairs
- ❏ Stays out of world affairs

How often are you asked for your opinion on foreign policy?

- ❏ Often
- ❏ Sometimes
- ❏ Never

Have you been abroad during the last two years?

- ❏ Yes
- ❏ No

Do you know, or are you learning, a foreign language?

- ❏ Yes
- ❏ No

Do you have any close friends or family that live in other countries?

❑ Yes

❑ No

Do you donate to any charities that help the poor in other countries?

❑ Yes

❑ No

Generally speaking, do you usually think of yourself as a Republican, a Democrat, an Independent or something else?

❑ Republican

❑ Democrat

❑ Independent

❑ Other _____

With which gender do you most identify?

❑ Male

❑ Female

❑ Transgender male

❑ Transgender female

❑ Gender variant/non-conforming

❑ Other _____

❑ Prefer not to answer

What race do you consider yourself?

❑ White/Caucasian

❑ Black/African American

❑ Hispanic/Latino

❑ Asian American

❑ Native American

❑ Other _____

❑ Prefer not to answer

Were you born in the United States or another country?

❑ United States

❑ Another country

Are you a citizen of the United States, another country, or are you a citizen of both the United States and another country?

❑ United States

❑ Another country

❑ United States and another country

How important is religion in your life?

❑ Very important

❑ Somewhat important

❑ Not too important

❑ Not at all important

What is your age? _____

Are you currently employed?

❑ Full-time employee

❑ Part-time employee

❑ Self-employed

❑ Unemployed

❑ Retired

❑ Student

❑ Homemaker

What are the first three digits of your zip code? (This will allow us to do a state-by-state breakdown of results.)

_____ _____ _____

Can you give us an estimate of your household income in 2018 before taxes?

❑ Below $30,000

❑ $30,000–$50,000

❑ $50,000–$75,000

❑ $75,000–$100,000

❑ $100,000–$150,000

❑ Over $150,000

❑ Not sure

❑ Prefer not to say

What is the highest level of education you have completed?

❑ Did not graduate from high school

❑ High school graduate

❑ Some college, but no degree (yet)

❑ 2-year college degree

❑ 4-year college degree

❑ Some postgraduate work, but no degree (yet)

❑ Post-graduate degree (MA, MBA, MD, JD, PhD, etc.)

Now we would like to ask you some ballot questions from previous years:

1. From 2008's "U.S.-China Economic relations": Does the fact that a product is made in China affect your decisions on whether or not to buy it?

- ❏ I buy products made in China
- ❏ I don't buy products made in China
- ❏ I don't care where the products I buy are made

2. From 2014's "China's foreign policy": How worried are you, if it all, that China could become a military threat to the U.S. in the future?

- ❏ Very worried
- ❏ Somewhat worried
- ❏ Not too worried
- ❏ Not at all worried

3. From 2013's "Trade": People debate whether the U.S. government should increase restrictions on imports, keep restrictions on imports at current levels or decrease restrictions on imports. What do you think the U.S. government should do?

- ❏ Increase restrictions on imports
- ❏ Keep restrictions on imports at current levels
- ❏ Decrease restrictions on imports

4. From 2009's "The Arctic age": Do you agree or disagree with the following statements:

The U.S. must develop a plan for its Navy based upon the premise that the Arctic region will be open for exploration, transport and trade in the next 10 years.
- ❏ Agree
- ❏ Disagree

The U.S. must do whatever is necessary to actively compete for resources in the Arctic.

- ❏ Agree
- ❏ Disagree

The U.S. must ensure all parties in the region take adequate environmental measures.
- ❏ Agree
- ❏ Disagree

5. From 2011's "Making sense of multilateralism": If the international community only has the time and commitment to cooperate on one of the issues below, which issue do you think most critically needs to be addressed at the global level?
- ❏ Nuclear proliferation
- ❏ Climate Change
- ❏ Global economic coordination
- ❏ Economic development
- ❏ Human rights

6. From 2013's "China in Africa": What should be the top U.S. priority in Africa?

- ❏ Peacekeeping
- ❏ Democracy building
- ❏ Humanitarian assistance
- ❏ Human rights
- ❏ Economic investment
- ❏ Natural resources
- ❏ Trade

7. From 2015's "The U.S. and Africa: The Rise and Fall of Obamamania": Do you think the amount of foreign aid the U.S. gives to African countries in general should be increased, kept the same, decreased, or stopped altogether?
- ❏ Increased
- ❏ Kept the same
- ❏ Decreased
- ❏ Stopped altogether

8. From Great Decisions 2014 "China's foreign policy": In dealing with a rising China, do you think the U.S. should…
- ❏ Undertake friendly cooperation and engagement with China
- ❏ Actively work to limit the growth of China's power

9. From 2017's "The future of Europe": Which of the following do you think poses the greatest challenge to the EU?
- ❏ Managing Brexit
- ❏ Immigration from non-EU countries
- ❏ Terrorist attacks
- ❏ Russian actions in Crimea and Ukraine

10. From 2017's "Trade, jobs and politics": How important were free trade agreements in your vote for president in 2016?
- ❏ Extremely important
- ❏ Somewhat important
- ❏ Not too important
- ❏ Not at all important

11. From 2016's "Korean Choices": How likely is it that the Korean peninsula will unify in the next decade?
- ❏ Very likely
- ❏ Somewhat likely
- ❏ Somewhat unlikely
- ❏ Very unlikely

Enter your answers online at www.fpa.org/ballot

Topic 1. Global Supply Chains and National Security

1. Have you engaged in any of the following activities related to "Global supply chains and national security" topic? Mark all that you have done or mark none of the above.

❑ Read the article on supply chains in the 2021 Great Decisions briefing book

❑ Discussed the article on supply chains with a Great Decisions discussion group

❑ Discussed the article on supply chains with friends and family

❑ Watched the GDTV episode on supply chains

❑ Followed news related to global supply chains

❑ Taken a class in which you learned about issues related to supply chains

❑ Have or had a job related to global trade

❑ None of the above

2. How interested would you say you are in issues related to Global supply chains?

❑ Extremely interested

❑ Somewhat interested

❑ Not too interested

❑ Not at all interested

3. How concerned were you regarding Global supply chains before the outbreak of the covid-19 pandemic?

❑ Overly concerned

❑ Somewhat concerned

❑ Not that concerned

❑ Not at all concerned

4. How concerned are you, post-outbreak?

❑ More concerned than before

❑ Less concerned than before

❑ About the same

5. In your opinion, which of the following industries is the most important for the U.S. to gain control over the global supply chain in…

❑ Rare Earth Elements (REE)

❑ Pharmaceuticals

❑ Power supply equipment

❑ Surveillance Technology (cameras, drones etc.)

❑ Other (Please specify)

❑ None

6. In your opinion, can the United States compete against China economically without a more a cooperative relationship between the public and private sectors?

❑ The U.S. needs more government/private sector cooperation to compete

❑ The U.S. can compete without strong government/private sector cooperation

❑ The U.S. cannot compete with China economically

❑ Unsure

7. Would you want to see the U.S. make a concentrated effort to build factories in order to increase manufacturing jobs?

❑ Yes, with little restriction

❑ Yes, with some restrictions (i.e.. Green power, increase minimum wage, etc.)

❑ Somewhat

❑ Not at all

8. Of the three policy options the author provides, which one would you like to see applied by the current administration?

❑ Renewed engagement

❑ Decouplement

❑ Industry policy adoption

❑ Keep current policy

9. Would you like to share any other thoughts with us about supply chains? If so, please use the space below.

. . . .

. . . .

. . . .

. . . .

. . . .

. . . .

. . . .

Enter your answers online at
www.fpa.org/ballot

Topic 2. Persian Gulf Security

1. Have you engaged in any of the following activities related to the "Persian Gulf Security" topic? Mark all that you have done or mark none of the above

- ❏ Read the article on Persian Gulf Security in the 2021 Great Decisions briefing book
- ❏ Discussed the article on Persian Gulf Security with a Great Decisions discussion group
- ❏ Discussed the article on Persian Gulf Security with friends and family
- ❏ Watched the GDTV episode on Persian Gulf Security
- ❏ Followed news related to Persian Gulf Security
- ❏ Taken a class in which you learned about issues related to Persian Gulf
- ❏ Traveled to the Persian Gulf
- ❏ None of the above

2. .How interested would you say you are in issues related to Persian Gulf security?

- ❏ Extremely interested
- ❏ Somewhat interested
- ❏ Not too interested
- ❏ Not at all interested

3. Do you agree with President Trump's decisions to strengthen ties with the Saudi regime?

- ❏ Strongly agree
- ❏ Somewhat agree
- ❏ Neither agree nor disagree
- ❏ Somewhat disagree
- ❏ Strongly disagree

4. In your opinion, which is the biggest threat to Persian Gulf security? (Please select one)

- ❏ Iran/Saudi Rivalry
- ❏ GCC instability
- ❏ Saudi Arabia itself
- ❏ Iran itself
- ❏ Religious tension
- ❏ Terrorism
- ❏ Outside intervention

5. In your opinion, should the U.S. seed economic authority in the Persian Gulf region to another country?

- ❏ Yes, the U.S. should completely remove itself from the region
- ❏ Yes, but the U.S. should keep some ties in the region
- ❏ Yes, but only if it is on "U.S. terms"
- ❏ No, the U.S. should not seed economic authority in the Persian Gulf region

6. Which of the two options do you think is best for the U.S. to use when dealing with Iran?

- ❏ Focus on handling Iran alone
- ❏ Focus efforts on a coalition of partners

7. In your opinion, what should be the U.S. number one priority in the region?

- ❏ Protecting trade (specifically oil)
- ❏ Containing Iran
- ❏ Containing Saudi Arabia
- ❏ Combating terrorism
- ❏ Ensuring peace between the Arab world and Israel

8. In your opinion, how important are the "Abraham Accords" to future Arab/Israeli peace negotiations?

- ❏ Especially important
- ❏ Somewhat important
- ❏ Not too important
- ❏ Not at all important

9. Would you like to share any other thoughts with us about Persian Gulf security? If so, please use the space below.

. . . .

. . . .

. . . .

. . . .

. . . .

. . . .

Topic 3. Brexit and the EU

1. Have you engaged in any of the following related to the "Brexit and the EU?" topic? Mark all that you have done or mark none of the above.

- ❏ Read the article on "Brexit and the EU" in the 2021 Great Decisions briefing book
- ❏ Discussed the article on "Brexit and the EU" with a Great Decisions discussion group
- ❏ Discussed the article on "Brexit and the EU" with friends and family
- ❏ Watched the GDTV episode on "Brexit and the EU"
- ❏ Followed news related to "Brexit and the EU"
- ❏ Taken a class in which you learned about issues related to "Brexit and the EU"
- ❏ Traveled to Britain in last 4 years
- ❏ None of the above

2. How interested would you say you are in issues related to "Brexit and the EU"?

- ❏ Extremely interested
- ❏ Somewhat interested
- ❏ Not too interested
- ❏ Not at all interested

3. Are you concerned that other nations that have threatened to leave the EU (Hungary, Italy) will do so after Brexit?

- ❏ Overly concerned
- ❏ Somewhat concerned
- ❏ Not too concerned
- ❏ Not at all concerned

4. Do you think the U.S. should "pick a side" in the Brexit/EU debate, or try and work with both sides?

- ❏ The U.S. should side with the EU
- ❏ The U.S. should side with the UK
- ❏ The U.S. should try and work with both

5. In your opinion, should the UK have held a second referendum on the Brexit vote?

- ❏ Yes, there should have been a second referendum
- ❏ No, the first vote was sufficient
- ❏ Not sure

6. How would you evaluate the ability of the European Union to react and respond to crises (i.e. Migration Crisis, Euro Crisis, Covid pandemic)?

- ❏ Excellent
- ❏ Good
- ❏ Fine
- ❏ Not good
- ❏ Awful
- ❏ Not Sure

7. Do you have a positive opinion of Brexit?

- ❏ Yes
- ❏ Somewhat
- ❏ No
- ❏ Unsure

8. Would you like to share any other thoughts with us about "Brexit and the EU?" If so, please use the space below.

. . . .

. . . .

. . . .

. . . .

. . . .

. . . .

. . . .

Topic 4. Struggles over the Melting Arctic

1. Have you engaged in any of the following activities related to the "Struggles over the melting Arctic" topic? Mark all that you have done or mark none of the above.

- ❏ Read the article on the Arctic in the 2021 Great Decisions briefing book
- ❏ Discussed the article on the Arctic with a Great Decisions discussion group
- ❏ Discussed the article on the Arctic with friends and family
- ❏ Watched the GDTV episode on the Arctic
- ❏ Followed news related to the Arctic
- ❏ Taken a class in which you learned about issues related to the Arctic
- ❏ Travelled to the Arctic
- ❏ None of the above

2. How interested would you say you are in issues related to the Arctic?

- ❏ Extremely interested
- ❏ Somewhat interested
- ❏ Not too interested
- ❏ Not at all interested

3. How important do you view the Arctic to U.S. national security?

- ❏ Extremely important
- ❏ Somewhat important
- ❏ Not too important
- ❏ Not at all important

4. In your opinion, should the U.S. risk antagonizing Russia and China by increasing their naval/military presence in the Arctic?

- ❏ Yes
- ❏ No
- ❏ Unsure

5. In your opinion, what should the U.S. main priority in the Arctic be?

- ❏ Environmental protection
- ❏ Ensure freedom of navigation
- ❏ Compete for territory with China and Russia
- ❏ Harvest as much natural recourses as possible
- ❏ Unsure

6. Are you concerned with the actions of China and Russia in the Arctic?

- ❏ Very concerned
- ❏ Somewhat concerned
- ❏ Not too concerned
- ❏ Not at all concerned

7. How likely do you think it is that the U.S. will have a sizable foothold in the Arctic region in the next 5 years?

- ❏ Very likely
- ❏ Somewhat likely
- ❏ Not too likely
- ❏ Not likely at all

8. Would you like to share any other thoughts with us about the Arctic? If so, please use the space below.

. . . .

. . . .

. . . .

. . . .

. . . .

. . . .

. . . .

Topic 5. China in Africa

1. Have you engaged in any of the following activities related to the "China in Africa" topic? Mark all that you have done or mark none of the above.

❑ Read the article on China in Africa in the 2021 Great Decisions briefing book

❑ Discussed the article on China in Africa with a Great Decisions discussion group

❑ Discussed the article on China in Africa with friends and family

❑ Watched the GDTV episode on China in Africa

❑ Followed news related to China in Africa

❑ Take a class in which you learned about issues related to China in Africa

❑ Traveled to Africa before 2020

❑ None of the above

2. How interested would you say you are in issues related to China in Africa?

❑ Extremely interested
❑ Somewhat interested
❑ Not too interested
❑ Not at all interested

3. .In your opinion, what is the most important concern facing the U.S. regarding China in Africa?
❑ China, as a supplier of weapons to African nations
❑ China's growing military presence in Africa
❑ China spreading communism to Africa
❑ China's growing economic presence in Africa

4. Should the U.S. do more to combat China's growing influence in Africa, and if so how?

❑ Increasing foreign aid to Africa

❑ Increasing campaigns for democratization

❑ Stepping up military presence in Africa

❑ Economic sanctions against African countries that support China

❑ Funding Human rights campaigns

❑ The U.S. should not do anything to combat China't

5. Do you view China's growing relationship with Africa as a 'win-win' for both parties?

❑ Yes, the current relationship will benefit both parties

❑ No, I think only China will benefit

❑ No, I think only the African nations will benefit

❑ No, I don't think it will benefit either party

6. Do you think that China will leverage its relationship with African nations in order to affect some African countries' domestic policies?

❑ Yes

❑ No

❑ Unsure

7. Do you think the covid-19 pandemic will hurt China's momentum in Africa?

❑ Yes

❑ No

❑ Unsure

8. Would you like to share any other thoughts with us about China in Africa ? If so, please use the space below.

. . . .

. . . .

. . . .

. . . .

. . . .

. . . .

. . . .

. . . .

. . . .

Topic 6. The two Koreas

1. Have you engaged in any of the following activities related to the "The two Koreas" topic? Mark all that you have done or mark none of the above.

- ❏ Read the article on the two Koreas in the 2021 Great Decisions briefing book
- ❏ Discussed the article the two Koreas with a Great Decisions discussion group
- ❏ Discussed the article the two Koreas with friends and family
- ❏ Watched the GDTV episode on the two Koreas
- ❏ Followed news related to the two Koreas
- ❏ Taken a class in which you learned about issues related to the two Koreas
- ❏ Travelled to the Korean peninsula
- ❏ None of the above

2. How interested would you say you are in issues related to "The two Koreas"?

- ❏ Extremely interested
- ❏ Somewhat interested
- ❏ Not too interested
- ❏ Not at all interested

3. Do you approve of the job President Trump has done with regards to combating North Korea's nuclear program?

- ❏ Approve
- ❏ Somewhat approve
- ❏ Neither approve nor disapprove
- ❏ Somewhat disapprove
- ❏ Disapprove

4. Do you think that North Korean leader Kim Jong-un would launch a nuclear attack preemptively?

- ❏ Very much so
- ❏ Somewhat
- ❏ Not so much
- ❏ Not at all

5. In your opinion, do you foresee a scenario where the North Korean government gives up on its nuclear weapons program?

- ❏ Yes, but only after pressure from China
- ❏ Yes, but only after lifting of all sanctions from the global community
- ❏ Yes, but only as part of a global denuclearization program
- ❏ Yes, but only as part of unifying Korea
- ❏ No, I don't foresee any scenario where N.K gives up its nuclear weapons

6. Which of these factors do you believe benefited South Korea the most when combatting the spread of covid-19 in the country?

- ❏ Ease of testing
- ❏ Culture of mask wearing
- ❏ Public-private cooperation
- ❏ Treatment practices
- ❏ Faith in government officials/information

7. Of these options, which do you think is the most likely scenario for the future of the Korean peninsula?

- ❏ Reignition of the Korean War
- ❏ Unification under a democratic government
- ❏ Unification under authoritarian regime
- ❏ Remains the same

8. Would you like to share any other thoughts with us about the two Koreas? If so, please use the space below.

. . . .

. . . .

. . . .

. . . .

. . . .

. . . .

. . . .

Topic 7. Role of the WHO

1. A. Have you engaged in any of the following activities related to the Role of the WHO topic? Mark all that you have done or mark none of the above.

- ❏ Read the article on the Role of the WHO in the 2021 Great Decisions briefing book
- ❏ Discussed the article on the Role of the WHO with a Great Decisions discussion group
- ❏ Discussed the article on the Role of the WHO with friends and family
- ❏ Watched the GDTV episode on the Role of the WHO
- ❏ Followed news related to the World Health Organization
- ❏ Taken a class in which you learned about issues related to the Role of the WHO
- ❏ Have or had a job related to healthcare
- ❏ None of the above

2. How interested would you say you are in issues related to the Role of the WHO?

- ❏ Extremely interested
- ❏ Somewhat interested
- ❏ Not too interested
- ❏ Not at all interested

3. In your opinion, how did the World Health Organization do in managing the early stages of the covid-19 outbreak?

- ❏ Excellent job
- ❏ Good job
- ❏ Adequate job
- ❏ Bad job
- ❏ Awful job

4. Would you support President Donald Trump's decision to withdraw the U.S. from the World Health Organization?

- ❏ Strongly support
- ❏ Somewhat support
- ❏ Somewhat oppose
- ❏ Strongly oppose
- ❏ Unsure

5. In your opinion, would the WHO have had a better response to the pandemic if it had more monetary support from the U.S.?

- ❏ Much better
- ❏ Somewhat better
- ❏ Not much better
- ❏ Not at all better

6. How trusting are you of health information coming from the WHO vis-à-vis the Center for Disease Control (CDC)?

- ❏ More trusting of WHO
- ❏ More trusting of CDC
- ❏ Don't trust either

7. Would you support the U.S. starting a counterpart to the WHO?

- ❏ Yes, I would support the U.S. backed org more
- ❏ No, I would prefer a stronger U.S. presence in the WHO
- ❏ No, I would prefer the U.S. stays out of global health agencies

8. After reading the article, has your opinion on the World Health Organization changed at all?

- ❏ Yes, for the better
- ❏ Yes, for the worse
- ❏ Only somewhat
- ❏ Not at all

9. Would you like to share any other thoughts with us about the Role of the WHO? If so, please use the space below.

. . . .

. . . .

. . . .

. . . .

. . . .

. . . .

Topic 8. The end of Globalization?

1. Have you engaged in any of the following activities related to the "End of globalization?" topic? Mark all that you have done or mark none of the above.

- ❏ Read the article on the End of globalization in the 2021 Great Decisions briefing book
- ❏ Discussed the article on the End of globalization with a Great Decisions Discussion group
- ❏ Discussed the article on the End of globalization with friends and family
- ❏ Watched the GDTV episode on the End of globalization
- ❏ Followed news related to the End of globalization
- ❏ Taken a class in which you learned about issues related to the End of globalization
- ❏ None of the above

2. How interested would you say you are in issues related to the End of globalization?

- ❏ Extremely interested
- ❏ Somewhat interested
- ❏ Not too interested
- ❏ Not at all interested

3. In your opinion, do you have a positive opinion on negative opinion, or no real opinion on globalization?

- ❏ Very positive
- ❏ Somewhat positive
- ❏ Somewhat negative
- ❏ Very negative
- ❏ No opinion

4. In your opinion, was Donald Trump's "America First" doctrine more beneficial to the economic health of the U.S. than engaging in globalization efforts?

- ❏ Much more beneficial
- ❏ Somewhat more beneficial
- ❏ Not too beneficial
- ❏ Not at all beneficial

5. Would you like to see future U.S. administration pull away from globalization in favor of more economic nationalism?

- ❏ Very much so
- ❏ Somewhat
- ❏ Not much
- ❏ Not at all

6. Do you trust AI firms with your data?

- ❏ Trust completely
- ❏ Trust somewhat
- ❏ Neither trust nor distrust
- ❏ Distrust somewhat
- ❏ Distrust completely

7. Please select the response that best fits your opinion toward the following statement:

"Globalization is better in theory than in practice"

- ❏ Strongly agree
- ❏ Somewhat agree
- ❏ Neither agree nor disagree
- ❏ Somewhat disagree
- ❏ Strongly disagree

"Isolationism is better for a countries populace, globalization is better for business"

- ❏ Strongly agree
- ❏ Somewhat agree
- ❏ Neither agree nor disagree
- ❏ Somewhat disagree
- ❏ Strongly disagree

"Economic nationalism is better in theory than in practice"

- ❏ Strongly agree
- ❏ Somewhat agree
- ❏ Neither agree nor disagree
- ❏ Somewhat disagree
- ❏ Strongly disagree

8. Would you like to share any other thoughts with us about the end of globalization? If so, please use the space below.

. . . .

. . . .

. . . .

. . . .

. . . .

. . . .

Become a Member

For nearly a century, members of the Association have played key roles in government, think tanks, academia and the private sector.

As an active participant in the FPA's Great Decisions program, we encourage you to join the community today's foreign policy thought leaders.

Member—$250
Benefits:
- Free admission to all Associate events (includes member's family)
- Discounted admission for all other guests to Associate events
- Complimentary **GREAT DECISIONS** briefing book
- Complimentary issue of FPA's annual *National Opinion Ballot Report*

Visit us online at

www.fpa.org/membership

Make a Donation

Your support helps the FOREIGN POLICY ASSOCIATION's programs dedicated to global affairs education.

Make a fully tax-deductible contribution to FPA's Annual Fund 2020.

To contribute to the Annual Fund 2020 visit us online at **www.fpa.org** or call the Membership Department at

(800) 628-5754 ext. 333

The generosity of donors who contribute $500 or more is acknowledged in FPA's *Annual Report.*

All financial contributions are tax-deductible to the fullest extent of the law under section 501 (c)(3) of the IRS code.

FPA also offers membership at the SPONSOR MEMBER and PATRON MEMBER levels. To learn more, visit us online at www.fpa.org/membership or call (800) 628-5754 ext. 333

Return this form by mail to: Foreign Policy Association, 551 Fifth Avenue, 30th Floor, New York, N.Y. 10176

ORDER ONLINE: WWW.FPA.ORG/GREAT_DECISIONS

CALL (800) 477-5836

FAX (212) 481-9275

❑ MR.　❑ MRS.　❑ MS.　❑ DR.　❑ PROF.

NAME _____

ADDRESS _____

_____ **APT/FLOOR** _____

CITY _____ STATE _____ ZIP _____

TEL _____

E-MAIL_____

❑ AMEX　❑ VISA　❑ MC　❑ DISCOVER
❑ CHECK (ENCLOSED)

CHECKS SHOULD BE PAYABLE TO FOREIGN POLICY ASSOCIATION.

CARD NO.

SIGNATURE OF CARDHOLDER

EXP. DATE (MM/YY)

PRODUCT	QTY	PRICE	COST
GREAT DECISIONS 2021 Briefing Book (FPA31705)		$32	
SPECIAL OFFER TEN PACK SPECIAL GREAT DECISIONS 2021 (FPA31699) *Includes 10% discount		$288	
GREAT DECISIONS TELEVISION SERIES GD ON DVD 2021 (FPA31706)		$40	
GREAT DECISIONS 2021 TEACHER'S PACKET (1 Briefing Book, 1 Teacher's Guide and 1 DVD (FPA 31708) E-MAIL: (REQUIRED)		$70	
GREAT DECISIONS CLASSROOM-PACKET (1 Teacher's Packet & 30 Briefing Books (FPA31709) E-MAIL: (REQUIRED)		$725	
MEMBERSHIP		$250	
ANNUAL FUND 2021 (ANY AMOUNT)			

SUBTOTAL $ _____
plus S & H* $ _____
TOTAL $ _____

For details and shipping charges, call FPA's Sales Department at (800) 477-5836.
Orders mailed to FPA without the shipping charge will be held.